TRANSFORMATION
COMPANY

TRANSFORMATION COMPANY

*Power To Become The Change Agent
You Were Positioned To Be*

UCHE EZECHIM

XULON PRESS

Xulon Press
2301 Lucien Way #415
Maitland, FL 32751
407.339.4217
www.xulonpress.com

Unless otherwise indicated, Scripture quotations taken from the King James Version (KJV) – *public domain.*

Scripture quotations taken from the Holy Bible, New International Version (NIV). Copyright © 1973, 1978, 1984, 2011 by Biblica, Inc.™. Used by permission. All rights reserved.

Scripture quotations taken from the Amplified Bible (AMP). Copyright © 1954, 1958, 1962, 1964, 1965, 1987 by The Lockman Foundation. Used by permission. All rights reserved.

Paperback ISBN-13: 978-1-6628-2213-1
Ebook ISBN-13: 978-1-6628-2214-8

DEDICATION

To the King Eternal, Immortal, Invisible, the only wise God, be glory and honor, forever and ever Amen!

To His Excellency, the Heavenly Governor, the Holy Spirit, who is the source of all truth and life for His continuous work of profound transformation in my life.

To the Institute of Discipleship and Transformation team that stands with me in my passion to impart and nurture positive change of mindset, mentality, and attitude by modelling truth in love

To my husband Pastor Ezekiel, and my children Glory, Covenant and Prince Emmanuel, my greatest investment on earth.

To the Transformation Company family and change agents all across the nations. We shall see the manifestation of God's word in our generation.

TABLE OF CONTENTS

PREFACE

VISION: WHAT DO YOU SEE? TWO PEOPLE were shown a tiny seed and asked what they saw? The first person quickly replied that it was just a small seed. The second person thought about it and replied that they saw a forest. That is right! A seed that can become a tree, which can produce more seeds that can grow into trees, thereby becoming a forest someday.

Vision is the ability to see things as they should be; not necessarily as they are. True vision is the capacity to see farther than your eyes can look. Eyes that look are common, but eyes that see are rare. True vision is not limited to natural sight; it is an internal revelation of a future occurrence. A leader is born when vision is captured. As a Visionary Leader, who is an innovative, risk taker, out-of-the-box thinker, I can see the possibilities for the future and empower others. This attribute of empowering is not only essential to one's development, but it is also important to the success of relationships.

"Seeing the forest" is essential in visionary leadership. The forest is the big picture. If the leader cannot see it all, they will not be able to lead to the highest-level outcomes. Let us go back to the scenario of the forest and the trees. If the forest is the big picture, let us look at the trees as the colleagues, associates, allies and employees.

These people are the "doers" that make it all happen. A Visionary Leader cannot get so caught up in seeing the big picture (the forest) that they lose sight of the people (the trees) who bring the vision to reality. In keeping this thought, to be a more effective visionary leader, one needs to have a good sense of their strengths, attributes, and growth opportunities to appropriately empower everyone to be a part of the big picture in a way that will be meaningful to them.

When empowering your team to be a part of the big picture, an effective visionary leader focuses on three key things:

- Listening with authenticity,

- Responding with integrity, and

- Leading with inspiration.

I learned a great deal about seeing the forest and the trees in my previous position as a pioneer and lead National Coordinator of the work of Wailing Women Worldwide in Canada. For over 13 years, I was fortunate to be surrounded by colleagues with numerous strengths that made our work together so powerful. It was uplifting for me to empower them to be all they could be. Today, strong functional teams of passionate intercessors are established in 6 Provinces of Canada. What about you…? How do you empower your team or how have you been empowered by a visionary leader?

INTRODUCTION

THE WORLD IS CURRENTLY CONTENTIOUS, CHA-
otic, painful, and there is untold suffering. Most people are
desperate for good leadership, the world is desperate for change.
Do you desire to make your world better? What is this concept of
transformation all about? Are you ready to be a catalyst to change
our community?

TRANSFORMED BY HIS LOVE

Have you experienced love that is so powerful that it totally
changes your life? Can you say that you have experienced a life
change that has finally given you peace, fulfillment, and joy? You
are destined for transformation as you accept this profound love.
We throw the word 'love' around rather carelessly. It is used in a
lot of different ways: to describe the food we eat and the places we
enjoy, our favourite sports teams and our day off. We use love to
describe relationships that are friendly, family, or romantic. There
is a love that is so powerful that it changes everything. This love
that comes from God is one that defines the very nature of God:
God is love (1 John 4:8). This word appears in the New Testament
numerous times and is the Greek word agape. Since God revealed
His agape love personally to me, my whole life-worth has been
drastically and consistently transformed. Experiencing God as my

own Father, and lover of my soul, realigns my entire identity and purpose for existence with His. Knowing I am the one Jesus Christ loves has transformed me; how about you? Knowing that God, the God of the entire universe loves me and accepting that incredible love, has given me eternal life. God's love is transformational. There is no doubt about it.

HOW DO WE DESCRIBE AGAPE?

It is perfect. There are no flaws or shortcomings in it. This kind of love finds perfection of expression and perfection of application.

It is unconditional. That means it is not earned but given. It does not depend on what we do; it depends on the nature of the giver. Since God is love and is perfect and gracious, He lavishes this love on us. We cannot do anything or go anywhere that would cut off God's love from us.

For I am convinced that neither death nor life, neither angels nor demons, neither the present nor the future, nor any powers, neither height nor depth, nor anything else in all creation, will be able to separate us from the love of God that is in Christ Jesus our Lord (Romans 8:38–39).

It is powerful. This is the love of God that seeks after mankind in order to bring us into relationship with Him, and it can totally transform a life. Transformation is a powerful word and it is something that is desperately needed in every life.

WHAT IS TRANSFORMATION?

In molecular biology and genetics, transformation is the genetic alteration of a cell by the introduction or uptake and incorporation of a DNA that is originating externally. God wants to introduce his DNA into us. That is how He is going to transform us like Mary (Luke chapter 1:34), overshadowing us by the power of His Holy Spirit and He is going to enable us to bring forth impactful change.

INTRODUCTION

Metamorphosis is a process which means transformation; change or alter the form of, change in shape or nature; for example, egg/ovum-larva/caterpillar-pupa/chrysalis-butterfly/adult. The egg and larva stages are very unlike the butterfly; it becomes vulnerable but as it develops a thick covering, the butterfly is forming, transformation is going on. Then, it is cocooned into the shelf before the beautiful butterfly emerges. We must allow God to cocoon, prune, and work on to transform us, until we come out as a beautiful butterfly.

In Mathematics, transformation is a function that changes the position or direction of the axis of a coordinate system.

In general Physics, transformation is to convert from one form of energy to another; example, energy to light. We should not be in a hurry to leave His presence. Every day, for at least 30 minutes, do nothing, lay down and meditate on God. Once a week, keep one day for the Lord, to build intimacy and to be taught by the Holy Spirit as the Holy Spirit is the transformer. Without holiness we cannot see God. It is one of the preconditions for transformation. We are asked not to adopt the ways of the world, do not think like the world; do not conform to its ideals and standards. God wants to recreate our mentality, recondition, and regenerate our mind; He is looking for those who are radically transformed, and filled with the Spirit of God to ignite and spark off this trans-generational change. God is about to drop a mantle, as well as double the anointing which we must position ourselves to catch and receive like the mantle from Elijah to Elisha.

As followers of Christ, we need metamorphosis. Our spiritual growth requires radical change. Consider, for a moment, the biological process of metamorphosis, which can be seen in a variety of creatures, such as toads and dragonflies. As the process begins, their bodies are altered, their cells are reconfigured, and even their behavioural patterns are modified. The process is an astonishing clear evidence of the ingenuity and artistry of our Creator. It is a fitting analogy of God's desire for human life.

The apostle Paul spoke often of such transformation, using the Greek word metamorphosis. Paul urges Christians to "be transformed by the renewing of your mind" (Romans 12:2). The salvation that Jesus offers us is much more than a "get out of hell" card. It involves a moral, spiritual, and mental transformation that takes place in this life. However, living a transformed life may seem complicated as *we* cannot do it. Though we try our best, we may fail. That is because a transformed life is something that *God* does in us. When we give God control of our lives, He begins reshaping and transforming us into someone new and wonderful.

Therefore, the Bible talks about our *being* transformed. God is the agent of transformation, not us. Paul says that, through God's power, we "are *being* transformed into his [Christ's] likeness" (2 Corinthians 3:18).

If God is the agent, then what is the mechanism of this change? In Romans 12:2, Paul explains that transformation comes through the renewal of the mind. The Greek word for *mind* refers to our understanding, attitude, and entire way of thinking. In some ways, the word 'mind' here could be translated as "worldview"; the mental lens through which we view, interpret, and respond to the world around us. As followers of Christ, we need to memorize Bible verses as well as think biblically. We must instill in ourselves a passion for soaking up Scripture and let it dictate the way we think about God, suffering, poverty, sex, love, justice, forgiveness, truth, healing and what it means to be human.

When we talk about being transformed, we are talking about something very strong. It is not a word to throw around because it means a real change in our nature or character or appearance. It signifies a turning point, something permanent, not temporary. So, what would you identify as the transformational points in your life? What person or situation or event has made a truly significant difference in your life for the better? If you think carefully about it, my guess is that the transformational points in your life came because of love. Love has the power to transform us. When you think about transformation, one of the best examples in nature is the butterfly. The butterfly undergoes a transformation when it emerges from the cocoon that it had woven for itself when it was a caterpillar. For example, getting to know Jesus Christ and accepting his gift of salvation certainly transforms our nature, does it not? The Bible says that we become new creations in Christ; the new has come, the old has gone. The love of God transforms us like no other love ever could. When this love captivates our hearts, we are similarly transformed. We are changed from the inside out. It starts with a changed heart. When we allow God to transform us with His love, He changes our heart. He removes all the sins and guilt, as we receive His grace. We become captivated first in our hearts by His great love.

Then He begins to work on our minds. He changes the way we think about things and people. He enables us to love unconditionally just as He loves. Our attitudes begin to change as we yield to Him. Compassion and forgiveness replace judgment and retribution. When our attitudes and thoughts change, our actions follow close behind.

A FOUNTAIN OF LOVE

The Bible says that God is love. Human love is an intense affection for another person that is based on feelings and can change at any given moment, but agape love is unconditional; it is based on God's nature. God's nature is consistent, and so is His love for us. The best example of the nature of God's love is the story of The Prodigal Son. The father's love did not change, even though his son left home, wasted his wealth, and ended up destitute. When he saw his son returning home, he ran to him and hugged him; that showed that he never stopped loving him. As followers of Christ, we can only give God's kind of love once we have received it ourselves. For me, the revelation ...

OUR TURN TO GIVE BACK

Love from God is expressed in so many ways. When we love with this great love of God, it comes out over and over. When His transforming love is made real in our daily lives, we are everything He wants us to be. Considering the magnitude and authenticity of the love of God which we receive, we express the same kind of love to people and circumstances around us.

Romans 12:10: *Be devoted to one another in love. Honour one another above yourselves.*

Matthew 22:37 – 39: Jesus replied: *"'Love the Lord your God with all your heart and with all your soul and with all your mind.' This is the first and greatest commandment. And the second is like it: 'Love your neighbour as yourself.'*

Is there someone in your life right now who is trouble for you? It could be a co-worker or a boss, a child or a mate, a friend or foe. You know what they need? Love! I know they are probably not very lovable, but that does not change the fact that they need love. What could you do today to show love to that person – undeserved, unconditional love? Maybe it is a phone call or a note or a gift or a listening ear. Maybe it is a lack of criticism and condemnation, a willingness to love them as they are, in their unlovable condition.

However, here is the roadblock that we often encounter: How can you love someone when you do not feel it? How can you show love when someone does not love you back; when they are not lovable, when they may not deserve your love? This is where God's love in us has to kick in, and the good news is God's kind of love is expressed in actions, not necessarily in feelings.

In 1 Corinthians 13, we have the definitive description of how you love someone, whether you feel it or not. We are given specific actions and behavior that we can choose to exhibit whether or not we feel them. Consider these love actions:

➢ *Love is patient and kind.* Does patience come easy for you? It does not for me; but when you and I choose to be patient with someone, we are showing love. When we are kind to someone who is not kind to us, we love them. You do it by choice, not by feelings, but you do it and it is credited to you as love.

➢ *Love does not envy or boast; it is not arrogant or rude.* Well, that's pretty practical and down to earth, isn't it? For example, if you hear that your friend just got a raise or a great new job or a new house or got married, and you choose to rejoice with them instead of envying them, you have chosen to love them. If you intentionally refrain from boasting about yourself or your accomplishments, you love others. If you are not rude to that person who just cut in line in front of you, even though you want to say something, you have chosen the path of love.

➢ *Love does not rejoice in wrongdoing but rejoices with the truth.* This pretty much eliminates gossip, doesn't it? A loving person simply does not get any joy in passing along bad news about other people, but instead assumes the best instead of the worst and is never part of gossip or malicious talk.

➢ *Love bears all things, believes all things, hopes all things, and endures all things.* Love simply hangs in there with people, never giving up, always hoping for the best, listening when you don't want to listen anymore, believing that God can turn any person, any situation around.

I encourage you; indeed, I challenge you to read 1 Corinthians 13 every day for a month. Just begin each day reading this incredible definition of what true love is and what you can do every day to be a lover of people. It would take you maybe five minutes to read it, and likely memorize it after thirty days, and it will transform your thinking. Learning to see love as actions, not feelings will make a huge difference in you, and it will transform the way you see others, which will in turn transform the way you treat others, as well as the way they respond and react to you. It could start a "trickle-down effect" that will astonish you.

I find that I must become intentional about expressing love; I must remember to do it. I often take for granted the love I receive from others, my family, and friends without focusing on the expressions of love they need from me. Love is transformational and we can become God's agents of change to people in our lives by simply taking time each day to give love and love can be given in many ways, as we have seen from 1 Corinthians 13:

> If I speak in the tongues[a] of men or of angels, but do not have love, I am only a resounding gong or a clanging cymbal. 2 If I have the gift of prophecy and can fathom all mysteries and all knowledge, and if I have a faith that can move mountains, but do not have love, I am nothing. 3 If I give all I possess to the poor and give over my body to hardship that I may boast, [b] but do not have love, I gain nothing."

Here is how you can start practicing love and becoming an intentional lover. It begins when you allow God's love for you to fill up the emptiness inside you. When your need to be loved is met as you understand more that your identity is found in Jesus' love for you. When you daily remind yourself that you are the one Jesus loves. That is what gives you value and significance. Knowing you are loved by the one true God, gives you the ability to love others, and in turn receive their love which comes back to you. So, not only does God's love fill you up and satisfy you, but as you start giving love to others, that love comes back to you and fills you up, so that you are overflowing with the knowledge that God loves you and you are enriched by the love you receive from others. Who is in your life today? How can you give them love? Here are some suggestions:

➤ Purpose in your heart to find something good about that person or people in your life today and express it in words to them.

➤ Listen to someone's story without criticizing or lecturing them even without giving advice.

➤ Call someone who is needy and say, "I'm here for you if you need me."

➤ Compliment someone on a job well done, an attractive outfit, a kindness offered.

➤ Smile!

It does not take much to share love with someone else. We just must remember to do it. So, of course, we need to pray that God will help us to become lovers; people who willingly and frequently share his love with others. Remember, love begets love. Try it!

Let me share one more truly incredible truth about God's love for you, from Romans 8:

Who shall separate us from the love of Christ? Shall trouble or hardship or persecution or famine or nakedness or danger or sword? As it is written "For your sake we face death all day long; we are considered as sheep to be slaughtered." No, in all these things we are more than conquerors through him who loved us. For I am convinced that neither death nor life, neither angels nor demons, neither the present nor the future, nor any powers, neither height nor depth, nor anything else in all creation, will be able to separate us from the love of God that is in Christ Jesus our Lord.

As God's love becomes more and more real to you, through Jesus Christ and what He has done for you to redeem you, you will become more and more able to love others. Love is powerful. It never fails. So, I hope you will bask more in the all-surpassing good news that God loves you and nothing can separate you from His love. Then you will become more and more intentional about loving others. It has the power to transform you, your relationships, your attitude, your productivity, love transforms us. Believe me, it's true.

MY PASSION: For over 25 years of intimate walk with the Lord, the Holy Spirit is continually transforming my eyes to see the invisible, ears to hear the inaudible, hands to touch the intangible and my heart to comprehend the incomprehensible. As a change agent, my ultimate desire is to extend the blueprint of what a transformed person, marriage, family, professional, business, nation, Kingdom, and globe look like. My passion is a Call to Action.

This uncommon passion is inspired by prominent Bible characters who were agents of change and transformation. Their lives and service to God are mirrored in different modules of this book. They are:

Abraham: A righteous man who lived a prosperous and active life. He was so faithful that he agreed to sacrifice his only son to God.

Deborah: Prophetess, Apostle, Virtuous Woman, Spiritual Mother, and Intercessor

Daniel: Bold, Courageous and Devoted to God regardless; wise Kingdom political hero and prophetic diplomat

Joseph: A man of divine governmental authority/administrator

Mary: Chaste, Consecrated and set apart for special use

CHANGE MY WORLD OPPORTUNITIES INCLUDE:

➢ Legislate, repeal, and replace unrighteous laws in the Courts of Heaven

➢ Ongoing Possession of the gates of every community, nation, and institution where I dwell/work

➤ Pulling Down and demolishing every existing ungodly altars everywhere I dwell/work

➤ Raising Godly altars at every place/institutions where I dwell/work

➤ Pioneer Moral Instructions for educators/students

➤ Initiate/supervise Character Building Clubs in School

➤ Ongoing Prayer/intercession to maintain the presence of God

➤ Providing spiritual support for colleagues, students, and their parents.

➤ Spreading the love of Jesus Christ and modelling compassion.

➤ Champion peaceful rallies to speak up against injustice

➤ Distributed, collected, and submitted signed petitions to stand up for righteousness and justice

➤ Regular small group prayer, Bible study and fellowship in the marketplace

As a change agent, my ultimate desire is to extend the blueprint of what a transformed person, marriage, family, professional, business, nation, Kingdom, and globe look like. My passion is to call you, the reader to action.

The Institute of Discipleship and Transformation has developed a divinely inspired system to repair these damages and achieve a mindset change in order to raise sons and daughters of righteousness in every sphere of the society.

Vision–Transform active followers of Christ into resilient leaders, and metamorphose them into dynamic, radical change agents who will bring forth the Kingdom of God here on earth.

Mission Statement–We inspire and embolden current and future generations to discover and unleash their true God-given potential and leadership ability through discipleship, coaching, mentorship, personal development, and prayer.

What if we all cared about transforming our culture? What if we take dominion over the educational system like we are supposed to? What about enthroning Jesus Christ as head over every sphere of influence in our society? We must come into agreement and unity like never.

What if we collaborate with one another? How about professionals, intercessors and prophets hearing the current Word of the Lord about the strategic plans and blueprint He wants to download for our domain of society? Clarity is Power! Action cures fear!

ANSWER THESE QUESTIONS TO GET YOU STARTED:

1. What makes you upset that stirs up "holy anger" in your spirit? The injustice you see in the world that burdens your spirit.

2. What breaks your heart? The compassion you have deep inside; it has to be heart-centered.

3. What is the big problem you want to solve? It has to stem from who you are.

God is saying, dream again! He has plans that you are the most qualified to pursue to change the world system within your sphere. This is a call for true Disciples of Christ everywhere, students, moms, dads, teenagers, young adults, children, and grandparents, everyone, to come together. We can all be a part of this change.

MY MOTTO: Togetherness and Collaboration–If you want to go fast, go alone but, if you want to go far, go together! One is too small to achieve greatness, team work makes the dream work.

I see a great company of:

> Faithful Fathers like Abraham–All father figures: biological, spiritual, Foster, adoption, potential

> Men like Joseph–Divine Governmental Authority/ Administrators

> Women like Deborah–Prophetess, Apostle, Mothers in our nations, Virtuous wives, singles, grandmothers, spiritual mothers, and intercessors

> Young Men like Daniel – Bold, Courageous and devoted to God regardless, wise Kingdom political hero, prophetic diplomats

> Young Women like Mary – Chaste, Consecrated and set apart for special use.

OUTCOME – WHAT IS IN IT FOR ME YOU MAY WONDER…?

> Discover the Creator's divine motivation, design, and mandate for His creation and your role in that

creation. After reading this manual and obtaining your Discipleship certificate, you will be equipped with the knowledge to answer some of the questions addressing the heart cries of humanity in our search for a better world. Is there hope for mankind? This handbook will address that concern as well as:

➢ Reintroduce the concepts, principles, and nature of true authentic kingdom worldview as presented by the Creator.

➢ Show the superior and advantageous nature of the Kingdom as compared to any religion, political ideology, government system, or social program.

➢ Explore and understand the precepts and principles of the Kingdom.

➢ You will be helped to identify your gift and or talent, use it within your sphere of influence so that you can fulfill the specific and unique purpose why God endowed you in this season.

➢ Accomplish your unique part in obedience to the Great Commission as we are preparing for the biggest harvest the world has ever seen.

➢ You will practically experience the Kingdom of God being established in/with/through you.

➢ Create a biblical alignment of leaders for redeeming the culture of our local society.

➢ Coaching leaders to live and work in alignment with their purpose and values, enabling them to re-ignite passion and bring out the best in themselves and others.

➢ Working with team members to strengthen their relationships and collaborate creatively across differences.

> Enabling leaders to make strategic decisions to overcome challenges, manage change and fulfill their organizational mission.

> The secret to a full and fulfilled life is discovery, understanding, and application of the Kingdom of Heaven on earth. God's desire for you is that you enter the Kingdom life now and experience, explore, apply, practice, and enjoy living with the benefits, promises, and privileges of Heaven on earth. Let the adventure begin!

THE FACT:

> A good number of Spirit-filled committed believers are in every sphere of life.

> Most of them are completely dissatisfied with how ungodliness and evil have prevailed so far from the top.

> Many earnestly desire for a change which they individually feel incapable of effecting.

THE TRUTH:

> You are called to impact your culture thereby influencing the whole society for Christ.

> You are an embodiment of solution to the world's challenges.

> There is a destiny only you can fulfill.

> If only believers would disregard our personal interest, yield to the Holy Spirit and network with other believers, we can take dominion over every area of our society.

> The Lord is set to raise global marketplace ministers who understand and will discharge their everyday job/career as a ministry.

- ➤ There is no such thing as a part-time Christian as we have erroneously believed. We are all in full-time ministry, on a divine assignment or project to administer. Each believer associated with any of these spheres is placed there for the transformation of your domain.

- ➤ The Kingdom of God must work in you first, before it can work through you to affect your environment.

- ➤ From the Lord's point of view, there is no difference between being called to be a pastor and a businessman, a nurse, farmer, teacher, lawyer, artist, doctor, social worker, and a host of other professions.

- ➤ In addition to praying for transformation and revolution in the society, it is time to live it. YOU ARE A PARTAKER! JOIN A COMPANY TODAY!

PART 1

SUITABLE FOR ALL COMPANY

MODULE 1

DEFINE THE PROBLEMS

Proverbs 6:9-10, Matthew 13:24-28a, Proverbs 24: 30-32

WORLDVIEW: A WORLDVIEW IS A BELIEF system about reality; what is good, what is important, what is sacred, what is real. The values and behaviors of a culture stem directly from its worldview.

WHAT WORLDVIEW IS DIRECTING THE CHRISTIAN COMMUNITY IN OUR GENERATION?

One great concern is that the professing church has drifted into a salvation-focused gospel rather than a kingdom-focused gospel. Salvation, of course, is deeply and eternally important, but salvation is not the goal of the Christian life; it is just the beginning of it. Through Christ, we are heirs of the kingdom of God. A strategic look at scripture reveals that from the beginning, God created mankind to be the earthly stewards of his kingdom. It is essential we understand this. God's kingdom is his authority. It is his rule, lordship, and sovereignty. It is the reality that God is the creator and king of all things. The centrality of the kingdom of God is evident by the fact that when Jesus announced His ministry, He proclaimed the good news that the time had arrived for God to re-establish his kingdom on planet earth.

Jesus came into Galilee, preaching the gospel of God, saying, 'The time is fulfilled, and the kingdom of God is at hand; repent and believe in the gospel. Mark 1.14-15.

Many tend to think the gospel is primarily the message of salvation. It is the good news that the kingdom of God has come in the person and ministry of Jesus. Obviously, salvation is an integral and essential element of the gospel, but it is only a part. The central focus of the gospel is the kingdom of God.

Jesus did not bring the kingdom to save us; rather, he saved us so that we can serve the kingdom. Salvation is for a purpose. Jesus came to live in us and through us so that we can serve as heirs and agents of his kingdom. We were saved to reflect his character and represent his kingdom in everything we do. We were saved to make a difference in the world.

Christians individually and corporately as the church are to live and work in a manner that makes God and his kingdom known to a watching world. As a supernatural community of redeemed and transformed people, the church is called to be the living example of the presence of the kingdom. We are called to be the earthly embodiment of the love and lordship of Jesus Christ.

To help us see this great truth, here is a big picture view of how the kingdom plays a central role in God's purpose and plan. It can be summarized in four key actions:

> ➤ **Creation:** The kingdom is established, and life is given.

> ➤ **Fall:** The kingdom is rejected, and life is lost.

> ➤ **Redemption:** The kingdom is re-established, and life is restored.

> *Transformation:* The kingdom is at work in and through the Christian community. Christians live life and do work as agents of the kingdom of God.

The challenge is that the church has traditionally focused on the fall and redemption but has largely ignored creation and transformation. One of the consequences of the neglect of creation and transformation is that the Christian community embraces being redeemed from the fall, but we are not nearly as committed to being stewards of creation and agents of change. Not surprisingly, managing creation and being agents of transformation require hard work, whereas receiving redemption is mostly a matter of "faith." But when removed from the context of the whole plan, receiving redemption can become very self-oriented and out of alignment with authentic biblical faith.

It is critically important to understand that the gospel is more than redemption. We must not get stuck on salvation. We must not tell a half-gospel. We must not be directed by a half-story. We must not follow an abridged version. We must be faithful to declare and live out the whole story of God's plan for planet earth.

Christ's death and resurrection not only save us from something, but also restore us to something. In Christ, God redeems us from sin, restores his image in us, and calls us to be agents of the work of his kingdom during a fallen and broken world. Being saved is not the goal of the Christian life. Rather, being saved is the beginning of our participation in God's work of restoration and transformation in our lives and in the world until Jesus returns.

"For by grace you have been saved through faith. And this is not your own doing; it is the gift of God, not a result of works, so that no one may boast. For we are his workmanship, created in Christ Jesus for good works, which God prepared beforehand, that we should walk in them." (Ephesians 2.8-10

So, while the church, the ecclesia sleeps, the devil is damaging souls with the world system. An occultist, who died 65 years ago, crafted

5

a strategy and the system she designed is still dragging people to hell till today.

Alice Bailey is known as one of the founders of the New Age Movement. She was a writer who lived between 1880 and 1949 and she is the person who is known for creating the term "New Age" in her books which mostly focus on the subject of theosophy.

Britannica describes theosophy as *"an occult movement originating in the 19th century with roots that can be traced to ancient Gnosticism. The term theosophy is derived from the Greek theos ("god") and sophia ("wisdom") and is generally understood to mean "divine wisdom." ... The international New Age movement ... originated among independent theosophical groups "*

Alice Bailey is known as one of the prophetesses of the New Age Movement. Her teachings and writings are viewed as foundational and authoritative within the New Age Movement. She described most of her work as having been telepathically dictated to her by a Master of Wisdom, or spirit entity identified as Djwal Khul.

1 Timothy 4:1
Now the Spirit expressly says that in later times some will depart from the faith by devoting themselves to deceitful spirits and teachings of demons.

This bible verse reveals that mankind can receive teachings from demons or deceitful spirits. Since Alice Bailey claimed to receive inspiration for her New Age / theosophy writings from a spirit being by the name of Djwal Khul, it is evident there is a demonic inspiration to the New Age philosophies and practices.

Part of the main agenda of the New Age Movement is to become the dominant religion or lifestyle within the entire world. Therefore, for New Age philosophies to become dominant, then all other religions, especially Christianity, must either be destroyed or become less of a spiritual influence within society and in the individual lives of people. It is from this desire to see the dominance of the New Age movement that Alice Bailey wrote a 10-Point Plan / Charter to destroy Christianity so that New Age philosophies may become the one world religion for the world.

The main purpose of the 10-Point Charter / Strategy is to either destroy Christianity or to convert the nations to New Age philosophies.

The 10-Point Charter by Alice Bailey is as follows:

1. Take God and Prayer Out of The Education System

2. Reduce Parental Authority Over the Children

3. Destroy the Judeo-Christian Family Structure or The Traditional Christian Family Structure

4. If Sex Is Free, Then Make Abortion Legal and Make It Easy

5. Make Divorce Easy and Legal, Free People from The Concept of Marriage for Life

6. Make Homosexuality an Alternative Lifestyle

7. Debase Art, Make It Run Mad

8. Use Media to Promote and Change Mindsets

9. Create an Interfaith Movement

10. Get Governments to Make All These Law and Get the Church to Endorse These Changes.

Let us bear in mind that the above 10-Point Plan was formulated in the early 20th Century; many decades before such a strategy was even conceivable within culture and society at the time.

If one makes an objective observation, it would be easy to conclude that this 10-Point Plan is being implemented at the highest cultural, spiritual, and political levels within the world.

Why? Probably because Alice Bailey is regarded by New Agers and occultists as one of the "prophetesses" of the New Age Movement.

Ephesians 6:12 says: *For we do not wrestle against flesh and blood, but against the rulers, against the authorities, against the cosmic powers over this present darkness, against the spiritual forces of evil in the heavenly places.*

In this module, we will try to unpack the 10-point charter as well as find out what the Bible has to say about each. As God's legislators, my team and I carried out prophetic actions and made some specific declarations regarding this charter as the Lord instructed us by a word of prophesy. In this module, we will continue declaring and enacting the changes we want to see in every facet of our society. A great eye opener, it is all about creating awareness and making the average believer become cognizant of this Charter, as well as informing others in their circle of influence. Suggestions and recommendations of how trainees will apply their knowledge in various organizations will be included. In addition, participants will be fully equipped, empowered to respond, and deal with the Charter, using the appropriate spiritual tools. In other words, they will receive a tool kit that will remain relevant in handling similar issues in the future.

Let us take a closer look at the 10-point charter, find out what the Bible has to say about each, as well as recommend strategies to reverse them.

POINT #1: TAKE GOD AND PRAYER OUT OF THE EDUCATION SYSTEM

She said: "Change the curriculum to ensure that children are freed from the bondage of Christian culture. Why? Because children go to school to be equipped to face life, they are willing to trust and value what is being given to them. If you take God out of education, they will unconsciously form a resolve that God is not necessary to face life". They will focus on those things the school counts worthy to be passed on and they will look at God as an additional, if one can afford the additional".

The attempt to remove God and prayer out of the education system is a spiritual attack on the young generation. It is the devil's attempt to change the minds of the young and lead them away from God and from prayer. Instead, we notice that teachings such as the theory of evolution are taught to children to remove the concept of God from children's minds. Today, they introduce transcendental Meditation (TM) in schools which takes children to altered states of consciousness to meet with demons (spiritual guides) of New Age. As of the year 2020, the children of our nations are inundated with liberal ideologies, atheistic teaching, and postmodern principles in our public schools and in most universities (including many Christian institutions). Put simply; they are being indoctrinated with often false, biased, and anti-biblical information.

REVERSE–BRING GOD AND PRAYER BACK INTO THE EDUCATION SYSTEM

At one time, the education system unapologetically incorporated the Bible, prayer to the God of the Bible, and biblical values in every aspect of school life. Not coincidentally, this system produced a people that produced the most powerful and prosperous nation the earth has ever seen. A re-introduction of biblical truth and Bible-centric values is the key to renewal and restoration in our failing educational system. **Proverbs 9:10** says:

The reverent fear of the Lord (that is worshiping Him and regarding Him as truly awesome) is the beginning and preeminent part of wisdom (its starting point and its essence), and the knowledge of the Holy One is understanding and spiritual insight.

The Bible is clear that prayer is essential in the life of every human being. We have access to God 24 hours a day and 7 days a week. The Bible says that we should "pray without ceasing" (1 Thessalonians 5:17). What if we take dominion over the educational system like we are supposed to? What about enthroning Jesus Christ as head over our Education sector? We must come into agreement and unity like never. What if we helped each other? How about professionals, intercessors and prophets hearing the current Word of the Lord about the strategic plans and blueprint He wants to download? God is saying: Dream again! He has plans that you are the most qualified to take up to change the educational system in your region. This is a call for the educators everywhere, as well as students, moms, dads, and grandparents to come together. We can all be a part of this change.

POINT #2: REDUCE PARENTAL AUTHORITY OVER THE CHILDREN

She said: "Break the communication between parent and child."

(Why?) So that parents do not pass on their Christian traditions to their children and liberate children from the bondage of their parent's traditions.

(How?) **2a: Promote excessive child rights; Child rights legislation** – UNICEF Charter; Today a child is able to say to parent 'I do not want to hear that; I don't want to (or have to) do what you are telling me. If you beat me, I will call child protection services.

(1997-1998 South Africa introduced Child rights legislation – UNICEF Charter; Teachers cannot talk to children, children step up and say I have my rights, you cannot talk to me like that). Reducing parental authority over children is an attack on the family.

Proverbs 13:24 says:

Whoever spares the rod hates his son, but he who loves him is diligent to discipline him.

When parental authority is undermined and reduced, this will gradually create an undisciplined young generation that does not respect authority. Respect for authority by children begins at parental level. It is therefore the responsibility of parents to exercise godly or Biblical authority over their children and to also train the children in the values and principles of the Lord (Proverbs 22:6). There is the need to restore parental responsibility to exercise Godly authority over their children.

2B) ABOLISH CORPORAL PUNISHMENT

Abolish corporal punishment; (this has been made law). On the other hand, the Bible says *'Do not withhold correction from a child, for if you punish them with a rod, they will not die. Punish them with the rod and save them from death.'* (Proverbs 23: 13-14) Educators are no longer able to discipline children physically [in some cases by talking to them either]. NOTE: Jesus said in the last days – wickedness will increase, there will be rebellion and children will not obey their parents. It is not a trend-it is organized (Matt 10:21) (this has been made law).

2C) SCHOOLS ARE THE AGENTS OF IMPLEMENTATION (because where do most children spend most of their awake time?) – Teachers tell children "You need to discover yourself"; self-expression, self-realization, self-fulfillment are all buzz words. Teachers tell children, "Your parent has no right to force you to pray or read the Bible, you are yourself, and have a right of your own. In the West, at a very young age, the system, through the teachers, begins to teach to the child "you have a right to choose whether you want to follow the faith of your parents or not, parents are not allowed to enforce their faith upon you." Question is, what type of decision can a child make?

REVERSE: RE-ESTABLISH/INCREASE PARENTAL AUTHORITY OVER THE CHILDREN

PARENTS HAVE A GOD-GIVEN AUTHORITY OVER THEIR CHILDREN

In the Bible, parents have the responsibility of raising children; they have a God-given authority over their children. The fifth commandment requires a child to honour their father and mother (Exodus 20:12). This was quoted by Jesus and by the Apostle Paul. Parents are expected to exercise loving discipline over their children. As part of this, most parents use physical chastisement such as smacking. Discipline can be progressive, loving and must not be harsh. Fathers are asked to instruct children according to what is good and not to exasperate their children.

Ephesians 6:4 says:

Fathers, do not provoke your children to anger [do not exasperate them to the point of resentment with demands that are trivial or unreasonable or humiliating or abusive; nor by showing favoritism or indifference to any of them], but bring them up [tenderly, with lovingkindness] in the discipline and instruction of the Lord.

That discipline can be painful is clearly accepted in Scripture.

Hebrews 12:7-11 says:

You must submit to [correction for the purpose of] discipline; God is dealing with you as with sons; for what son is there whom his father does not discipline? [8] Now if you are exempt from correction and without discipline, in which all [of God's children] share, then you are illegitimate children and not sons [at all]. [9] Moreover, we have had earthly fathers who disciplined us, and we submitted and respected them [for training us]; shall we not much more willingly submit to the Father of spirits, and live [by learning from His discipline]? [10] *For our earthly fathers disciplined us for only a short time as seemed best to them; but He disciplines us for our good, so that we may share His holiness. 11 For the time being no discipline brings joy but seems sad and painful; yet to those who have been trained by it, afterwards it yields the peaceful fruit of righteousness* [right standing with God and a lifestyle and attitude that seeks conformity to God's will and purpose]. **Hebrews 12:10-11**

However, attempts to make the administration of reasonable chastisement a criminal offence should be strongly resisted as should other moves which usurp the authority of parents. Christians ought particularly to be concerned by any proposals which weaken the moral protections for children. Jesus gave a serious warning of judgment against those who cause children to sin (Matthew 18:6). This is an apt warning in these days when children have their innocence stolen from them.

POINT #3: DESTROY THE JUDEO-CHRISTIAN FAMILY STRUCTURE OR THE TRADITIONAL CHRISTIAN FAMILY STRUCTURE

She said: "Liberate the people from the confines of this structure. It is oppressive and the family is the core of the nation. If you break the family, you break the nation."

WHY: So that the youth will not grow up with a sense of belonging, identity, or structure.

HOW: A) PROMOTE SEXUAL PROMISCUITY – free young people to the concept of premarital sex, let them have free sex, lift it so high that the joy of enjoying it (sex) is the highest joy in life, fantasize it, that everybody will feel proud to be seen to be sexually active, even those outside of marriage. This is contrary to the word of God which says:

... But fornication and all uncleanness or covetousness, let it not even be named among you, as is fitting for saints... for this you know, that no fornicator, unclean person, nor covetous man, who is an idolater has any inheritance in the kingdom of Christ and God. Ephesians 5: 3-5.

3b): USE ADVERTISING INDUSTRY, MEDIA T.V., MAGAZINES, AND FILM INDUSTRY TO PROMOTE SEXUAL ENJOYMENT AS THE HIGHEST PLEASURE IN HUMANITY. (PROPAGANDA)

Have they succeeded? Have they done it? If you want to see whether they have succeeded or not, go to the advertising industry; it does everything to catch your attention and today almost no advert comes out without a sexual connotation Even when they advertise ice cream, they must show you the thigh of a woman and a bikini, they must do something to set off a trail of thoughts. They will show you more thighs than ice cream. Even cleaning supply is sexy these days! Why? Because that is what must be in the minds of the people.

There have been many blatant and subtle attempts to destroy the traditional Christian family. Examples are the promotion of sexual immorality which leads to a growth in teenage pregnancies, adultery, fornication, and the like. Sexual immorality destroys marriages, creates a growth in single mothers, and increases divorce rates.

Other examples include the promotion of same-sex marriages which are clear attempts to destroy the traditional Christian family.

The traditional Christian family structure is being destroyed. The families have been under constant and prolonged attack. Today, the assailants are fatherlessness, divorce (50% rate in secular and Christian marriages), abuse, homosexual marriage, pornography, and other negative influences have brought great dysfunction to the family life.

REVERSE: *GO BACK TO THE BIBLE AND REBUILD THE FAMILY STRUCTURE ACCORDING TO THE WORD OF GOD*

FAMILY -In any functional society, the family is the 'building block'. The family is the core of the nation and whatever breaks the family breaks the nation. Throughout the Bible, you will find familial examples that portray how we ought to live our lives today. God desires that men, women, and children within a family be united in His love. After all, He is the ultimate Father (Romans 8:14-17).

God is calling fathers and mothers (both spiritual and biological) to bring order to the chaos that the enemy has unleashed against families. He also wants to bring healing to marriages and relationships within families to maintain a moral foundation for children to stand upon in the future. The Bible teaches us that since the creation of the first man and first woman, marriage is between a male and a female (Genesis 2:18-25). Within the traditional Christian family, the husband has a role; the wife has a role and so do the children (Ephesians 5:22-33).

Since 2016, Family Prayer Network Canada has been empowering individuals and families to discover, activate, and operate at their maximum God-given potentials. Our mandate is to rescue, recover, reconcile, rebuild, reposition, and restore families to the original purpose of God. Our goals include:

- Keeping the church simple,

- Building strong Godly families,

15

- Linking every family to God,

- Raising God-fearing children,

- Networking the families together to form Godly communities,

- Networking the communities to form a strong Godly nation, and

- Networking the nations to form the kingdom of God; for righteousness, peace, joy in the Holy Ghost is the kingdom of God.

The family is the bedrock of the kingdom of God. So, join Family Prayer Network Canada today.

FACTORS OF SUCCESS IN RAISING CHILDREN– SUMMARY ABOUT JEWISH SUCCESS

Environment = 50% 1 Corinth 15:33 do not be misled: "Bad company corrupts good character."

Character = 40% Proverbs 22:1 choose a good reputation over great riches; being held in high esteem is better than silver or gold.

Knowledge = 10% Proverbs 18:15 -The heart of the prudent acquires knowledge, and the ear of the wise seeks knowledge.

GROWTH THROUGH PAIN: PEOPLE LEARN THROUGH PAIN- TWO TYPES OF PAIN WE LEARN FROM:

Voluntary Pain – self-inflicted for growth; this is the pain of discipline which is about 2 grams of weight.

Involuntary Pain–reality inflicted pain; this is the pain of regret for failing to discipline oneself which is equivalent to 2 tons of weight.

THE IMPORTANCE OF CREATING A GODLY ENVIRONMENT – COMPARE MAX JUKE AND JONATHAN EDWARDS' FAMILY LINEAGE:

In the early 1700s, two men started families: Jonathan Edwards and Max Juke.

JUKE: Was not a Christian and lived an ungodly life. He married a woman of similar character.

- 1,026 descendants' lives were studied: 300 died prematurely, 67 died of syphilis, 190 public prostitutes, 100 alcoholics, 280 lived in abject poverty, 140 received government aid, 150 were criminals of which 7 were murderers, and incarcerating 150 of them cost the state more than 1.2 million dollars. Juke himself made no contribution to society.

EDWARDS: Was a godly man and married a woman of like character.

- 729 of their descendants' lives were studied, 300 were ministers, 65 were college professors, 13 were university presidents, 60 authored books, 3 were Congressmen, and one was Vice President of the United States. The family has not cost the government a single dollar. Edwards was used to spearhead one of the most influential moves of God in American History, "The Great Awakening". The decisions we make today in our personal lives have a "Domino Effect" for years to come. What is going to be the "Domino Effect" of your marriage and family?

REVERSE: PROMOTE SEXUAL PURITY–WHAT DOES THE BIBLE SAY ABOUT SEXUAL PURITY?

God declares that sexual relations should be only for a man and a woman in a marriage and should stay between those married people for a lifetime. Ephesians 5:31 says:

For this reason, a man will leave his father and mother and be united to his wife, and the two will become one flesh.

God designed sex to be pleasurable, but also instructed that it is reserved for marriage. Despite what many cultures today advocate, sexual purity is for our own benefit. Within the boundaries of marriage, sex is a pleasurable and beautiful gift. Sexual activity outside of marriage is a perversion of something God made to be good. There are many Scriptural passages about sexual purity, but 1 Thessalonians 4:3–5, 7 summarizes much of God's directive on the subject: "For this is the will of God, that you be sanctified [separated and set apart from sin]: that you abstain and back away from sexual immorality; that each of you know how to control his own body in holiness and honor [being available for God's purpose and separated from things profane], not [to be used] in lustful passion, like the Gentiles who do not know God and are ignorant of His will…For God has not called us to impurity, but to holiness [to be dedicated, and set apart by behavior that pleases Him, whether in public or in private]".

Sanctification is being set apart for a holy reason for God's purposes. When we accept Jesus as our Savior, we are made holy and become a new creation (2 Corinthians 5:17–19). We can live by faith, instead of by our old sinful nature (Galatians 2:20).

The Bible seems to set the lack of sexual purity somewhat apart from other sins. In the first book of Timothy passage above, sexual purity is listed as the first evidence, or step of sanctification. Self-control over this aspect of life shows that we rely on and allow the Holy Spirit's work (Galatians 5:22–23). We are told to honor God with our bodies because they are the temple of the Holy Spirit (1 Corinthians 6:18–20). It is the Holy Spirit who helps us honor Him.

Sex joins two people as one. God knows this should be reserved for marriage. 1 Corinthians 6:15–18 asks:

Do you not know that your bodies are members of Christ? Shall I then take the members of Christ and make them members of a prostitute? Never! Or do you not know that he who is joined to a prostitute becomes one body with her? For, as it is written, 'The two will become one flesh.' But he who is joined to the Lord becomes one spirit with him. Flee from sexual immorality. Every other sin a person commits is outside the body, but the sexually immoral person sins against his own body.

God designed and created us, so He knows what is best for us. His rules, boundaries, and discipline are designed for our benefit and His glory. Sex is the most intimate and venerable of acts. This type of intimacy is precious within the committed relationship of a married man and woman. Remaining sexually pure protects that gift. Sexual purity is not only something those who are single need to be concerned about, but it is also intended for married couples to remain faithful to each other. Sex is unique to marriage, and sexual purity does much to maintain the integrity and strength of the marriage bond. No matter your marital state, we are all called to be sexually pure in both our actions and our thoughts. When we follow God's instruction about sexual purity, our lives and relationships will be better for us and honor Him, and our marriage bed will be kept pure (Hebrews 13:4).

POINT #4: IF SEX IS FREE, THEN MAKE ABORTION LEGAL AND MAKE IT EASY

She said "Build clinics for abortion: Health clinics in schools. If people are going to enjoy the joy of sexual relationships, they need to be free of unnecessary fears." In other words, they should not be hampered with unwanted pregnancies. 'Abortion as told by Christians is oppressive and denies our rights. We have a right to choose whether we want to have a child or not. If a woman does not want the pregnancy, she should have the freedom to get rid of that pregnancy as painless and as easy as possible'. Besides, if you carry the unwanted pregnancy, then give them up for adoption. That system is so unkind to them; so, just get rid of them and spare them that life and the hindering of yours. This also ties into the strategy to curb population control together with the use of condoms and 'pill'.

Today, it is not only accessible; it is legalized in most nations. Today, abortion is a strategy to reduce population, together with the use of condoms and 'pill'.

According to statistics, more than 40 million unborn babies are aborted every year around the world. This is clear evidence just by the statistics alone that abortion in this world has become easier and "convenient" due to its legality in many countries. But is abortion biblical? No! God does not support abortion. The Bible says that God knows us whilst we are in our mother's womb (Jeremiah 1:5). An unborn child is a unique person even though they temporarily reside in the mother's womb.

The promotion of sex through the media and the like has contributed to sexual immorality in the world. It has removed the principle that sex is only to be conducted within the confines of marriage. Sex outside of marriage which ironically is supported by Alice Bailey's 10-Point Strategy is likely to create more "unwanted" pregnancies which result in increased abortions which the 10-Point Strategy also supports. Pro-abortionists try to "dehumanize" unborn children by referring to them as merely "lumps of tissue" or "products of conception"; however, biblically, as well as biologically, you and I are unique human beings from the moment of conception. The result of conception (the "product" that is conceived) is known as a baby, as Scripture (and science) tells us:

The babies jostled each other within her. Genesis 25:22.

When Elizabeth heard Mary's greeting, the baby leaped in her womb. Luke 1:41.

Some abortion supporters go so far as to claim that early religions did not bar abortion; a claim that is contrary to the truth. God speaks very clearly on the value of the unborn in the Scriptures, the basis for both the Jewish and Christian faiths. An unborn baby is still a human life that God has created and which He values very much (Psalms 139:13-18). However, every year, more human lives (though unborn) die because of abortion alone, than any disease in the world.

REVERSE: *GO BACK TO THE BIBLE AND TEACH SEXUAL PURITY, VIRGINITY, AND CHASTITY.*

WHY SHOULD WE VALUE LIFE?

According to the Scriptures, Life is a gift created by God and is not to be taken away by abortion. God is "pro-choice," but He tells us clearly the only acceptable choice to make:

I have set before you life and death, blessings and curses. Now choose life, so that you and your children may live. Deuteronomy 30:19.

Know that the Lord Himself is God; it is He who has made us, and not we ourselves; we are His people and the sheep of His pasture Psalm 100:3.

Thus, says the Lord, your Redeemer, and the One who formed you from the womb, 'I, the Lord, am the maker of all things, stretching out the heavens by Myself, and spreading out the earth all alone... Isaiah 44:24.

But now, O Lord, thou art our Father, we are the clay, and Thou our potter; and all of us are the work of Thy hand Isaiah 64:8.

WHO IS THE CREATOR OF THE PREBORN?

"For you formed my inward parts; you covered me in my mother's womb. I will praise you, for I am fearfully and wonderfully made;

21

marvelous are your works and that my soul knows well. My frame was not hidden from you, when I was made in secret, and skillfully wrought in the lowest parts of the earth. Your eyes saw my substance, being yet unformed, and in your book they all were written, the days fashioned for me, when yet there were none of them" Psalm 139:13-16.

"Before I formed you in the womb, I knew you, before you were born, I set you apart; I appointed you as a prophet to the nations" Jeremiah 1:5.

ARE THE PREBORN HUMAN BEINGS?

"When Elizabeth heard Mary's greeting, the baby leaped in her womb, and Elizabeth was filled with the Holy Spirit... [Saying] 'As soon as the sound of your greeting reached my ears, the baby in my womb leaped for joy" Luke 1:41, 44.

The Lord Jesus Christ began his incarnation as an embryo, growing into a fetus, infant, child, teenager, and adult: "While they were there, the time came for the baby to born, and she gave birth to her firstborn, a son Luke 2:6-7.

WHO IS RESPONSIBLE FOR LIFE AND DEATH?

Then God spoke all these words, saying..."*You shall not murder"* Exodus 20:1, 13.

"I call heaven and earth to record this day against you, that I have set before you life and death, blessing and cursing: therefore, choose life, that both thou and thy seed may live" Deuteronomy 30:19.

ARE HUMANS PERMITTED TO TAKE LIFE
BEFORE BIRTH?

"If men who are fighting hit a pregnant woman and she gives birth prematurely but there is no serious injury, the offender must be fined

whatever the woman's husband demands and the court allows. But if there is serious injury, you are to take life for life, eye for eye, tooth for tooth, hand for hand, foot for foot, burn for burn, wound for wound, bruise for bruise" Exodus 21:22-25.

The Bible says of our Creator, "In His hand is the life of every living thing and the breath of every human being" (Job 12:10). God, the giver of life, commands us not to take the life of an innocent person: "Do not shed innocent blood" (Jeremiah 7:6), and He warns us, "Cursed is the man who accepts a bribe to kill an innocent person" (Deuteronomy 27:25). The Sixth Commandment, written in stone by the finger of God, commands, "You shall not murder" (Exodus 20:13).

God speaks very clearly on the value of the unborn in the Scriptures, the basis for the Christian faith. The unborn baby is undeniably alive and growing, and taking its life is clearly murder, as the prophet Jeremiah points out: "He did not kill me in the womb, with my mother as my grave" (Jeremiah 20:17). God vowed to punish those who "ripped open the women with child" (Amos 1:13). In ancient Israel, the unborn child was granted equal protection in the law; if he lost his life, the one who caused his death must lose his own life: "If men who are fighting hit a pregnant woman and she gives birth prematurely but there is no serious injury, the offender must be fined...But if there is serious injury, you are to take life for life" (Exodus 21:22,23).

SHOULD A CHILD WHO MIGHT BE BORN DEFORMED OR DISABLED BE ABORTED?

"So, the Lord said to him, 'Who has made man's mouth? Or who makes the mute, the deaf, the seeing, or the blind? Have not I, the Lord?'" Exodus 4:11.

"Woe to him who quarrels with his Maker, to him who is but a potsherd among the potsherds on the ground. Does the clay say to the potter, 'What are you making?' Does your work say, 'He has no

hands?' Woe to him who says to his father, 'What have you begotten?' or to his mother, 'What have you brought to birth?' This is what the Lord says the Holy One of Israel, and its Maker: Concerning things to come, do you question me about my children, or give me orders about the work of my hands?" Isaiah 45:9-11.

"Yet, to shame the wise, God has chosen what the world counts folly, and to shame what is strong, God has chosen what the world counts weakness" 1 Corinthians 1:27.

HOW SHOULD A WOMAN VIEW HER BODY AND THE PREBORN LIFE GROWING IN HER WOMB?

"Behold, children are a gift of the Lord; the fruit of the womb is a reward" Psalm 127:3.

"Or do you not know that your body is a temple of the Holy Spirit who is in you, whom you have from God, and that you are not your own? For you have been bought with a price: therefore, glorify God in your body" 1 Corinthians 6:19-20.

DOES GOD FORGIVE THOSE WHO HAVE HAD ABORTIONS?

"In Him we have redemption through His blood, the forgiveness of our trespasses, according to the riches of His grace." Ephesians 1:7.

"I, even I, am the one who wipes out your transgressions for my own sake; and I will not remember your sins" Isaiah 43:25.

POINT #5: MAKE DIVORCE EASY AND LEGAL; FREE PEOPLE FROM THE CONCEPT OF MARRIAGE FOR LIFE

She said: Love has got a mysterious link called the love bond. It is like an ovum that comes out of the ovary, as it travels through your system, it clicks a love favour in you and there is one other person in the world who can respond to that love bond. When you see that person, everything within you clicks, that is your man/woman. If you miss him, you will never be happy until that love bond cycles past, for many years; so, for you to be happy get that person at whatever cost. If it means getting them out of that marriage, get them. That is your man/woman. It is a mistake for them to be elsewhere. And if you go together for some time and find that love has died, do not be held in bondage by the Christian values. It will never come back. What you need is an easily arranged divorce and allow another love bond to come forth, just like an ovum comes up, and when it comes forth, you will enjoy life again.

WHY? So, the youth will not feel they must stay tied down to one person. This will also promote multiple sex partners. We must be free to enjoy life, not tied to one person for eternity. This will also produce broken homes and possibly broken children who will carry the brokenness forward.

HOW: Degrade the value of marriage over time. Decrease the difficulty of getting a divorce by advertising divorce law and making it an easy and understandable process to obtain one.

Note: People enter marriage, having signed contracts of how they will share their things after divorce. In other words, people enter with one foot and another behind. Divorce is way more common today than it was, say, 50 years ago. Marriage is now treated like a high school relationship – easy come, easy go! In the past, divorce was unthinkable. It is one thing for a marriage to fail but it is another thing for people to enter marriage with an intention to enjoy if it was enjoyable and to walk out of it, if not.

Divorce rates worldwide continue to rise. Indeed, as we look at our world today, the institution of marriage is no longer sacred or respected. Many couples continue to lose their sense of commitment to each other. Yet, the Bible says that God hates divorce (Malachi 2:16). Marriage parallels Christ's relationship with the Church. Jesus Christ is the bridegroom, and the Church is the bride (Ephesians 5:25-30). Therefore, an attack on marriage is an attack on God who created the institution of marriage. In the beginning, God created marriage when He created Adam and decided that it was not good for the man to be alone, but that man should have a helper comparable to him. This is why God created Eve and created marriage so that the man and woman would become one flesh (Genesis 2:18-25).

REVERSE: HOW SHOULD A CHRISTIAN VIEW MARRIAGE AND DIVORCE?

God, the Creator of humanity and of marriage itself, has laid out His plan for marriage as a lifelong union. God knows this design is the best. When we stray from His plan, as we have seen in the studies mentioned above, the results are damaging on many levels. Unfortunately, the divorce rate in the church is comparable to that of the society at large. Many Christians see nothing wrong with divorce, at least in their own situation. But the Bible clearly addresses marriage and divorce. Marriage is the first institution created by God. God made the first man, Adam, but declared that it was not good for Adam to be alone. He then brought to Adam all the animals, which Adam named, but "no companion suitable for him" was found (Genesis 2:20). God was revealing to Adam his incomplete nature. God then created a woman, Eve, for Adam. He blessed them and their union and gave them the earth to rule over. (Genesis 1:27-28). The creation of marriage occurred prior to the entrance of sin into the world. It was a part of God's perfect design for mankind.

Through the prophets, God emphasized three principles: Marriage is sacred, God hates divorce, and Marriage is designed to produce children of good character. (Malachi 2:13-16).

Jesus underscored the importance and sacredness of lifelong marriage in His own teachings. (Matthew 19:6).

The apostle Paul further taught that the marital relationship is to be an ongoing demonstration of the sacrificial love that Christ showed His church. (Ephesians 5:21-33).

Let us look at this issue more closely. Specifically, what does the Bible tell us about divorce? Malachi 2:13-16 gives us a clear look into God's heart for marriage:

Another thing you do: You flood the Lord's altar with tears. You weep and wail because he no longer pays attention to your offerings or accepts them with pleasure from your hands. You ask, "Why?" It is because the Lord is acting as the witness between you and the wife of your youth, because you have broken faith with her, though she is your partner, the wife of your marriage covenant. Has not the Lord made them one? In flesh and spirit, they are His. And why one? Because He was seeking godly offspring. So, guard yourself in your spirit, and do not break faith with the wife of your youth. "I hate divorce," says the Lord God of Israel.

Jesus Christ reiterated the importance and permanence of marriage. Matthew 19:3-6 says:

Some Pharisees came to Him to test Him. They asked, 'Is it lawful for a man to divorce his wife for any and every reason? Haven't you read, He replied, *that at the beginning the Creator 'made them male and female,' and said, for this reason a man will leave his father and mother and be united to his wife, and the two will become one flesh? So, they are no longer two, but one. Therefore, what God has joined together, let man not separate.*

This is because, says an attorney, "I've represented many people going through divorce, I understand why God says, "I hate it!" Divorce is the tearing apart of the foundation of all stable societies – the family. Sometimes, it is necessary. Sometimes, it is even unavoidable. (In Colorado, for example, if one spouse files for divorce, the other cannot stop it from occurring.) Nonetheless, it is important that we in the Body of Christ encourage those in troubled marriages to seek counseling and restoration because most divorces are neither necessary nor unavoidable.

But are there any cases in which the Bible *allows* divorce? Many Christians disagree about whether the Bible allows divorce and/or remarriage. If you are concerned about whether you have biblical grounds for divorce, you will need to commit the matter to prayer and study. You should also seek out counsel from an authentic God-fearing wise pastor and a licensed bible believing counselor. The question of sin cannot be taken lightly, but biblical grounds may exist:

> ➢ One spouse is guilty of sexual immorality and is unwilling to repent and live faithfully with the marriage partner. Jesus' words in Matthew 19:8-9 indicate that divorce (and remarriage) in this circumstance is acceptable. That passage reads: "Why then," [the Pharisees] asked, "did Moses command that a man give his wife a certificate of divorce and send her away?" Jesus replied, "Moses permitted you to divorce your wives because your hearts were hard. But it was not this way from the beginning. I tell you that anyone who divorces his wife, except for *marital unfaithfulness,* and marries [or, 'to marry'] another woman commits adultery." (Emphasis added) However, divorce is not *required.* If your spouse has committed adultery, divorce is morally *allowed,* but not required. Many couples have been able to rebuild their marriages even after such a devastating blow.

> ➢ When one spouse is not a Christian, and that spouse willfully and permanently deserts the Christian spouse (1 Corinthians 7:15).

According to Focus on the Family, divorce and remarriage appear to be justified in Scripture only in a few instances. There is a third instance in which they believe remarriage is acceptable in Scripture. That instance is when an individual's divorce occurred prior to salvation.

If you are a follower of Jesus Christ, please pray carefully about your decision to divorce, and be open to God's leading. (God's heart is to heal marriages.) If your spouse is the one deciding on divorce, you may not be able to stop him or her through current divorce laws. However, you can try to persuade your spouse to consider a legal separation first, which would give you both more time to consider the issue. Pray that God will open the lines of communication between you and your spouse and that He will restore the love in your relationship; pray for patience and a forgiving spirit. Try to resist the temptation to say angry words to your spouse or do things that would push him or her further away. Restoration does occur even in the most hostile circumstances, but it is more difficult when harsh words have passed between you.

DIVORCE & REMARRIAGE

God hates divorce. He hates it because it always involves unfaithfulness to the solemn covenant of marriage that two partners have entered into before Him, and because it brings harmful consequences to those partners and their children (Mal. 2:14-16). Divorce in the Scripture is permitted only because of man's sin. Since divorce is only a concession to man's sin and is not part of God's original plan for marriage, all believers should hate divorce as God does and pursue it only when there is no other recourse. With God's help, a marriage can survive the worst sins.

In Matthew 19:3-9, Christ teaches clearly that divorce is an accommodation to man's sin that violates God's original purpose for the intimate unity and permanence of the marriage bond (Gen. 2:24). He taught that God's law allowed divorce only because of "hardness of heart" (Matt. 19:8). Legal divorce was a concession for the faithful partner due to the sexual sin or abandonment by the sinning partner, so that the faithful partner was no longer bound to the marriage (Matt. 5:32; 19:9; 1 Cor. 7:12-15). Although Jesus did say that divorce is permitted in some situations, we must remember that His primary point in this discourse is to correct the Jews' idea that they could divorce one another "for any cause at all" (Matt.

19:3), and to show them the gravity of pursuing a sinful divorce. Therefore, the believer should never consider divorce except in specific circumstances, and even in those circumstances it should only be pursued reluctantly because there is no other recourse.

THE POSSIBILITY OF REMARRIAGE

Remarriage is permitted for the faithful partner only when the divorce was on biblical grounds. In fact, the purpose for a biblical divorce is to make clear that the faithful partner is free to remarry, but only in the Lord (Rom. 7:1-3; 1 Cor. 7:39).

Those who divorce on any other grounds have sinned against God and their partners, and for them to marry another is an act of "adultery" (Mark 10:11-12). This is why Paul says that a believing woman who sinfully divorces should "remain unmarried, or else be reconciled to her husband" (1 Cor. 7:10-11). If she repents from her sin of unbiblical divorce, the true fruits of that repentance would be to seek reconciliation with her former husband (Matt. 5:23-24). The same is true for a man who divorces his wife in an unbiblical manner (1 Cor. 7:11). The only time such a person could remarry another is if the former spouse remarries, proves to be an unbeliever, or dies, in which cases reconciliation would no longer be possible.

The Bible also gives a word of caution to anyone who is considering marriage to a divorcee. If the divorce was not on biblical grounds and there is still a responsibility to reconcile, the person who marries the divorcee is considered an adulterer (Mark 10:12).

THE ROLE OF THE CHURCH (ECCLESIA)

Believers who pursue divorce on unbiblical grounds are subject to church discipline because they openly reject the Word of God. The one who obtains an unbiblical divorce and remarries is guilty of adultery since God did not permit the original divorce (Matt. 5:32; Mark 10:11-12). That person is subject to the steps of church discipline as outlined in <u>Matthew 18:15-17</u>. If a professing Christian violates the marriage covenant and refuses to repent during the process of church discipline, Scripture instructs that he or she should be put out of the church and treated as an unbeliever (v. 17). When the discipline results in such a reclassification of the disobedient spouse as an "outcast" or unbeliever, the faithful partner would be free to divorce according to the provision for divorce as in the case of an unbeliever departing, as stated in <u>1 Corinthians 7:15</u>. Before such a divorce, however, reasonable time should be allowed for the possibility of the unfaithful spouse returning because of the discipline.

The leadership in the local church should also help single believers who have been divorced to understand their situation biblically, especially in cases where the appropriate application of biblical teaching does not seem clear. For example, the church leadership may at times need to decide whether one or both of the former partners could be legitimately considered "believers" at the time of their past divorce, because this will affect the application of biblical principles to their current situation (<u>1 Cor. 7:17-24</u>). Also, because people often transfer to or from other churches and many of those churches do not practice church discipline, it might be necessary for the leadership to decide whether a member's estranged or former spouse should currently be considered a Christian or treated as an unbeliever because of continued disobedience. Again, in some cases, this would affect the application of the biblical principles (<u>1 Cor. 7:15</u>; <u>2 Cor. 6:14</u>).

PRE-CONVERSION DIVORCE

According to <u>1 Corinthians 7:20-27</u>, there is nothing in salvation that demands a particular social or marital status. The Apostle Paul, therefore, instructs believers to recognize that God providentially allows the circumstances they find themselves in when they come to Christ. If they were called while married, then they are not required to seek a divorce (even though divorce may be permitted on biblical grounds). If they were called while divorced, and cannot be reconciled to their former spouse because that spouse is an unbeliever or is remarried, then they are free to either remain single or be remarried to another believer (1 Cor. 7:39; 2 Cor. 6:14).

REPENTANCE AND FORGIVENESS

In cases where divorce took place on unbiblical grounds and the guilty partner later repents, the grace of God is operative at the point of repentance. A sign of true repentance will be a desire to implement 1 Corinthians 7:10-11, which would involve a willingness to pursue reconciliation with his or her former spouse, if that is possible. If reconciliation is not possible, however, because the former spouse is an unbeliever or is remarried, then the forgiven believer could pursue another relationship under the careful guidance and counsel of church leadership.

In cases where a believer obtained a divorce on unbiblical grounds and remarried, he or she is guilty of the sin of adultery until that sin is confessed (Mark 10:11-12). God does forgive that sin immediately when repentance takes place, and there is nothing in Scripture to indicate anything other than that. From that point on, the believer should continue in his or her current marriage.

POINT #6: MAKE HOMOSEXUALITY AN ALTERNATIVE LIFESTYLE

She said: Enjoying sexual intercourse is the highest pleasure in humanity. No one must be denied or restricted in how to enjoy themselves. People should be allowed to experience sex, however they want, whether it is homosexuality, incest, or bestiality, as long as the two agree.

WHY: To demolish the restraint of tradition that establishes sex between a man and woman, to further the agenda of population control, to abolish creation roles and to incorporate the satanic Mantra "do what thou wilt".

HOW: Preach tolerance and acceptance. Give the homosexuals a voice in numbers, as the numbers grow tolerance and acceptance will too. Pass laws and implement legislation that legalize gay marriage and shun "hate speech". Silence the voice of the preacher in the pulpit through 501c3. Put it everywhere it is now forbidden on TV, on billboards, in church. Advertise it! Encourage foods that increase estrogens in males (like soy). Males will no longer grow to be strong fathers in a traditional home as they will have no desire.

Alice Bailey preached (over 65 years ago) that sexual enjoyment is the highest pleasure in humanity; no one must be denied, and no one must be restricted how to enjoy themselves. People should be allowed in whichever way they want, whether it is homosexuality or in incest or bestiality, as long as the two agree. In the world today, so many laws have been made that promote homosexuality and give so much freedom to gay rights, that a time will come when it is illegal for a preacher to mention homosexuality as an abomination in the eyes of God, or to read scriptures publicly that talk about homosexuality. On the international scene, Western nations now sanction African countries that have resisted homosexuality, with threats of withdrawing foreign aid and investments. Today, many churches marry gays/lesbians and ordain gay priests. According to the Bible, this is an abomination before the eyes of God.

"Thou shalt not lie with mankind, as with womankind: it [is] abomination." Leviticus 18:22.

"If a man also lies with mankind, as he lieth with a woman, both of them have committed an abomination: they shall surely be put to death; their blood [shall be] upon them. Leviticus 20:13.

Even though Alice Bailey wrote her 10-Point Charter many decades before homosexuality became accepted by the world, the push to make homosexuality an alternative lifestyle has gained momentum. The gay rights movement is a very powerful movement in the world today.

Even churches are ordaining homosexuals as priests or pastors, thereby accepting homosexuality within the church itself. However, the Bible does not change; God's word remains the same in relation to sexual immorality and homosexuality.

BIBLICAL PERSPECTIVE ON HOMOSEXUALITY AND SAME-SEX MARRIAGE – FOCUS ON THE FAMILY INTERVIEW:

Question: Is it true that the Scriptures do not really have anything to say about homosexuality and the legalization of gay marriage? We have heard this argument advanced many times so often, in fact, that we have become seriously confused about the issue. What is your perspective?

Answer: As an evangelical Christian ministry committed to the authority of Scripture as the inspired Word of God, Focus on the Family believes that sex is given by God as an expression of love to be shared and enjoyed exclusively between a husband and wife. Further, we are convinced that the Bible leaves no room whatsoever for confusion or ambiguity where homosexual behavior is concerned. The Scripture both explicitly and implicitly regards it as falling outside of God's intention in creating man and woman as sexual beings that bear His image as male and female.

"There is no place for hatred, hurtful comments, or other forms of rejection toward those who experience same-sex attraction or identify themselves as gay, lesbian or bisexual."

To this, we would add the crucial observation that, here as elsewhere in the Christian life, the example and commandment of Christ places us under obligation to proclaim both God's truth *and* His redemptive grace. We must "speak the truth in love" (Ephesians 4:15). There is no place for hatred, hurtful comments, or other forms of rejection toward those who experience same-sex attraction or identify themselves as gay, lesbian, or bisexual. As humans, we are made in the image of God, Jesus teaches us to regard all humanity as having inherent value, worth and dignity, including those affirming or adopting labels or behaviours which we believe the Bible associates with sexual sin. The priority of love for the Christian is unquestionable, and the cause of love is advanced by telling the truth with grace and compassion.

As for same sex "marriage," we see no place for it within the context of a Christian worldview. According to the Bible, marriage is heterosexual. Jesus, when expressing his understanding of the scriptural foundation for the divine purpose and design in marriage, referred to its origins in the Creation account: "From the beginning of creation, God made them male and female. For this cause a man shall leave his father and mother, and shall cleave to his wife, and the two shall become one flesh..." (Mark 10:6-8, quoting Genesis 2:24).

We realize that not everyone shares our perspective. Even within the ranks of professing Christians, there are those who do not believe that God's Word and created order affirm heterosexual marriage as the one and only legitimate context for sexual expression. A careful study of this stance shows that its adherents either discount the authority of the Scripture or adopt interpretive methods that create the latitude to ignore or distort the plain and obvious meaning of its words.

"The Bible prohibits all kinds of sexual promiscuity – heterosexual as well as homosexual."

In our opinion, the clarity of God's truth on this matter remains unchanged despite hermeneutical methods designed to justify homosexual behaviour. The Bible prohibits *all* kinds of sexual promiscuity heterosexual as well as homosexual. Logical consistency demands that individuals and groups who want to reinterpret Scripture to sanction free sexual expression among homosexuals should extend the same concession to heterosexual singles; and, in fact, some have already taken this next step. But none of this can alter the facts: there is simply no scriptural support for endorsing sexual immorality (i.e., sexual activity outside the bond of hetero-sexual marriage) for *anyone,* no matter what his or her personal sexual *feelings* may be.

We hope these thoughts help to clarify these issues in your own mind. You may also want to view our articles concerning revi-sionist theology. For further information on our perspective, we invite you to visit two other areas of our website, Sexuality and Understanding Homosexuality

POINT #7: DEBASE ART, MAKE IT RUN MAD

She said: The arts are one of the primary keys to changing culture.

WHY: To break down social norms of what is acceptable and for-bidden. To encourage creative expression of self outwardly and inwardly in whatever way is pleasing to the individual. To corrupt the minds of the youth into accepting what was once forbidden as normal.

HOW: Promote new forms of art which will corrupt and defile the imagination of people because art is the language of the spirit, that which is inside, you can bring it out in painting, music, drama etc.

Note: Look at the quality, spirituality and message of the art, music and the films that are coming out today, and the films out of Hollywood and think about how that has changed drastically in provocative ways throughout history.

Today, we live in a world where pornography and nudity are viewed as an 'art' or a form of artistic expression. We live in a world where promiscuity and immorality of all kinds are promoted and cele-brated in music and film. What is Alice Bailey's goal with debasing art? The purpose of art should be to glorify God and edify others. However, debasing art will lead to corrupt minds and a corrupt form of expression. Instead of people being edified by art, they are defiled by it.

The plan of "debasing art" and making it run mad is an expression of the defilement that is already in the soul of man. The Bible says that the heart of man is desperately wicked and who can understand it? (Jeremiah 17:9). In Mark 7:20-23, Jesus says the following... "*What comes out of a person is what defiles him. For from within, out of the heart of man, come evil thoughts, sexual immorality, theft, murder, adultery, coveting, wickedness, deceit, sensuality, envy, slander, pride, foolishness. All these evil things come from within, and they defile a person.*"

It is therefore the case that the kind of art that we see in the world today is an expression of what is in the heart of men. It is therefore evident that the form of artistic expression we see in music and film is just as the vices and sins that Christ mentions in Mark 7:20-23 (Exodus 31:1-5.)

THE ARTS

The arts are a very wide range of human practices of creative expression, storytelling and cultural participation. The term "the arts" includes, but is not limited to music (instrumental and vocal), dance, drama, folk art, creative writing, architecture and allied fields, painting, sculpture, photography, graphic and craft arts, industrial design, costume and fashion design, motion pictures, television, radio, film, video, tape and sound recording, the arts related to the presentation, performance, execution, and exhibition of such major art forms, and all those traditional arts practiced by the diverse peoples of this country. By definition, the arts themselves are open to being continually re-defined.

POINT #8: USE MEDIA TO PROMOTE AND CHANGE MINDSET

She said: The greatest way to change human attitude is media (again, the arts).

WHY: To foster groupthink around normalizing deviant behavior; to encourage pleasure over social norms; to revise the social norms in accordance with the New World Order.

HOW: Use the press, the radio, T.V, cinema, any form of public media to influence people in the way you want them to think! Break up the traditional home by using media to encourage females to be independent and to "have their own" or to "not need a man". This will further deteriorate the traditional "long-term" family structure.

Note: So much money is pumped into media and advertising and the spreading of violence, pornographic material, and other sources. Sex outside of marriage is thrown in your face 80-90 times more than sex in marriage through media. Promiscuity is being promoted as natural, you watch gay sex on TV in homes where children's minds (and yours) are being neutralized to sensitivity to these things. Everything is promoted in a sensual way, even cleaning supplies is advertised on TV by using sex. So, those who believe it is just art, it is art, but with an agenda.

We can tell today how successful they have been in implementing the plan over 65 years via media as well as advertising agencies, billboards, and magazines. Who controls media? (New Age). We wonder why newspapers, TV, etc. do not record much about Christian activities. In our world today, the media is mostly controlled by people who are not born-again Christians. Even before the television had become a device that was owned in every household and well before the Internet and social media platforms existed, Alice Bailey understood the power of the media in the future and how it could be promoted to change mindsets.

The media can be used as an instrument for both good and bad. However, because most of the media is controlled by unbelievers or people who support Alice Bailey's New Age beliefs, the media is being used to support the New Age agenda.

MEDIA

Media is the term we use to refer to different types of media that **provide us with important information and knowledge. The media has always been part of our society, even when people used paintings and writings to share information.** The goal of the media is to convey an advertising message to the audience through the most appropriate media channel for their product. As time passed, people came up with different modes to provide news to the public. Based on the type of medium, their role may be different, but they all exist to communicate to the audience and affect their perceptions.

Today, we do not have to travel oceans or wait for a pigeon to get the latest news. Media is critical, which includes the air waves, newspapers, websites, television stations, networks, and telephones, radio stations, and magazines. It influences each person in our nations negatively or positively. Media increases its stamina with each new breakthrough in technology. News media which was originally to be an objective citadel of honor and truth (John 8:32) in our society, has fallen from its foundation, into subjective criticism, which is distasteful and derogatory in nature, as reporters seem to care more about getting their image in the camera than what comes out of their mouth. The current day "reporting" on a governmental level is repulsive to many and it is better not seen and not said, as person after person, item after item, line upon line, is castrated before the public. The Satanic goal is the tearing down, instead of building up, and who can find the most effective dirt on the individual involved in a situation.

REVERSE: PROMOTE BIBLICAL/GODLY CONTENT THROUGH MEDIA

Media is one of the fastest ways to change people's mindsets on a massive scale. The media has enormous power to persuade and change perceptions and even cultures Romans 12:2 says:

Do not be conformed to this world, but be transformed by the renewal of your mind, that by testing you may discern what is the will of God, what is good and acceptable and perfect.

Therefore, we are not to conform to the mindset of the world, but instead we should allow God's word and teachings to transform our thinking so that we know the will of God. It is time for changing one's worldview. God has a plan for good for His people, and we all have that seed of God implanted within us. There is recovery hope for different types of Media; Print Media, Broadcasting Media, and Internet Media.

Internet Media: Nowadays, we are relying on the Internet to get the news a lot more often than traditional news sources. Websites provide information in the form of video, text, and audio. We can even choose the way we want to receive the news.

Types of Internet Media: **Social networks or websites** – Facebook, Instagram, Twitter, YouTube, Tumblr, LinkedIn, Snapchat, Quora, Reddit, Pinterest, etc. They are user-friendly and widely used by people around the world. Although we can find any news here, they may be misleading because of the lack of regulations on the content shared. Social media can be an awesome tool, but it can also be a terrible temptation. It is a mixed bag that gives people a platform to say whatever they want – the good, the bad, and the ugly – whenever they want, with little to no consequence. Before sending on an online message, let us try to ask ourselves; is this true or false? Does it build up or tear down? Does it amplify or diminish Christ's gospel? We must take entertainment discernment seriously, approach choices from a biblical worldview, and train children to make Christ-honoring media decisions.

If you are looking for alternatives to Facebook, Twitter, or YouTube or for new ways to express your faith on social media, try out the following:

THE ECHO PRAYER APP: The Echo Prayer App is an exciting tool that allows you to create prayer lists. But beyond that, the app gives you the ability to create virtual prayer groups with friends and family.

YOUVERSION BIBLE APP: If you are looking for a Christian social network that focuses exclusively on scripture, look no further than the Youversion Bible app. The app not only offers multiple versions of the Bible, but it also allows you to connect with other Christians to see what scriptures they are reading, commenting on, and pondering.

SHINE CHRISTIAN SOCIAL NETWORK: The SHINE Christian Social Network is a Christian Facebook alternative that looks to be relatively new. The app offers sharing capabilities among other elements and dubs itself the "world's first fully-functional, family-friendly, Christian social media app."

MYPRAIZE: myPraize describes itself as a "free value-based social network with the best of Facebook, Instagram, Pinterest & YouTube." The Christian social media site, a Christian Facebook alternative that allows users to import Facebook contacts, pledges to be different from other platforms like it.

CHRISTIANSLIKEME.NET: The site ChristiansLikeMe.net is yet another Christian social network that offers Christians the opportunity to both share and grow their faith. Based on forum discussions, the platform, like other Christian networking sites, allows for free-flowing discussion about an array of faith topics.

GODTUBE: YouTube has become the world's most popular Christian social media site for video-sharing, but there is a Christian social network that is also worth checking out: GodTube. The site is filled with inspiring, faith-based video clips.

CROSS.TV: For people looking for another Christian social network that allows for video consumption, look no further than

<u>Cross.tv</u>, "a multi-lingual, faith-based, online social media community." It is a "family-friendly online network featuring various media sharing functionalities."

PURE FLIX: Stream clean and enjoy access to thousands of faith and family-friendly movies, original shows, engaging documentaries and more. God-honoring and inspiring media on any device at any time, Pure Flix takes great care in previewing and selecting content so that you can rest assured that it is free of violence, sex, and language surprises.

RECLAIM MEDIA: Reclaim Media is an online media ministry focused on building spiritual leaders and disciples. By releasing biblically-based, Spirit-filled content, we are engaging a generation of believers who desire to grow spiritually and fulfill the call of God. Reclaim Media is an official member of the Encounter TV Network.

It is my hope that, as believers, we effectively communicate the gospel, be an example of evangelism and are actively living out and sharing our faith with others. In the height of the pandemic, there are more churches that are having services virtually, with the chance to reach more people than ever. What an amazing opportunity for the Word of God not just to be viewed but spread! When we share on our social platforms, we are inviting others to join us and be encouraged and inspired by the message. When we share, we are leveraging our relationships and evangelizing by compelling others to come and join to hear the message of hope. Here are some practical ways to encourage believers to share their faith through social media and beyond: Your testimony, scripture, posts from your church, burdens, prayers and praise, resources to meet needs, your love through social media, opportunities to connect in an online community group, share in giving, and the invitation of Jesus Christ.

DISCIPLESHIP OF ARTISTS

Let us look at the artist in spiritual community. Our focus will be the discipleship of the artist shaped by a kingdom view. It will encompass the calling, mentoring, training, empowerment, and support of artists as uniquely gifted and vital parts of the Body of Christ who like us all are called to work under the lordship of Christ, the creative Head of the Body which is the church.

To understand discipleship for artists as participants in the church's mission in the world, we need to understand with more empathy and perspective some of the key issues that affect their involvement. Among the issues to be considered are:

➤ Attitudes of the church toward the arts and of artists toward the church

➤ The struggles of the artist with authority, freedom, and accountability

➤ The nature of artistic language (the way art "speaks")

➤ The inspiration or empowerment of artists by the Holy Spirit

➤ How we understand the nature of the creative process itself

➤ The impact of "non-contextual" attempts at mission on indigenous art.

The church today faces a different kind of world – one that has undergone profound changes in the past fifty years and continues to change at a rapid pace. Few people anywhere can avoid the realities of the information and artistic media that shape our everyday environment. At a time when communication has abandoned the age of the orator, we now find ourselves, culturally speaking, in the age of the artist.

TRANSFORMATION OF ARTISTS

With spiritual and cultural transformation as desired outcomes, let us examine the place of the arts within culture, the importance of indigenous and contextualized artistic expression, the role of the arts in evangelism and missions, the need for Christians to practice their art in the marketplace, and the significant contribution the arts can make to the process of personal healing and social change. Let us realize that art cannot transform; only Christ can transform the human condition. With that clarification as context, we can show that the arts allow for diversity as they "witness" in verbal and nonverbal ways to the truth about the human condition and God's redemptive purposes. They can also draw people to Christ when linked to acts of compassion and service.

The arts enable cross-cultural and cross-generational communication and contextualization. Social and economic barriers can be overcome through collaborative art making, and arts used in therapies can invigorate health and healing.

Jesus consistently invited people to use their imaginations, to allow the images He presented to come alive, and to find meaning within those imaginings. He recognized that words or commands were insufficient. For people to make changes, they must first be able to imagine what is possible. Human transformative activity depends upon a transformed imagination. We will illustrate that this is especially true in at-risk and impoverished communities or groups of displaced and broken people, where the arts can reinvigorate a sense of personal and social responsibility. Healing can come through safe, accepted, and celebrated personal and communal expression.

CHRISTIAN ART OR CHRISTIAN ARTISTS

The commonly used phrase "Christian art" is plagued with a host of meanings that can either help or hinder our understanding. To avoid confusion, we will prefer to talk about art that contains a Christian worldview, and we suggest that such art will in some way resonate with the narrative of Scripture. It will speak the truth about the world and the human condition with or without content that is recognizably or overtly Christian in nature and it will be done with integrity and imagination. While some artistically-gifted believers like to be called "Christian artists" (mostly in the contemporary

Christian music arena), other Christians, particularly artists who work in the marketplace, consider it an unhelpful and inaccurate designation that implies that their creative work will contain only Christian symbolism and subject matter. Such phrases can unintentionally reinforce the notion that a work of art is only valuable in relation to its usefulness, particularly in the cause of gospel proclamation – an idea we do not want to endorse.

POINT #9: CREATE AN INTERFAITH MOVEMENT

She said: "Promote other faiths to be at par with Christianity and break this thing about Christianity as being the only way to heaven; by that Christianity will be pulled down and other faiths promoted."

WHY: To increase the levels of tolerance & acceptance among men that all religions are equal, thereby promoting a false peace; to employ the thought that all religions/spirituality lead to God; to lay the groundwork that will usher in the one-world religion.

HOW: Promote the importance of man in determining his own future and destiny". Humanism:

"Tell man he has the right to choose what he wants to be and he can make it happen, and that he has the right to determine his cause; this takes God off His throne." Interfaith movements are rising everywhere in the world today.

Alice Bailey's advice to create an interfaith movement is one of the main agendas of the New Age, which may eventually lead to the creation of a one world religion. An interfaith movement promotes the notion that all faiths or religions must become one and look for "common ground" and discard their differences. It is the ecumenical view that all religions in the world can unite and become one. It is certain in this day and age that there is a subtle but emerging movement that exists within different faiths from Christianity to Buddhism to Hinduism, which seeks to promote ecumenism at the expense of the truth.

Therefore, in the name of unity, Christians are advised to compromise God's truth for the purpose of being united. False doctrines will always divide people between those who believe the truth and those who believe what is false. Furthermore, the authentic gospel of Jesus Christ will also divide people.

1 Corinthians 1:18 says: *For the message of the cross is foolishness to those who are perishing, but to us who are being saved it is the power of God.*

Jesus Himself knew that His message and His arrival on earth would divide many people because the truth will always divide people between those who follow the truth and those who follow a lie (Matthew 10:34-39).

RELIGION/FAITH/BELIEF SYSTEM

Every society has some type of belief in a superior being or beings. In the east, religions tend to be polytheistic (many gods) or outright idolatrous (such as Hinduism and Buddhism). Although these religions are thousands of years old, they nonetheless continue to thrive today. In the west, Christianity and Catholicism are predominant, but postmodern views are increasingly being accepted and the concept of God is being rejected. This is especially true in Europe.

The Christian Church is described in the Greek language as the ecclesia. Literally translated, the word ecclesia means "governing body." The church mentioned 113 times in the New Testament, is always defined as Ecclesia, except for one time. That was a political term used by Jesus, taken from the Greek, to mean those who sit at the city gates and determine what is done within the city, by a raised hand vote. Therefore, the church has failed many nations. We have so far failed to take the dominion mandate of Genesis 1 and enforce the Kingdom of God. So, we invite you to partake of what God wants to do in this area, and let it unfold before us as we work toward taking back our dominion. Please, take this to the Lord regarding aligning with the Institute of Discipleship and Transformation, that is leading action movements to establish the Kingdom of God in our midst.

POINT #10: GET GOVERNMENTS TO MAKE ALL THESE [POINTS] LAW AND GET THE CHURCH TO ENDORSE THESE CHANGES.

She said: "the church must change its doctrine and accommodate the people by accepting these things and put them into its structures and systems."

HOW: Mainly through the implementation of the points 1-9 and 501c3s; convince people to grow numbers and the rest will come.

WHY: To usher in the new world order in an almost seamless effort.

Have they succeeded? Today, some may wonder why our governments are legislating laws contrary to the Bible and why the church is compromising the Word of God. It is the process of implementing this 10-Point Plan – a 50-year strategy of the New World Order to fulfill its goal to establish a One World Government, a One World Economic system, and a One World Religion. Today, the strategy, almost in its entirety, has been adopted by the United Nations and today a lot of it is already law in many nations. This deception has crept up by increments, unobserved by most people. It can best be illustrated through the well-known analogy of the frog in the pot of water. If you put a frog in a pot of boiling water, it is smart enough to know that it is in terrible danger and will immediately jump out to safety. But if you turn up the heat very slowly, a little at a time, it does not notice the changes that are taking place and will slowly cook to death. Many people today are slowly cooking to death and do not seem to realize how far they have come from where they once were.

NOTE: Today, the First World Nations are not struggling to resist these points because the New World Order and the New Age Movement focused there primarily from its inception.

It is recorded that they say they have succeeded in the task in the First World nations but suddenly they realize Christianity has spread to the rest of the world, so now they have to use every resource in the First World nations to deal with the rest of the world. In Africa, South Africa is the number one state; it is changing at such a rapid pace. They are saying give to African countries a financial package with conditions to; **legalize abortion and take God and prayer out of school.**

The Third World nations' governments are so attracted to this package that they cannot say no to it, they need the money, and they ask the church to find an answer. These are done secretly. Christianity is 5%, the rest is Hinduism, Buddhism, and Spiritism. New Age is being taught to teachers; they are being taught to teach this in schools. Today, governments all over the world are legalizing such things as abortion, homosexuality, bestiality, same sex marriage and even addictive drugs, such as marijuana. Even though the Bible disagrees with such lifestyles, there is a growing trend where governments are legalizing lifestyles that directly oppose the scriptures. This is because the influence of the New Age movement is growing as it seeks to achieve Alice Bailey's 10-Point Plan agenda.

REVERSE: We can all have a power of influence as we unite in arms to take back the government in our region from the enemy's hands. We must go individually and corporately to the Court of Heaven in the Spirit realm and confess our sins as God's people. The battle must be won in the heavens before it will happen on the earth. Intercessors, prophets, and apostles all need to be involved to hear the current word of the Lord as to what was written in the "volume of the book" about this sphere and put it in place. This transformation can happen quickly once the court of heaven is called into session. Ungodly earthly and political behavior within the body of Christ must be identified and repented for. Jesus Christ is our attorney in these cases. A verdict must be given by the Judge of the Court; and appropriate "documents" received, and the verdict enforced. The long-term goal is that God's Ecclesia rule at the gates of this arena and decree who does and who does not have political office.

United, we can become a mighty governmental force to be reckoned with in our nations. People do not really know much about us yet, but one by one individuals and churches will come into alignment in this region once apostolic and prophetic leadership are authorized and in place. Those who hold a governmental position, and who feel called to champion teamwork on this mountain, please contact us. We call forth those in the military also who are born again and are true followers of Jesus Christ. Military forces will be involved in setting structures in place in what is shortly to come. Is your umbilical cord tied securely to the Kingdom of God and His purposes?

If you have no experience of dealing within the courts of heaven, there is a module on that coming up; please, register to participate. This is a new walk for all of us; we have never walked this way before. I perceive that all believers are called to participate. We do not live in normal times. We have all been set here in this period to accomplish God's tasks through us.

SUGGESTED EXERCISES

Based on Points 3 and 4 of Bailey's 10-Point Agenda, teach your children/wards about sexual immorality and abortion. Give them the following exercise:

- **List at least 3 Bible verses that forbid fornication and adultery.**

1. _____

2. _____

3. _____

- **Is abortion permitted by God? Support your answer with Bible verses.**

_____

_____

_____

_____

- **On what grounds is divorce permissible?**

_____

_____

_____

_____

- **List and explain 5 social media apps that can help grow your Christian faith.**

1. _____

2. _____

3. _____

4. _____

5. _____

PART 2

STRATEGIES TO REVERSE
THE 10-POINT CHARTER

MODULE 1.1

GOD USES
BROKEN VESSELS

HAVE YOU EVER FELT YOU WERE TOO BROKEN, weak, and flawed for God to use? Have you wanted to serve God in ministry or in any capacity, but wonder if you are just too much of a mess for Him to even want to make use of? Biblical history has shown that God uses broken people throughout Scripture. God uses the weak things of the world and chooses flawed people to achieve great things. I will share my thoughts as to the reason: God Can Achieve Great Things Through You.

God Uses Broken People But Am I Too Broken?

We sometimes fall into the trap of comparing **ourselves to other people.** I think we all do that at one time or another; everyone else seems to have this deep walk with God, while we are **feeling like a mess.** It feels like they must all live these wonderful, God-filled lives of perfection, with perfect marriages, perfect kids, perfect friends, with cloud floating and harp playing. Then, you begin to wonder how God is ever going to use you in the capacity you feel called to, when you have **all these issues** in your life, not just prior to being saved but well after. You would ask "Who am I to write and give other people encouragement or advice or teach anyone anything when I have made so many mistakes in my life and been such a mess myself? So many times, I felt I disappointed God?" You may have felt like you were somehow the only one that was messed up and did not have your life together. You may have this 'head-knowledge' that God uses the weak and that God uses the broken. You may have read the stories. He has done it throughout history, but surely, He didn't mean **you,** anyone but you, right?

God Uses Broken People and He Handpicked You!

In the place of prayer and **Bible study**, may God bring you to a very important revelation. May you hear His voice clear in your spirit: "It is because of the mistakes that I use you, not in spite of them." God uses the weak of this world, God uses the broken of this world and God chose you. The weakness, brokenness and those mistakes give you **a voice to reach** those people who maybe feel like they **do not measure up.** Those that perhaps feel that **their mistakes** render them unusable, or that they are **too far gone** to have a relationship with Him. It's because of the mistakes you made that God would use **you.**

God Uses Broken People and, Like Broken Vessels, He Puts Them Together Again

You see, in the Bible, God did not choose people who were perfect. No, not even close.

He did not choose the **righteous and religious elite of Jesus' days** to be His disciples; far from it!

No, all throughout the Bible, God uses broken vessels; God uses weak people, imperfect people, the flawed, and the "messed up". Let us face it; most of Jesus' disciples had shortfalls. No one is too broken for God. We all have broken pieces and God uses all our broken pieces and puts them together again in ways only He could. He solidifies them in His **refining fire** and molds us into what He knows we can be. He makes us the perfect vessel that He can work through and use.

He Chooses the Least Likely

When you are tempted to ask "Lord, am I broken, am I flawed too much for you?" just remember; He chose a brash, bigmouthed man, He chose a King who committed adultery with Bathsheba and then had her husband killed to cover up his sin, He chose a Hebrew with a supposed speech impediment, He chose a prostitute, He chose a persecutor of believers, He chose a tax collector… and on and on. How come God uses flawed people like these?

Why God Uses the Weak, Broken, and Flawed People of the World

> ➤ *He chooses flawed people because that is who we can most identify with. We relate to those people. We cannot relate to the holy and righteous Pharisees…no, but we relate to Peter.*

> ➤ *He chooses flawed people because their flaws make them see their need for a Savior.*

> *He chooses flawed people because they have no cause to boast. They have to rely on grace. If He chose a skilled orator and leader to lead the children out of Israel, he might have assumed to have done it through his own skill and leadership and not given the glory to God. Had Peter been a righteous and holy man, he may not have seen his need to lean on God and might have taken the credit for himself. There is no question, when you are flawed, that it was God who did the work through you and not you on your own.*

> *God chooses and uses broken people to show us that He can equip anyone to do His work. We can look at Moses and see that we do not need to be a great speaker or a skilled leader to do God's work.*

God Uses the Weak and Yes, He Will Use You

If you feel called to be a writer, you don't have to have years of experience. Write! If you feel called to be a speaker, you don't need a communications degree and years under your belt at Toastmasters. Speak! In other words, if God calls you to something, you can trust Him to equip you for it. You don't need to rely solely on your own talents, skills, abilities. God will equip you for it, as long as you make yourself available. When God equips you, you don't feel boastful or haughty in your own abilities. A flawed person is open to God's work in them. God uses the weak, broken people, not because they are capable. He uses them when they are yielded, available, and pliable to Him.

God Uses the Broken So That No One May Boast

"You were not delivered by your own actions; therefore no one should boast."

EPHESIANS 2:9

It is not our own works; God is working through us and that leaves us **no room to boast**. It **should** leave us **praising God** for the wonderful works He has performed through us. So if you feel flawed, that's ok. You're in great company. Remember it is not about you and what you can do. It is about Him and what He can and will accomplish through you. All you have to do is make yourself available, not capable. He will take care of that part. We should all be thankful that God uses the broken things of this world, as every person in one way or another is imperfect. It is in our weakness that, through Him, we are made strong.

2 Corinthians 12:10

"For Messiah's sake, then, I delight in weaknesses, in insults, in distresses, in persecutions, in calamities. For when I am weak, then I am strong."

God Uses the Weak – Examples from the Bible

Gideon: In the Book of Judges Chapter 6, we meet Gideon. Gideon was anything but a warrior. In fact, he was quite the opposite. The Israelites were under constant torment by the Midianites and the Amalekites. The Bible tells us they "ravaged the land" and left them nothing. They had no sustenance; their sheep and cattle were taken. They cried out to the Lord, but God sent them a prophet. They wanted a Savior, but God sent them a sermon. They needed to get right in their relationship with God. Israel had gone through yet another cycle of obedience-rebellion-judgment-redemption. However, God had a plan, as He always does. He sent His angel, and He calls to Gideon and says in Judges 6:12

"Then the angel of Adonai appeared to him and said to him, "Adonai is with you, O mighty man of valor..."

Mighty man of valor, He is calling into being the warrior in Gideon according to Romans 4:17:

"...who gives life to the dead and calls into existence that which does not exist."

God was not just referring to the Gideon in his current state; He saw the potential of who Gideon could become with God in him. Gideon went on to obey the Lord in spite of all his fear; he defeated Israel's enemies by obeying God and became the mighty warrior God called him to be. Since people knew Gideon was not a war- rior but a frightened, weak man, there was no doubt it was God at work. At this point in your life, God is calling you, not by who or what you are now in your weakness, but in who He sees you can be, if you could make yourself available to Him.

Jael: In Judges Chapter 4, we learn of Sisera; the commander of the Canaanite army. He was a very cruel man who oppressed the Israelites for twenty years. Jael was the wife of Heber the Kenite. Not much detail was written about her, but that she was a Bedouin, a nomadic people who dwelled in tents. Sisera, despite coming against Deborah and Barak with extreme might, was losing and chose to flee on foot. He ran right to Jael's tent. Jael (Yael in Hebrew) sees Sisera coming and tells him not to worry. She brings him into the tent and covers him up to warm him.

Judges 4:19-21:

He said to her, "Please give me a little water to drink, for I am thirsty." So she opened a skin of milk and made him drink some and covered him. Then he said to her, "Stand at the entrance of the tent, and if anyone comes and asks you saying, 'Is there a man here?' then you will say, "There's no one". Then Yael, Heber's wife, took a tent pin and got a hammer in her hand, approached him cautiously and drove the pin into his temple until it pierced through into the ground for he was exhausted and in a deep sleep. So he died. This ruler mighty man fell to a woman with a common household item, a tent peg. To the world, this was a woman with a common household tool, but God uses the weak to accomplish great things. God uses the weak and God uses broken people to achieve His purposes. What is God calling you to? Have you felt God's call on you but felt too unqualified or weak to heed that call?

In the last half century, the American society for instance, has seen profound erosion in the moral fiber of our society. Here are some shocking facts on this adverse shift we are seeing in our culture today: Since 1963, premarital sex increased 500 percent, unwed pregnancy was up 400 percent, sexually transmitted disease was up 200 percent, suicides were up 400 percent, and violent crime was up 500 percent. What we are witnessing today is a systemic decline of Christian influence in North America and most nations; in which many have been blinded by a joining together of secularization, pluralization, and post-modernism.

Nations are witnessing a tipping point in our culture today, where truth is victimized in the name of tolerance. In the light of this moral devastation, God is calling us to be His change agents. The primary duty of a change agent is to bring change to a problem entrenched in our society. For instance, Joseph solved a problem for his employer Pharaoh by providing a solution to a famine in the land, and in the process, he became a prominent leader. Moses solved a problem for God and the Israelites by freeing his people from slavery. Paul solved a problem by bringing the gospel to the Gentiles.

What problems are you born to solve?

A good place to start is answering this question: **What is the one aspect of this broken world that, when you see it, touch it, get near it, you just cannot stand it?** As change agents, we are called to change culture. This starts by small acts of influence growing on a daily basis. Begin influencing yourself, then your circle of family and friends, then on an organizational and community level. You will soon find yourself to be a profound influencer. It is important to be intentional about your level of influence.

MODULE 1.2

The Person Of The Holy Spirit

THE NATURE OF THE GOVERNOR

A person left to himself will self-destruct.

W E HAVE SEEN THAT THE PRESENCE OF THE
Governor is essential for transforming the world into the
kingdom of Heaven. It is now vital that we consider in more depth
the nature of the Holy Spirit because, though the Governor is the
most important person on Earth, he is also the most misunder-
stood and ignored.

People who are not yet in the kingdom do not understand the Holy Spirit's indispensable role in their lives because they have been led to believe that he is mysterious and unknowable. Or they think he is a kind of apparition because of our modern connotation of the word *spirit* and the use of the term *Holy Ghost* for Holy Spirit in the King James Version of the Bible. Even people who have received the Governor have misconceptions regarding who he is. I said earlier that some think he is a sensation or a thrill whose purpose is to make them feel good. Let us explore the nature of the Governor starting with what he is not.

WHAT THE HOLY SPIRIT ISN'T

NOT AN "IT"

The Holy Spirit is not an "it" or a "thing." Some people refer to him as a non-personal object, saying, "Do you feel it?" Or "Do you have it?" The Holy Spirit is a person with a personality. We will discuss more of his personal characteristics in the next section.

NOT A UNIVERSAL "FORCE" OR "COSMIC MIND"

The Holy Spirit is not some force or cosmic mind that we can "tap into" to receive the power and knowledge of the universe. He is not the sum total of the consciousness and inhabitants of earth. To some people, these metaphysical ideas have become synonymous with God's Spirit. However, no one can control the Holy Spirit or "siphon off" his knowledge or power. Neither is he part of our consciousness. He is a distinct Being who grants us knowledge and power when we have a relationship with the King and are yielded to the will of the kingdom. Instead of demanding or taking it for granted, we are to be grateful for the power with which he works in our lives to further the purposes of the kingdom and to strengthen us as children of the King.

NOT A CLOUD OR MIST

Some people think of the Holy Spirit as just a kind of smoke or mist or cloud that comes in to a place and sometimes causes people to fall down on the floor. I am not saying that there are not legitimate times when the Holy Spirit will manifest his presence in a physical way, but I believe that people who are always looking for such manifestations are susceptible to imaginings and fabrications.

Rather than referring to the Spirit as a kind of ethereal mist, Jesus talked about the Spirit using the word *he*. In fact this statement of his could not be clearer:

But when he, the Spirit of truth, comes, he will guide you into all truth. He will not speak on his own; he will speak only what he hears, and he will tell you what is yet to come. He will bring glory to me by taking from what is mine and making it known to you.

John 16:13-14

Jesus could have said, "When the Holy Spirit comes." He kept repeating the word he, however, as if he wanted to make sure we knew the Holy Spirit is not just a force or cloud.

NOT A FEELING OR SENSATION

The Holy Spirit is also not just a "feeling." Again, I think we have often relegated him to a kind of strange, goose-pimple raising experience. I think part of the reason for this is that some people come to corporate worship experiences so pent up with frustration about their lives that, when they cannot take it anymore, but they sense an accepting environment, they run around screaming, roll on the ground, and call it the Holy Spirit. They are simply releasing tension.

You do not need to make noise to experience the Holy Spirit. You do not need loud drums and cowbells and screaming, shouting, and clapping. If you read the Bible carefully, most of the time when the Spirit manifested himself, it was in quietness, not feelings. The prophet Elijah had this experience:

A great and powerful wind tore the mountains apart and shattered the rocks before the Lord, but the Lord was not in the wind. After the wind there was an earthquake, but the Lord was not in the earthquake. After the earthquake came a fire, but the Lord was not in the fire. And after the fire came **a gentle whisper**. When Elijah heard it, he pulled his cloak over his face and went out and stood at the mouth of the cave. Then a voice said to him, "What are you doing here, Elijah?"

1 Kings 19:11-13

Let me add this statement, however: The Holy Spirit is not a feeling, but his presence can certainly affect your emotions as you experience his peace, joy, and comfort.

WHO IS THE HOLY SPIRIT?

THE HOLY SPIRIT IS GOD EXTENDED

The most important thing we must know about the nature of the Holy Spirit is that he is God. I like to use the term "God extended." He is God extended to a person and/or situation to work the purpose and will of his kingdom in the person's life or in the circumstance.

ONE WITH GOD

Earlier, we talked about the fact that Jesus is fully God, even though he is also fully human. God the Son became Jesus of Nazareth for the purpose of his redemptive task in the world. His dual nature never diminished His oneness and equality with the Father. The Scripture says that Jesus, "being in the form of God, did not consider it robbery to be equal with God, but made Himself of no reputation, taking the form of a bondservant, and coming in the likeness of men."

Philippians 2:6-7

You do not need to grasp for something that you already have. Jesus is equal with God, even though he is distinct in personality and function from God the Father and God the Spirit. The Scripture tells us that Jesus was sent from the Father through the Spirit. The heavenly messenger told Mary, the mother of Jesus:

"The Holy Spirit will come upon you, and the power of the Most High will overshadow you. So the holy one to be born will be called the Son of God."
Luke 1:35

And Jesus spoke of his oneness with the Father, saying:

"I and the Father are one."
John 10:30

"If anyone loves me, he will obey my teaching. My Father will love him, and we will come to him and make our home with him."
John 14:23

The word *Father* in relation to God does not mean father the way one is related to a human father, or in the sense of someone who is "greater" or "older." God is not "older" than Jesus Christ. Jesus is eternal, as God the Father is eternal. Rather, the word *Father* refers to God's being the Source from which Jesus was sent.

Likewise, the Holy Spirit is God, and he is equal to the Father and the Son. John wrote in his gospel:

"God is spirit, and his worshipers must worship in spirit and in truth."
John 4:24

Jesus spoke of the Spirit as *"another* Counselor" who would continue his work on earth. So God is one, but he expresses himself in three distinct personalities and dimensions.

Jesus told his disciples:

"When the Counselor comes, whom I will *send to you from the Father*, the Spirit of truth who *goes out from the Father...*"
John 15:26

Both Jesus and the Spirit proceeded from the Father to accomplish the work that needed and still needs to be done on earth. Jesus was sent by the Father to **redeem** us; the Spirit was sent by Jesus to **empower** us. Jesus was sent to **restore** us; the Spirit was sent to **release** us into a new kingdom life.

I like to describe the concept of the **Triune God** by the analogy of water. Water, in its liquid state, is like God the Father; it is the natural source. If you were to take some water and freeze it, it would become solid ice. Ice is like Jesus, the Word who became flesh; he was tangible, someone who could be seen, heard, and touched. If you were to take the same ice, put it in a pot, and heat it to boiling, it would become steam. Steam is like the Holy Spirit, the invisible influence that generates power. Ice and steam can return to their original liquid state. All three are in essence water, although in different forms.

RECEIVES THE SAME HONOR AS GOD

Another confirmation that the Holy Spirit is God is Jesus' statement about the consequences of blaspheming him.

"*I tell you the truth, all the sins and blasphemies of men will be forgiven them. But whoever blasphemes against the Holy Spirit will never be forgiven; he is guilty of an eternal sin.*"
Mark 3:28-29

The only sin Jesus said you can never be forgiven of is a sin against the Holy Spirit. Why did he say this? I believe that he was saying it is the Holy Spirit who (1) convicts people of their need to be cleansed from sin by the work of Christ, and (2) who enables us to be spiritually reborn and brings us into the heavenly kingdom. Therefore, if someone totally hardens himself to the Spirit and his work, he will not be drawn to forgiveness through Christ, and he will not be able to receive the regenerating work of the Spirit in his life.

Jesus Christ cleanses us, the **Father forgives** us, and the **Spirit renews** us. The writer of the book of Hebrews wrote, quoting Psalm 95:

"As the Holy Spirit says: 'Today, if you hear his voice, do not harden your hearts as you did in the rebellion.'"
Hebrews 3:7-8

In other words, if you hear his voice, if you feel his conviction, if you hear him saying, *"It's time,"* then do not harden your heart because there is going to come a day when he will stop calling you. The Scriptures speak about God as longsuffering or patient; it does not say that he is *forever*-suffering. He will allow foolishness for a long time, but only for so long.

The term *apostate* refers to someone who has entered a state where he cannot hear the Spirit of God anymore. You don't want the Holy Spirit to stop convicting you. If the Holy Spirit convicts you about your need to repent, receive forgiveness, and enter the kingdom of God, you should run to him! Why? Because that means you are still in good relationship with him, and he is able to talk to you. Don't let your pride prevent you from responding because you wonder what people will say. You should rather worry that the Spirit will stop talking!

I hope that you will listen to the most important person from heaven, who is the most important person on earth! He is vastly more important than angels, which many people hope to see. Angels, however, work for the government, but he *is* the government.

THE HOLY SPIRIT IS A PERSON WITH QUALITIES, CHARACTERISTICS, AND A WILL

So the Holy Spirit is first of all "God extended." Second, as we have seen, the Holy Spirit is a *person*. A person has qualities and characteristics that distinguish him from others, so that he is a separate being. The Governor has a distinct personality, characteristics, and will. As the Representative of heaven, the Resident Governor in the colony, his main desire is for us to fulfill the King's purposes on earth.

Jesus described the person and work of the Holy Spirit, revealing at various times that among his characteristics are his abilities to teach and guide. A feeling or a force cannot be a governor. A mist cannot teach or guide. Most citizens of the kingdom have no real relationship with the Governor because they have not realized they have someone invaluable dwelling in them. Some*one*.

THE SPIRIT HAS SPIRITUAL SENSES

The Holy Spirit also has "senses" that are part of his personality. By this, I mean that he has spiritual senses similar to the way human beings have physical senses. Spiritually speaking, the Holy Spirit sees, hears, feels, and smells or discerns in his dealings with the earth and its inhabitants.

THE SPIRIT HAS FEELINGS OR EMOTIONS

Paul wrote:

"Do not grieve the Holy Spirit of God, with whom you were sealed for the day of redemption."
Ephesians 4:30

We can grieve the Spirit when we actively resist him, behave in ways that are contrary to the kingdom of heaven, or neglect him.

I want to focus on the area of neglect. Think about this: When you ignore someone, he generally stops talking to you. And the more you ignore him, the more he will ignore you. For example, if you do not acknowledge me, eventually I'll conclude that I'm not important to you and that you don't have any regard for me. Or, if you keep ignoring me when I talk to you, then, eventually, I should have a little sense to say, "He really doesn't want to listen to me." Jesus said that the Holy Spirit will teach us all things. I used to be a teacher in the classroom, and let me tell you, there is no worse experience for a teacher than to have a group of students who have no interest in learning.

We must realize that the Holy Spirit is a person who knows when we are ignoring him. If we disregard his teaching and leading, we are not treating him with the respect and devotion he deserves. We also miss opportunities to learn and serve in the kingdom. And it is not only us who are negatively affected by this. Suppose the Governor prompts you five times to bring food to a neighbor. Finally, he stops speaking to you about it. Two things happen: You miss a blessing, and your neighbor may go hungry.

Or suppose the Governor prompts you during the night to get up and pray for someone, but you say, "I'm tired, and I've had a long day, so I need to sleep." The Holy Spirit says, "Yes, but someone is in need of help, and I need a human vessel through whom to intercede because this is the way the kingdom of heaven works on earth." You think, "That's just my imagination; I'm tired." So you stay in bed and no longer sense his prompting. You find out the next day that someone was in a dangerous or troubling situation, and your prayers were urgently needed.

We listen to other people more than we listen to the Spirit of God. We seek other people's advice more than we seek his. Sometimes, he withdraws our sense of his presence in order to get our attention.

Some people have not heard the voice of the Holy Spirit for a long time. Why? They get up in the morning and do not acknowledge him at all before plunging into the day. They never refer to him when they make decisions, invest their finances, work at their jobs, run their businesses, or go to school. Therefore, he is quiet toward them.

You literally have to learn to fellowship with and listen to the Holy Spirit. He speaks to us through the Scriptures, through our thoughts, and through promptings and impressions. We need to practice hearing his voice and not ignore him but acknowledge him as a person who is intimately interested in who we are, what we do, and how we fulfill our role in the kingdom.

THE GOVERNOR'S NATURE EXPRESSED TO US

Let us now look at how the Governor attends to us in fulfillment of his nature. The Scriptures describe and define particular roles and responsibilities of the Holy Spirit on earth. Again, in all his works, the Governor acts only according to the word of the King.

"The Spirit of truth," Jesus said, "…will not speak on his own; he will speak only what he hears, and he will tell you what is yet to come. He will bring glory to me by taking from what is mine and making it known to you."
John 16:13-14

COUNSELOR AND COMFORTER

Jesus told his disciples,

"But the Counselor, the Holy Spirit, whom the Father will send in my name, will teach you all things and will remind you of everything I have said to you."
John 14:26

"And I will ask the Father, and he will give you another Counselor to be with you forever."
John 14:16

The Greek word for *Counselor* in both these statements is *parakletos*, which means "an intercessor, consoler," "advocate, comforter." Some Bible translations use the word "Helper." It refers to one who comes right alongside us to assist us. Jesus promised his followers that he would return to be with them in the person of the Governor to enable them to live the life they were called to:

"In a little while you will see me no more, and then after a little while you will see me."
John 16:16

I've heard people say, "I want to become a believer [citizen of the kingdom], but I'm not strong enough. When I have enough strength to stop doing this and start doing that, I'm going to commit to the kingdom." These people still have not made a commitment because they think they have to be strong *first*. You may be struggling with the same issue because you're trying to change yourself on your own. The King is telling us, "Look, if you're going to learn kingdom culture, you need help from the home country." Receiving the Governor into your life will enable you to change. He will show you how to transform your thinking and how to live.

Likewise, some of you are discouraged because, even though you are citizens of the kingdom of heaven, you feel as if you keep falling back into the attitudes and actions of the kingdom of darkness. But the Governor says to you, "I'm going to help you up again." This is his job! He won't give up on you.

Jesus emphasized the King's commitment to you through his analogy of a shepherd who leaves his ninety-nine sheep in the fold while he goes off to look for the one that is lost. This doesn't give us a license to keep going back to the behavior of the kingdom of darkness. Once we are in the kingdom of Heaven, we're not supposed to keep returning to our old ways intentionally. Some people purposely do what is contrary to the kingdom, and then they want to be automatically forgiven by the King. This does not reflect a true transformation into a kingdom citizen. If we really desire to live by heavenly standards, even though we sometimes may slip up, the Governor will help us to live them out. He wants us to succeed.

GUIDE AND TEACHER

Jesus also said about the Governor,

"But when he, the Spirit of truth, comes, he will guide you into all truth. He will not speak on his own; he will speak only what he hears, and he will tell you what is yet to come."
John 16:13

As we have seen, governors were placed in colonies not just to give information, but also to train the citizens to think, act, and live the standards, the customs—the entire culture—of the home country. This involved both general teaching and individual training.

Because the governor of a colony was sent from the throne of the sovereign, he knew the sovereign's intent. In the same way, the Governor from heaven is the only one who can enable us to understand the truth of the statements that Jesus made and the instructions he left for us. The Holy Spirit is the only one who can reconnect us to original information about the King and his kingdom. He protects us from error and from others' opinions that are not according to the mind of the King.

One of the jobs of a governor in a colony is to interpret for the citizens what the sovereign means by the words he delivers to them. We saw in the last section that the Holy Spirit is called the Counselor. The word *counsel* has to do with one who interprets law, and the Governor reveals and explains the laws of the King to us, bringing those words to life.

The prophet Isaiah said of Jesus:

"The Spirit of the LORD will rest on him—the Spirit of wisdom and of understanding."

Isaiah 11:2

We, too, have this Spirit of wisdom and understanding living within us. Knowledge is information, and wisdom is how to apply it. In other words, wisdom is the proper use of knowledge. The Governor shows us how to take our knowledge and apply it to life. He is the one who makes us practical people in the world. In some religious circles, this has been reversed. The Holy Spirit is considered to be the one who makes people act in strange ways. However, the Governor couldn't be more sensible. He shows us how to apply our knowledge to family, business, community, nationally, and to worldwide issues.

HELPER AND ENABLER

When the King-Son was on earth, he quoted from the prophet Isaiah concerning himself,

"The Spirit of the Lord is on me, because he has anointed me to preach good news to the poor. He has sent me to proclaim freedom for the prisoners and recovery of sight for the blind, to release the oppressed, to proclaim the year of the Lord's favor."
Luke 4:18-19

When a sovereign declared what he wanted for a colony, it was the governor's job to make sure it happened, encouraging the citizens to work toward its fulfillment. As the Holy Spirit carries out the will of God in the world, we are to be in unity with his desires and intent for the earth in carrying out our role as vice governors over the territory. We are not here to establish *our* kingdoms. We are here to establish the kingdom of our Sovereign, whom we represent.

IN FULFILLING THE PURPOSES OF THE KINGDOM

The above passage from the book of Isaiah emphasizes the focus of the kingdom on earth: telling the inhabitants about the promise of the Father, freeing them from the kingdom of darkness, and showing them the nature of the kingdom and how to enter in to it. It is the Governor who helps us to do all these things.

It is the King's ultimate purpose, as spoken through the prophet Habakkuk, that:

"The earth will be filled with the knowledge of the glory of the LORD, as the waters cover the sea."
Habakkuk 2:14

We can take this statement as an instruction concerning the kingdom. Again, the glory of God refers to the nature of God. Jesus said that, under the Governor's direction, we are to:

"Go and make disciples of all nations, baptizing them in the name of the Father and of the Son and of the Holy Spirit, and teaching them to obey everything [Jesus has] commanded."
Matthew 28:19-20

In this way, the prophecy will be fulfilled.

The Governor calls upon us to bring the culture of the kingdom into the foreign culture that has taken over the earth—the culture of the kingdom of darkness. We saw earlier that to disciple means to teach kingdom philosophy and values, so that the students are immersed in the mind-set of the King. The term *nation* is the Greek word *ethnos*, referring to races or people groupings. Every special grouping of people on earth is to be converted into kingdom culture.

The royal governor of the Bahamas used to appoint local commissioners, or council people, from the colony, and he would empower them to do different improvement projects, such as fixing the roads. Likewise, the Governor empowers us to do good works in the world on behalf of the government. As Paul wrote:

"For we are God's workmanship, created in Christ Jesus to do good works, which God prepared in advance for us to do."
Ephesians 2:10

IN RECONNECTING TO OUR GIFTS

Every human being is born with gifts from God, but in order for these gifts to reach their maximum potential in service for the kingdom, they need to be reconnected to their original source. No one really knows the true essence of his gifts unless he reconnects with the Spirit of the Creator. Moreover, the Governor activates our gifts to a level that we wouldn't naturally bring them. Paul wrote, quoting the prophet Isaiah:

"'No eye has seen, no ear has heard, no mind has conceived what God has prepared for those who love him'—but God has revealed it to us by his Spirit. The Spirit searches all things, even the deep things of God."
1 Corinthians 2:9-10

The Governor reconnects you to the source of your gifts so that you can understand what you have been given—not just the value of your gifts, but also the magnitude of them. In other words, no one's intellect alone can discern or understand the gifts that the King has placed within him for the purposes of the kingdom. This is why, if you want to know what the Spirit of God really created inside you, you have to connect to the Governor.

Paul also said:

"We have not received the spirit of the world but the Spirit who is from God, that we may understand what God has freely given us."
1 Corinthians 2:12

This statement tells us that we don't even realize what we *have* until the Holy Spirit reveals it to us. This truth is vital for fulfilling your purpose and potential. There are things about yourself that you will never know unless the Holy Spirit reconnects you to the deep things in the mind of the Creator and enables you to use your gifts most effectively.

Paul likewise wrote,

"The man without the Spirit does not accept the things that come from the Spirit of God, for they are foolishness to him, and he cannot understand them, because they are spiritually discerned." **1 Corinthians 2:14**

Without the Governor, we can never recognize what has been placed deep within us. We cannot know who *we* are without the Spirit of God. This is why many of us are living far below our potential.

We should note here that there are gifts we are born with and additional gifts that we are given when we receive the Spirit. I believe there is a distinction between these two types of gifts, and we will talk more about "gifts of the Spirit" in the coming chapters. However, the gifts I'm referring to here are the gifts you were born with to fulfill a specific purpose on earth for the kingdom. And the Holy Spirit empowers us to execute these gifts. This empowerment is not necessarily to give us the ability to *do* them because that ability already exists within us. Rather, he empowers us by revealing them to us fully and even introducing us to gifts we didn't even know we had. Moreover, he shows us how to use them for the kingdom rather than for selfish purposes because the gifts our King gives us are always given to benefit other people.

CONVICTER

Jesus told his disciples concerning the Governor,

"When he comes, he will convict the world of guilt in regard to sin and righteousness and judgment: in regard to sin, because men do not believe in me; in regard to righteousness, because I am going to

the Father, where you can see me no longer; and in regard to judgment, because the prince of this world now stands condemned."
John 16:8-11

The word *world* in the above statement is not referring necessarily to people but to a *system* or *mind-set*. It is the system based on the kingdom of darkness that influences the behavior of humans. Therefore, it is the Governor who convicts those outside the kingdom that they need to be forgiven and connected to their Father in the heavenly government. He also convicts the citizens of the kingdom of attitudes and actions that are contrary to the nature of the kingdom. It is the Governor who works through our consciences so that we will choose to live according to kingdom standards.

We should realize that the Holy Spirit is not given to us to "take over" our lives. He prompts us, but he never forces us. In other words, he makes all the citizens *conscious* of the expectations, the standards, the laws, the regulations, and the customs of the kingdom, and he also convinces them of the benefits of these things.

The King-Father is not in the business of controlling his citizens. He wants his children to *desire* what he desires. He respects our wills. The Governor shows us what the Father's will is and helps us to fulfill it as we look to him for wisdom, strength, and power.

DRAWER TO GOD

In accordance with being Convicter and Convincer, the Holy Spirit is heaven's divine attraction to the throne of the King. As the Governor works in people's lives, he draws them to the Father in a gentle way. Again, he is not overbearing. The prophet Hosea gave a beautiful illustration of this approach when he recorded these words of the King to his people:

"I led them with cords of human kindness, with ties of love."
Hosea 11:4

COMMUNICATOR

A true governor would never communicate anything to the people that violated the king's wishes. Likewise, as we have seen, the Holy Spirit communicates only what comes from the heavenly throne. Jesus said:

"He will not speak on his own; he will speak only what he hears, and he will tell you what is yet to come."
John 16:13

This statement reminds me of a practice we observed when the Bahamas was still under the kingdom of Great Britain. Every year, the people would gather at Clifford Park in Nassau to hear the royal governor read a document, sent from the queen in England, known as The Speech from the Throne. To ensure that everyone heard the speech, the whole country had a holiday; everything was shut down.

The royal governor would sit in a chair, surrounded by local government officials, and he would read the mind of the queen of England for our colony. That speech became the plan and the mandate for the New Year. We were gathered together to be reminded of the sovereign's desires for the kingdom and the colony, and her expectations from the colony. It was a review of the laws, customs, and standards of the kingdom, and it also expressed her plans for the future of the colony.

Similarly, the Holy Spirit regularly brings us The Speech from the Heavenly Throne as we set aside the busyness of life to listen to him. The Governor's words will never disagree with the King's words or bring a message that is contrary to them. He will remind us of what the King has already said and what he desires, and he will also speak prophetically of the future of the kingdom.

SANCTIFIER

Paul wrote to the first-century kingdom citizens in the city of Thessalonica:

"From the beginning God chose you to be saved through the sanctifying work of the Spirit and through belief in the truth."
2 Thessalonians 2:13

As Sanctifier, the Governor helps free us from things in our lives that are contrary to the nature of the King and that diminish our capacity to maximize our gifts for the kingdom. Earlier, we saw that to be sanctified or holy means to be both pure (integrated, whole) and set apart. The Holy Spirit therefore eliminates hindrances to our development and progress. It is like separating the chaff from the wheat. The chaff is no good to us. The separation involves some painful "winnowing," but it is for our benefit. The King does not want anything to stop us from fulfilling our potential and accomplishing our purpose.

The Governor also sanctifies us in the sense of setting us apart for the service of the heavenly kingdom, and for the day when the King will once more return to the earth to live forever with his people with the creation of a new heaven and earth. When the queen of England was going to visit the Bahamas, the royal governor would require everyone to prepare for it. We would have to sweep the roads, clean the lampposts, and plant trees and flowers. We even had to mow our own private yards, even though the queen would never see them. It is the Holy Spirit's job to prepare every aspect of our lives for the King's coming.

These, then, are the major ways in which the Governor attends to us according to his nature. In the next chapter, we will take a closer look at the culture of the kingdom that the Governor desires to instill in us.

Exercise: Why do we need the Holy Spirit?

_____

_____

_____

INITIAL CHANGE

The Holy Spirit's ministry is essential in the creation of the life of every believer. He is the change agent that makes us new creations in Christ Jesus. This means that anyone who belongs to Christ has become a new person. The old life is gone, a new life has begun. It begins when we accept Jesus Christ as Lord and Savior. At this point, the Holy Spirit comes and joins with the spirit of the new believer. He immediately replaces the sinful nature of man, (the nature you were born with) with the righteous nature of Christ. Christ' nature makes you righteous which means that you are now in right standing with God. This righteousness is not based on anything that you have done to earn it but, based on the completed work of Christ. The exchange of nature means that you are born again and now a new creation. The indwelling of the spirit produces the life of Jesus Christ in your life Romans 8:1 – 2. Being the agent of change is a first and continual ministry of the Holy Spirit. He is always shaping and changing us to be more and more like Christ. That way, you will expect and receive all of the promises of God in your life.

CONTINUAL CHANGE

The Holy Spirit's ministry of change continues through a process called sanctification. Sanctification, which means 'set apart for a holy purpose', is the process of maturing in your faith. It occurs as you yield more and more of your life to the Holy Spirit's teaching, witness, and direction. He leads you into truth. When the Holy Spirit is ministering to you, he is changing you (Ephesians 4:23 to

24). Instead, let the spirit renew your thoughts and attitudes. Put on your new nature, created to be like God truly righteous and holy.

Sanctification, a spiritual maturity, occurs as the Holy Spirit reveals the truth of God's word to you. As you learn, your lifestyle begins to mirror the change that has taken place on your inside. Your actions and lifestyle become the pool of the new creation that you have become. You will begin to live in victory, and you will see the promises of God come alive in your life.

Romans 8:5-6: Those who are dominated by the sinful nature think about simple things, but those who are controlled by the Holy Spirit think about things that please the spirit. So, letting your sinful nature control your mind leads to death. But letting the spirit control your mind leads to life and peace.

CHOOSE TO CHANGE

You have probably heard the saying that God is a gentleman; He will not force you to do what you do not want to do. This is very true. He gives us free will so that we can choose Him and choose how closely we will follow Him. The choice to change and become more like Christ is ours to make; the choice to believe Him and receive His promises are ours to make. You have to choose to change, and you have to continually embrace the change that God is trying to bring to you (Romans 12:1-2). You will continually have to make the choice to spiritually mature. That choice is proved out by the way you develop spiritual disciplines. Spiritual disciplines, like setting time aside to pray and read your Bible, applying what you learn in your everyday life, fellowshipping with other bible believing Christians, seeking to please the Lord by obeying His words regarding serving in His Kingdom, demonstrate your willingness to yield to the sanctification process. You can be saved and not grow to spiritual maturity. There are churches that are full of immature Christians who act the same way that they did the day they were saved. That is not God's desire for us. He wants us to get to develop a relationship with Him so that we will trust and believe Him and His word.

CHANGE AGENT (AGENT OF CHANGE)

A change agent, or agent of change, is someone who promotes and enables change to happen within any group or organization. In business, a change agent is an individual who promotes and supports a new way of doing something within the company, whether it is the use of a new process, the adoption of a new management structure or the transformation of an old business model to a new one. A change agent is sometimes also called an agent of change or change advocate. Overall, a change agent serves as a liaison between the organization's leadership that sponsors a change initiative and the people impacted by the change. He or she helps articulate reasons for the change, answers question and persuades others on the necessity of the initiative, while also bringing concerns voiced by the organization to the attention of leadership.

INTERNAL VERSUS EXTERNAL CHANGE AGENTS

Managers and executives are often expected to be change agents within their organizations. However, change agents are not limited to high-ranking employees. A change agent can be a lower tier worker with the right mix of skills, characteristics, and authority to shepherd others through the transformation. A change agent can also be someone outside the organization; an external change agent is often a consultant hired to help with a change effort. However, a change agent can come from various positions within or outside an organization, a successful change agent is generally one who is well-respected by the individuals impacted by the organizational change, and one who is well-informed about the various facets of the project, the organization and the individuals involved.

WHAT CHANGE AGENTS DO

Regardless of the actual position or job title a change agent holds, an individual who takes on the task of being an agent of change assumes responsibility for:

➢ Promoting the value of the transformation that is being undertaken by the organization.

➢ Formulating how the transformation will happen.

➢ Guiding and supporting others through the transformation.

➢ Ensuring that the new processes, procedures, structures, etc., are implemented in ways that deliver the expected value that the organizational change was to produce.

CHANGE AGENTS' ROLES AND RESPONSIBILITIES

To achieve those objectives, a change agent generally assumes several responsibilities that should start once leadership decides to undertake an initiative. That way, a change agent can contribute to the initiative's implementation strategy and decision-making process. In addition, by assigning a change agent at the start of the initiative, the change agent's objectives, responsibilities, and metrics for success can be incorporated into the project plan.

THE SPECIFIC TASKS THAT CAN FALL TO AN AGENT OF CHANGE INCLUDE:

➢ Explaining why change is taking place and who will be affected

➢ Advocating for the change initiative

➢ Disseminating information

➢ Highlighting potential benefits and drawbacks of proposed initiatives

➤ Anticipating and evaluating areas of potential dispute or disruption

➤ Developing strategies to counteract those potential areas of dispute or disruption

➤ Obtaining feedback to share with leadership and conveying responses back

➤ Serving as a point person who is available to hear others' concerns, ideas, and questions

➤ Advising stakeholders, as well as the impacted individuals

➤ Mediating points of contention

➤ Tracking and managing objectives of the project established for the change agent

CHARACTERISTICS OF CHANGE AGENT

To help ensure success, organizational leaders should choose a change agent based on a variety of characteristics that are commonly identified as the most effective for the role. Those characteristics include:

➤ Diversified knowledge

➤ Experience in the business discipline impacted by the change effort

➤ A willingness to ask tough questions

➤ Flexibility, creativity, and openness to new ideas

➤ A strong network

➤ Trustworthiness and credibility

➤ An understanding of the business culture

➤ Courage

➢ Excitement for new opportunities and potential

➢ Comfortable working through uncertainty

IMPORTANT SKILLS: Similarly, a change agent must have specific skills in order to be successful. These generally include:

➢ The ability to prioritize

➢ The ability to build relations

➢ Strong communication skills

➢ Good people skills

WHY AGENTS OF CHANGE ARE IMPORTANT.

A change agent serves a distinct role within a change initiative as a proponent of the change, as well as a conduit between leadership and the rest of the people. A successful agent of change can help smooth resistance to change and address the issues before they derail an initiative and thus, can help ensure the successful implementation and adoption of a new project.

STEPS TO BEING AN EFFECTIVE CHANGE AGENT

The only constant is change and change is difficult for most of us humans and organizations alike. However, change is necessary for growth and when harnessed properly, leads us to being more efficient and maximizing our potential. That is why it is important to learn how to be a change agent. The purpose of change management is to implement strategies for effecting change, controlling change, and helping people to adapt to change. A change agent is a person or group that facilitates the change process in an organization. The change agent is viewed as that entity that motivates, inspires, catalyzes, and potentially leads the change process in hopes of a positive outcome.

WAYS TO BE AN EFFECTIVE CHANGE AGENT

EMBRACE THE RESISTANCE.

The source of most of the anxiety when it comes to change management is people. People will be resistant, know it, appreciate it, and be comfortable with it. Then determine ways that you can slowly overcome this resistance. The first step is to identify your allies. Find the long-standing personnel who have some degree of influence in the organization and partner with them. When colleagues recognize that a long-standing team member is on Team Change, they will be more willing to accept the changes rather than oppose them.

CO-CREATE THE VISION

Most change management books will highlight the importance of creating a powerful vision. This emphasis is necessary, and the advice is wise. However, it is more effective to have leadership and other influencers collaboratively working with you to craft your desired end-state. The vision needs to be a co-creation with everyone feeling like they contributed and own the result. Your vision needs to be easily understandable, to inspire action and to focus attention. Frequent and consistent communication of the vision is one of the key strategies that will help you further overcome the resistance that you will face. You and your allies can never talk about the vision too much.

GET COMMITMENT

Getting people to commit to the idea of changing is vital. Embracing the resistance and co-creating the vision would have helped you get your allies and leadership backing. However, you not only have to launch an awareness and feedback campaign for all affected, but you also have to ensure that the most senior leader is on Team Change and spreading the same good news. Change management initiatives have a very high probability of failure when the top leader is not on board. They must be bought in, actively communicating the vision, and demonstrating with their actions that they are supportive and enabling the change. Besides, colleagues that feel outside of the sphere of this great new change are more likely to exhibit even more steadfast resistance. Therefore, it is crucial for them to be heard and provide feedback on the path forward.

CREATE A TRACK RECORD

Once you have the vision in a solid state and there are enough people who have committed, then it is time to create your execution plan. Be mindful of time and deliverables in your action plan. People will not wait for nine months to see the effect of your plan. You need to produce, demonstrate, and constantly share tangible products to the organization every one to three months. This process will build the momentum; support and excitement for change that you will need to energize the successful execution of your plan. It also reduces the resistance you will face as you move forward.

MAKE CHANGE NORMAL

Not only do you have to embed the changes made on the path to the vision, but you must take steps to make change management a normal part of work life. Identify and use the devices available to you and your allies that can gently nudge people to continuously question and improve. In the end, change is not easy for most. Being a change agent means that you will force those around you to think more critically and hopefully re-evaluate their existing behavior and ways of doing things. Given that most people become set in their ways after a certain period, this may be difficult for some. As a change agent, you must be okay with this. For a change agent to earn a good reputation, recognize that steady and deliberate progress towards the end goal is the approach that will likely yield the most successful outcome. Being a change agent is hard and important work, be encouraged to know that the world needs you to keep going.

Exercise:

Are you a change agent? How?

_____

_____

_____

_____

_____

Explain 3 ways in which you can be an effective change agent.

_____

_____

_____

_____

_____

MODULE 1.3

Altars, Gates & Thrones

Culled from prophesy on July 2011 at Chicago USA.

Thy throne oh Lord is forever and ever; The Sceptre of Thy Kingdom is a right sceptre. Thou lovest righteousness and hatest wickedness. Therefore, God thy God, hath anointed thee with the Oil of gladness above thy fellows (Psalm 45:67)

It is only my throne that is forever. Every other throne shall be cast down:
Thrones of iniquity, thrones of unrighteousness, thrones of wickedness,
Traditional thrones, thrones in the galaxies, and thrones in the waters.
It is only the throne of God that stands forever. For it is the throne of justice and righteousness.
I am the Righteous King. It is only my throne that will judge other thrones.

ALTARS

Establish My Altars in every nook and cranny.

Let My Altar speak.
Where is the meeting point, the place where you will
access my power?
I want Altars. I want a meeting place. Where will I meet you by the
day, noon, or night? Where?
Have you not seen altars of unrighteousness spread out?
Why are you keeping quiet?
Why are you observing and watching?
Why won't your world be saturated with wickedness, iniquity,
abomination, and all kinds of evil, when you allow the wicked to
raise altars all over the place?

GATES

Daughters arise! It is time to possess the gates of the enemy!
How many are diligent gatemen? How many are manning the gates?
Can't you see that many gates are left open and unmanned?
Can't you see a thoroughfare of abominable transactions?
Can't you see the evil trend? These things are happening because
there is no gateman or gate keeper. The ones at the gate are sleeping
and snoring.
I say, rise! Arise and stand at your duty post!
Did I not say, "Whatever you allow is allowed? And whatever you
disallow is disallowed? Stand fast and man your gates! When the
gateman is not at the gate what happens?
Is it not a thoroughfare for all kinds of things?
Where are the watchmen? Do they see?
My watchmen have gone to sleep, and the enemy has entered.
You must wake up to pursue the enemy.
Pursue vigorously!
See lions, wolves, and leopards on the streets!
They are walking around freely; they are comfortable because there
is no one to disallow their entry and no one to question them.
The gate was wide open. See thieves that have come in at an
unguarded hour!
See hawks! See them around, they have come to hunt.
You must go out to the streets! Go and recover!!

Go to the byways, seaports, Go to the airports and borders.
You must cry aloud at the city gates.

TAKE DOMINION OVER THE MARKET PLACE

Who rules your marketplace? Who is in charge? Does it concern
or bother you?
Where is the dominion power and authority I gave to you?
Can't you see how hard those in the other world work?
They work hard to gain ground. Can't you see their speed?
They are swiftly populating their kingdom; can't you see the speed
with which they go?
But my people love sleeping and snoring. Many are in deep sleep
Wake them up to possess your gates and take over.

KINGDOM AUTHORITY

If you are the children of the kingdom, do you know the authority
that backs you up?
Do you even know the influence the kingdom exercises? Do you
know your jurisdiction? Who do you submit to? Who do you wor-
ship or prostrate to? Whose instruction do you take? At whose
service are you?
Do you realize that My Kingdom shall reign forever and ever?
Are you part of that kingdom?
Are you reigning with me?
Do you know you are subjects of that kingdom?
As subjects, what do you do to service and establish that kingdom?
Children of the kingdom, do you know what obtains in the kingdom?
Do you live the lifestyle of the kingdom?
Do you operate in the system of the kingdom to which you belong?
Every kingdom has its own rules and regulations. But all these
kingdoms are just a footstool to Me:
They are My footstool, yet My heart is sad that the citizens of these
kingdoms exercise more authority than My children. They are bold
and courageous.
Where are the children of the real kingdom?

THRONE

Do you service the throne where you belong?
My throne will rule in Righteousness and Majesty, overall.
I am the king who sits upon the throne in Royal Majesty.
I sit as King forever. Thrones come and thrones dissolve, but my kingdom and Throne are forever.
Nothing changes me.
As I was yesterday, I Am today and ever shall be. I rule over all things: principalities, powers, dominions.
I rule over all. You should know your authority.

SERVICE THE LAMB'S ALTAR

Where is your service? Bring service to the lamb's Altar where you belong.
Are you not made a priest?
Do you offer me incense and Sacrifice?
How do you service and man my altar?
Let your life be a living sacrifice unto me.
Will your life be a burnt offering unto me that I may consummate you?
Where is your sacrifice and service?
When I come to consume the sacrifice, I don't see any sacrifice.
Where is your offering unto me?
The sacrifice of your lips and of your praise, where is it?
The kingdom of darkness makes daily sacrifice to strengthen the throne of Satan.
Where are the children who have made a covenant with me by sacrifice?
Where are they that they may service my throne?
Where are those who will sustain the fire that burns on My Altar?
Your fire must burn continually. Repair your Altars, that there will be a fresh fire on them. Call upon the name of the Lord. Wherever My Name is called I will go there and answer by myself.
I am searching, looking for places where My Name will be called, that I will answer and show myself strong and mighty.

ALTARS

Be wise, I need altars:
Establish My altars in your subway, in your malls, in your eateries, in hospitals, in prisons, in schools.
Establish my altars in your families and in every nook and cranny.
Establish my altars so that you can draw strength daily.
Let incense be offered unto me continually.
How can you take the kingdom of darkness – when you have not raised living altars unto me? How can you win the battles when there are heaps of ashes on your altars?
Where is the meeting place, where will I meet you? Some of you don't even give me an appointment- You do not engage me; I have come to require it from you.
Rise up and man your gates!
Were you not sleeping when the enemies sowed tares?
How can you chase out the enemy when he has entered your turf already?
You have a carefree attitude. By your attitude you are saying, "It doesn't matter". "I don't care", "it's not my business", what concerns me with education?"
But your children go to those schools. They are taught by people loyal to the enemy. Yet you claim nothing concerns you.
What concerns you with business?
But you eat and buy from the markets controlled and manipulated by the enemy.
My daughters, the hour has come.
The hour of light that you will work like children of light.

COUNTER STRANGE ALTARS

Don't you see what the sons of the bond woman are doing?
They are establishing unrighteous altars in their trade and all their business affairs.
They raise altars everywhere they go. Do you not see what their feet are doing?
They are possessing grounds.

They have spread out themselves in nations, continents, and cities.
They consolidate their gains by forming cell groups.
They move in cells. Can't you see their sacrifice?
They burn their incense and call upon their gods. Do they give any breathing space?
They do their thing in minutes and seconds.
They are judicious in their use of time. That is why they control the economy. Can't you see their altars?

How else do you want to take over and dominate – when you are complacent and satisfied? How do you hope to make progress?
You say, it is an abomination to pray openly.
You have been so intimidated.
You are afraid of your life. If you are afraid and too careful about your life you will lose it; for whosoever will not take up his cross and follow me is not worthy to be my disciple.
Do not be ashamed of me for if you are, I will be ashamed of you.
You do not respect my throne or my kingdom.
You walk into My Presence carelessly and behave the way you like.
You approach my throne without reverence. You are lax in attitude.

I love righteousness and hate wickedness. The habitation of my throne is righteousness and justice (Psalm 89:14). My throne is holy and cannot condone iniquity, wickedness, and unrighteousness. Although I am a merciful God, I am a consuming fire. Whosoever comes unto me must come with fear, trembling and reverence.
Don't you respect and honor your earthly kings?
Don't you give them reverence?
But when you come to my throne, you come lackadaisically and nonchalantly.
You do not have regard for me or recognize me as King.

DO NOT PROVOKE ME TO ANGER.

You approach me with hands that are defiled thinking that the Lord does not know nor see. I am not like your earthly kings.

When you go to your earthly kings, do you not prostrate?
Do you not bow and call them their names?
Do you not tremble before them?
But when you come to me, you come carelessly and without fear.
Yet you call me "King of kings and Lord of lords".
Do you not respect my subjects more than me?
You think I do not see or observe?
I am a loving Father, but you must never forget that I am a consuming fire.
Bow before My throne in worship; in adoration.

GATES

"Lift up your heads oh ye gates and be thou lifted up ye
everlasting doors"
The King of kings is coming, and every gate/door must lift.
The King of kings is coming in His splendor. He is coming
in Majesty.
The King of kings is coming, let every gate open; Command every
gate to lift their heads. Who is this King of glory? The Lord, mighty
in battle!!
The Lord will make war with the kings of the earth for they have
forgotten that there is a King over them. They have spread out
themselves and are taken over by arrogance and pride. They have
questioned the authority of the Almighty.
The King of kings will come, and every king will know they
are subjects.
He will make war and overthrow them.
He will fight in the three kingdoms: the kingdom in the heavenlies,
the kingdom in the waters and the kingdoms on the earth.
He will fight these kings, overthrow, and cast down their thrones.
Then He will sit as the Ancient of Days.
But this will not happen until His children establish His Altars,
until His Altars are established.
There are many treasures locked up and caged in the waters by the
power that controls and rules in the waters.

But unto you I have given authority and Dominion because the earth I have given unto man (Psalm 115:16b).

My time to rule on the Earth has come; I have given unto my people authority.

Exercise your authority and Dominion.

Take over what belongs to you.

ANCIENT GATES

There are ancient gates:

These are the gates of culture and tradition; deal with ancient gates because they have influence.

THE GATE OF THE WOMAN

My daughters, do you know why I have called you as gate keepers? Because you are a gateway to life, no human comes into being without passing through the gate of a woman. By that authority, you have control over humanity.

Know the authority I have put upon you. It is time to exercise it judiciously. The gate of the woman is an important gate. It is the gate to all living, whether of humans or animals. For anyone born of a woman cannot fight a woman and go free, why?

You are the gate that brought them to life.

THE EYE GATE: Defilement and pollution come from the gate of the eyes; the eye gate guards against what your eyes see.

THE MOUTH GATE: The destructive gate is the gate of the mouth. It causes a lot of destruction and devastations. Many have built and pulled down through the mouth gate. Let there be a padlock for your mouth gate because from it goes out and comes in what causes destruction.

THE EAR GATE: How does the ear gate sieve information? How do you sieve information? Let there be a sieve that you will sieve what enters your ear gate.

THE FEET GATE: This is the gate of possession. Let your feet be used in an orderly manner. It can possess evil or good. That is why it is ordered: "Guard/mind the gate of your feet that it does not walk where Angels abhor". It is the gate of possession; with it you break things.

THE HAND GATE: Your hands are the gate of transfer; it carries current. It is a gate, but it transfers things, blessings, curses, and whatever you want it to transfer, and it also receives. Man the gate of your hands. Be sensitive to guard your senses, and your sense organs. Your sense organs are gates.

WHAT IS A GATE? A gate is anything that has entrance to give or receive and to check out or allow in. A gate is an exit. Battles are fought at gates. A gate is a place of decision making and gates have walls of defense. Nothing comes in without it being permitted at the gates. Man the gates. It is from the gate you chase out or welcome in. Gates are very important. A gate is a place of sending out and receiving.

Exercise

Illustrate the importance of Gates in a Christian's life using the eyes, mouth, ear, feet, and hands.

MANNING THE GATE: A coward cannot man the gate, the fearful cannot man the gate, and the chicken-hearted cannot man the gate. For fearful things happen at the gates. There are terrors at the gate. The gate is a place of sensitivity and alertness. They that sleep cannot man the Gate.

Man the gate of your Nation.
Man the gate of your Territory.
Man the gate of your Neighborhood.
Man the gate of your Community.
Man the gate of your Family.
Man the gate of your Life.

The Outer court represents the Gate. The Altar represents the Holy Place.

The Throne represents the Holy of Holies. I call you this day to be those that will turn the battle to the gates. I call you this day as My Gate Keepers. It's not a mean job but the most sensitive. It is those that are mature that can stand at the gate.

SECULAR GATES: There are gates of industry, there are gates of technology and gates of media. How many people man these gates? How many are interested in what comes in or what is released through these gates.

MEDIA

The gate of media is a major gate of deceit. It is the gate of pollution. It is a major gate that influences other domains, yet my people have no understanding. I am coming soon. Recover your losses.

Deal with fear. Fear has tormented a lot of my children. Fear has torment. My people are caged by the spirit of fear. Deal with this intimidating spirit for I have not given you the spirit of fear.
RISE up and take over.
Possess and inhabit.
Arise with courage for Everything Belongs to Your God and Your Kingdom but the enemy has stolen from you.
Refuse to surrender.
Recover all and overtake for I am coming very soon!

PREPARATION TO RAISE ALTARS – PLEASE READ ALL THE LISTED SCRIPTURES

1. Do a spiritual mapping to find out as much as you can about the place or area where you want to erect an altar. Pray and prepare yourself.

2. Decide on what type of Altar to raise, properly set up, or declared (Declared recommended for non-church setting).

3. **Pulling down Altars**

    ➢ Thanksgiving/Worship.

    ➢ Cover yourself and all that concerns you in the Blood of Jesus and God's armor.

    (Ephesians 6:10-18, Jeremiah 1:18)

    ➢ Invite the assistance of the Holy Spirit and Angels.

    ➢ Establish your authority to carry out this exercise (Revelation 5:10, Gen 1:27-28, 1 Pet. 2:9-10, Jeremiah 1:10).

    ➢ Repentance: Self, identification (Daniel 9:3-19; Nehemiah 1:4-8).

    ➢ Renunciation and breaking of covenants, dedications & curses identified with the environment.

    ➢ Take authority over any altar that is or has been in existence there (Deut. 12:1-3).

    ➢ Speak to every aspect of creation involved or connected with the altar; command them to repent and stop releasing their strength for evil.

    ➢ Reconcile them back to God through the Blood of Jesus (Colossians 1:20).

> Bind every demon along with Satan in connection with the altar (Jeremiah 10:11).

> De-robe and sack every priest serving, servicing, and supporting the altar (Zechariah13:1-2).

> Command the altar to be pulled down (Jeremiah1:10; 1 Kings 13:1-3).

4. **Raising an Altar**

> Determine the Name of the Altar to be raised (Genesis 28:18-19) e.g., Altar of Righteousness/ Truth/Warfare/Fire/Life/Preservation/Prosperity/ Fruitfulness/etc.

> Pray over the olive oil to be used to raise the altar.

> Anoint the point where the altar is to be raised as you declare that you are erecting the altar (of righteousness/etc.) in the name of the Father, the Son, and the Holy Ghost, Amen.

> Link the Altar to the Lamb's Altar in heaven (Revelation 8:3).

> Ask for Angels to man the altar (Genesis 28:12).

> Ask for a record to be kept of that altar in the annals of creation.

> Call for the Witnesses in heaven and on earth (1 John 5:7-8) to note what you have done.

5 **Dust yourself from the smoke and dust of war and thank the Lord.**

> Cut off every backlash, counterattack, and reprisal.

> Put a seal over the altar with the blood of Jesus Christ.

> Place an injunction of judgement on anyone who tries to destroy the altar.

MODULE 1.4

THE COURTS OF HEAVEN

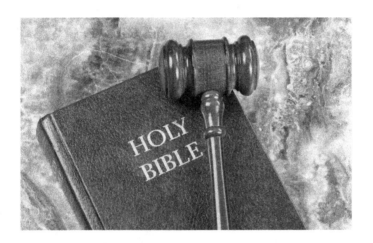

THE COURTS OF HEAVEN ARE A REAL PLACE where believers have access to, by way of prayer and petition, through intercession by the Holy Spirit, who intercedes for the believer. God governs His court system in Heaven as the sovereign judge. He hears our circumstances and answers us according to His governmental system.

Review the past for me, let us argue the matter together; state the case for your innocence. Isaiah 43:26.

Here are some of the legal terms in the Bible: **Law, Justified, Guilt, Penalty, Petition, Throne and Heaven's Court.** There is a legal battle over the rights of this earth, there is an accuser, and there is a <u>Righteous Judge</u>. The beauty of it is that we can come before the Judge, know His will, and petition in prayer. You do not need a law degree to understand the scriptures; you need the Holy Spirit. Likewise, digging into the roots of the Jewish faith, how governments and nations were set up at the time, also gives more understanding on the subject.

From the Old Testament to the New Testament, Heaven's court is mentioned throughout.

Daniel 7:9-10 says this…

"I watched till thrones were put in place, and the Ancient of Days was seated; His garment was white as snow, and the hair of His head was like pure wool. His throne was a fiery flame, its wheels a burning fire; a fiery stream issued and came forth from before Him. A thousand thousands ministered to Him; ten thousand times ten thousands stood before Him. The court was seated and the books were opened."

This vision is a manifestation of God the Father's splendor and the judgment.

Revelation 4 and 5 also illuminate the Throne Room of Heaven…

"…behold, a door standing open in heaven. And the first voice which I heard was like a trumpet speaking with me, saying, 'Come up here, and I will show you things which must take place after this.' "Revelation 4:1

The writing explains the majesty of God the Father's appearance and further discusses the scrolls being opened, revealing what is to come. **All these actions take place within the courts of Heaven. Many Christians steer clear of the book of Revelation and** passages like Daniel mentioned above. Some claim we cannot understand it, or there is too much symbolism.

But we need to remember what Jesus said:

"No longer do I call you servants, for a servant does not know what his master is doing; but I have called you friends, for all things that I heard from My Father I have made known to you." John 15:15

They bring clarity to the fact that, as Believers, we have access to this place in the spiritual realm. We have been granted the right to boldly approach Him, because of the blood of Jesus. We can then petition and become intercessors. Some argue this is in efforts to "change God's mind." It is clearly not about changing the mind of God; it is about having such an intimate relationship with Him that we can approach Him, and at the same time humbly grasp His sovereignty and authority. It is all about seeing the need to follow His protocol so that we can be used by Him to accomplish His will.

DOES SATAN HAVE LEGAL RIGHTS ON EARTH?

After the fall, sin entered the world. We have a choice to follow God and His authority or to go our own way and fall into temptation from the enemy. The fall allowed Satan to have access to this world.

Let us look at how God's Word describes this:

...the ruler of this world John 12:31
...the prince of the power of the air Ephesians 2:2
...the god of this world... 2 Corinthians 4:4
...the whole world is in the power of the evil one 1 John 5:19

Throughout the book of Job, we see the limited nature of Satan's power. God limited the enemy's affliction on Job.

THE POWER OF PRAYER IN THE COURTS OF HEAVEN

Believers, knowing the heart of God, are to come before the Judge and pray in **three realms of** prayer. He desires to be merciful and He wants us to approach Him, to seek and proclaim His mercy for others.

"When you step into these three dimensions, you are not approaching God with a prayer list. You are stepping into a spiritual sphere where you and God begin to move things in the spirt that shift things in the earth." Robert Henderson.

THREE REALMS OF PRAYER

1). Approaching God as Father opens the throne of Grace.

Let us therefore come boldly to the throne of grace that we may obtain mercy and find grace to help in time of need. Hebrews 4:16

2). Approaching God as Friend and stepping into the place of the counsel of the Lord.

And He said to them, 'Which of you shall have a friend, and go to him at midnight and say to him, "Friend, lend me three loaves; for a friend of mine has come to me on his journey, and I have nothing to set before him"; and he will answer from within and say, "Do not trouble me; the door is now shut, and my children are with me in bed; I cannot rise and give to you?" I say to you, though he will not rise and give to him because he is his friend, yet because of his persistence he will rise and give him as many as he needs. Luke 11:5-8

3). Approaching God as Judge opens the dimension of the courts of Heaven.

Then He spoke a parable to them, that men always ought to pray and not lose heart, saying:

There was in a certain city a judge who did not fear God nor regard man. Now there was a widow in that city; and she came to him, saying, "Get justice for me from my adversary." And he would not for a while; but afterward he said within himself, "Though I do not fear God nor regard man, yet because this widow troubles me I will avenge her, lest by her continual coming she weary me." Then the Lord said, 'Hear what the unjust judge said. And shall God not avenge His own elect who cry out day and night to Him, though He bears long with them? I tell you that He will avenge them speedily. Nevertheless, when the Son of Man comes, will He really find faith on the earth? Luke 18:1-8

TYPES OF COURTS IN THE COURTS OF HEAVEN

The Courts of Heaven operate similar to the legal system we see on Earth.

As a result of all the injustices happening in the world, God is releasing a new revelation about gaining justice through the Courts of Heaven. The Cross of Christ is our verdict but there are times we need to enforce this by entering the justice system of God. We operate in the Courts of Heaven through prayer and an intimate relationship with the Lord. Just like here on Earth, there is more than one type of court in the Courts of Heaven. You might be wondering: which ones are accessible to us? There are many different types of Courts mentioned in the Bible. Here are just a few that can help us understand and get started:

The Court of Mediation (Reconciliation): "Settling outside of court" the Court of Mediation should always be our first step in the process of gaining justice.

Now all things are of God, who has reconciled us to Himself through Jesus Christ, and has given us the ministry of reconciliation. 2 Corinthians 5:18

The Court of Petition: *Do not be anxious about anything, but in every situation, by prayer and petition, with thanksgiving, present your requests to God.* Philippians 4:6

We already operate in the Courts of Heaven when we bring our prayers and petitions to the Lord. Notice that Paul says we need to do it with thankfulness and not a spirit of revenge.

The Throne of Grace: *Let us then approach God's throne of grace with confidence, so that we may receive mercy and find grace to help us in our time of need.* Hebrews 4:16

Our interactions with the Lord in the Courtroom of Heaven are centered on prayer and intimacy. It is important to approach the Lord with grace and mercy toward others and ourselves. We need to know and have God's heart of love (1 John 4:8).

The Court of Mount Zion: The Throne of Grace and the Court of Petitions are linked to this court system. Most all your interactions take place here.

But you have come to Mount Zion, to the city of the living God, the heavenly Jerusalem. You have come to thousands upon thousands of angels in joyful assembly, to the church of the firstborn, whose names are written in heaven. You have come to God, the Judge of all, to the spirits of the righteous made perfect, to Jesus the mediator of a new covenant, and to the sprinkled blood that speaks a better word than the blood of Abel. Hebrews 12:22–24

Throughout the Bible, Mount Zion is a place of God's justice and judgment. This best describes the Courts of Heaven and how we can approach the Lord.

The Court of the Accuser: There are several verses in the Bible that show Satan accusing people in the Courts. The main one is:

For the accuser of our brothers and sisters, who accuses them before our God day and night, has been hurled down. Revelation 12:10

It is very important for us to not operate in the court of the accuser. It is best to learn to operate in a spirit of forgiveness and reconciliation.

The Court of the Ancient of Days (Supreme Court): The highest court in Heaven is the Ancient of Days court. This is equivalent to the Supreme Court in the U.S.

As I looked, "thrones were set in place, and the Ancient of Days took his seat. The court was seated, and the books were opened. Daniel 7:9–10

This is the highest-level court, and we cannot go in. One can be taken in through visions and dreams, but this is not a place to present our case, according to a lawyer, Elizabeth Nixon's insight on the Courts of Heaven. Elizabeth Nixon is a renowned attorney, author and speaker who teaches key spiritual principles that transform lives and launch people into their destinies.

WHICH COURT DO WE GO IN TO PRESENT OUR CASE?

There are other Courts of Heaven that require greater understanding to operate in, but these are the basic ones that are safe to operate in: The Court of Petitions, The Throne of Grace, The Court of Mount Zion, and The Court of Mediation. We always ask the Lord's permission before operating in the Courts of Heaven. Remember to mediate your case first and settle outside of the Courts of Heaven whenever possible, so we are not unnecessarily clogging up the heavenly courtrooms. We can pray more effectively once we understand some of the basic principles and protocols of the Courts of Heaven. You deserve justice from the Lord because the attacks of the enemy have been so great.

WHO IS WHO IN THE COURTS? Throughout the entire Bible, we see a pattern like a court of law. Many Greek and Hebrew words for God, Jesus and the Holy Spirit will confirm the roles of the lawgiver, advocate, intercessor, and witness. There are many verses in the Bible about this and I encourage you to search them out. I have provided a few verses below to illustrate the "roles" of "who does what" in the Courts of Heaven:

We are Petitioners: *Do not be anxious about anything, but in every situation, by prayer and petition, with thanksgiving, present your requests to God.* Philippians 4:6

God is our Judge but not a judge as we might think; remember God is also a loving Father and is not out to condemn us. *For the Lord is our judge, the Lord is our lawgiver, the Lord is our king; it is he who will save us.* Isaiah 33:22

Jesus is our Mediator (attorney): *For there is one God and one mediator between God and mankind, the man Christ Jesus.* 1 Timothy 2:5

Holy Spirit is our Witness: *The Spirit himself testifies with our spirit that we are God's children.* Romans 8:16

Satan is our Prosecutor: *For the accuser of our brothers and sisters, who accuses them before our God day and night, has been hurled down.* Revelation 12:10b

Let us then approach God's throne of grace with confidence, so that we may receive mercy and find grace to help us in our time of need. Hebrews 4:16

When we pray, we are already interacting in the Courts of Heaven at some level, but we may not have realized it. We are most familiar with intercession and spiritual warfare prayers. God is now releasing deeper understanding and revelation on this topic because the love of many has grown cold, which increases injustices. The Courts of Heaven are even more important now, as the enemy is over-attacking us, and we need justice.

NEW UNDERSTANDING

By the grace God has given me, I laid a foundation as a wise builder, and someone else is building on it. But each one should build with care. For no one can lay any foundation other than the one already laid, which is Jesus Christ. 1 Corinthians 3:10–11

Jesus opened the minds of His disciples, and they received a greater revelation of how He was fulfilling the Old Testament prophecies (Luke 24:45). We are no longer under the Law of Moses in the Old Testament. We now have the law of the Spirit of God in the New Testament (Romans 8:2). We have the finished work of what Jesus did for us on the Cross, which gives us access to all we need. But if you are not seeing the fullness of God's promises which include good health, financial blessings and answered prayers, then you might need to access the Courts of Heaven to change things. For deeper insight and revelation, I will be sharing much more in my upcoming online discipleship workshops. Please consider signing up.

MODULE 1.5

SEXUAL PURITY

G OD DECLARES THAT SEXUAL RELATIONS
should be only for a man and a woman in a marriage and
should stay between those married people for a lifetime (Ephesians
5:31). God designed sex to be pleasurable, but also instructed that
it was reserved for marriage. Despite what many cultures today
advocate, sexual purity is for our own benefit. Within the boundaries of marriage, sex is a pleasurable and beautiful gift. Sexual
activity outside of marriage is a perversion of something God
made good.

There are many Scripture passages about sexual purity, but 1
Thessalonians 4:3–5, 7 captures much of God's directive on the
subject: "For this is the will of God, your sanctification: that you
abstain from sexual immorality; that each one of you know how to
control his own body in holiness and honor, not in the passion of
lust like the Gentiles who do not know God. ... For God has not
called us for impurity, but in holiness."

Sanctification is being set apart for a holy reason for God's purposes. When we accept Jesus as our Savior, we are made holy and become a new creation (2 Corinthians 5:17–19). We can live by faith, instead of by our old sin nature (Galatians 2:20).

The Bible seems to set the lack of sexual purity somewhat apart from other sins. In the 1 Timothy passage above, sexual purity is listed as the first evidence, or step, of sanctification. Self-control over this aspect of life shows we rely on and allow the Holy Spirit's work (Galatians 5:22–23). We are told to honor God with our bodies because they are temples of the Holy Spirit (1 Corinthians 6:18–20). It is the Holy Spirit who helps us honor Him.

Sex joins two people as one. God knows this should be reserved for marriage. 1 Corinthians 6:15–18 says,

"Do you not know that your bodies are members of Christ? Shall I then take the members of Christ and make them members of a prostitute? Never! Or do you not know that he who is joined to a prostitute becomes one body with her? For, as it is written, 'The two will become one flesh.' But he who is joined to the Lord becomes one spirit with him. Flee from sexual immorality. Every other sin a person commits is outside the body, but the sexually immoral person sins against his own body."

God designed and created us, so He knows what is best for us. His rules, boundaries, and discipline are designed for our benefit and His glory. Sex is the most intimate and venerable of acts. This type of intimacy is precious within the committed relationship of a married man and woman. Remaining sexually pure protects that gift. Sexual purity is not only something those who are single need to be concerned about, but it is also intended for married couples to remain faithful to each other. Sex is unique to marriage, and sexual purity maintains the integrity and strength of the marriage bond. No matter your marital state, we are all called to be sexually pure in both our actions and our thoughts. When we follow God's instruction about sexual purity, our lives and relationships will be better for us and honor Him, and our marriage bed will be kept pure (Hebrews 13:4).

GUIDELINES FOR SEXUAL PURITY

According to Randy Alcorn "I have developed the following material and presented it to many young people and their parents over many years. When my now married daughters were teenagers, I enhanced it further for sharing and discussion with them and the young men who asked to date them. Until we had gone over these principles together (my wife and I, our daughter, and the boy) and made sure there was complete agreement, we did not allow a dating relationship to begin. We found that this was a great help not only to our daughters but also to the young men who wanted to date them. We made our expectations clear, gave them specific guidance and principles (not just rules), and told them we would be asking them if they were living up to these standards. This deepened our relationship, opened communication, and created healthy accountability. Though there were sometimes nervous fears as family members (and especially the young men) anticipated these sessions, in each case, the time together was strategic, encouraging and rewarding. Having consistently practiced this when they were dating, it was impossible for us and for our daughters to imagine them dating a young man without first openly addressing with him all the principles that follow. (Each time we did this, of course, it further reinforced these principles for our daughters and for us.) "It is God's will that you should be sanctified: that you should avoid sexual immorality; that each of you should learn to control his own body in a way that is holy and honorable, not in passionate lust like the heathen, who do not know God." (1 Thessalonians 4:3-5).

WHAT WE NEED TO KNOW

1. Sex is good. God created it, God called it "good," and it existed before there was any sin in the world.

Sex was not created by Satan, Playboy, Hollywood, HBO, rock musicians or the Internet.

- Sex was created by the holy God of heaven, where purity reigns.

- God made sex physically desirable by creating us with sexual drives, without which sex would not exist and neither would people. God's Word speaks openly of the pleasure of sex within the marriage relationship (Proverbs 5:18,19; Song of Solomon 4:5; 7:1, 6-9).

- We should not be ashamed to talk about what God was not ashamed to create. However, God requires us to address the subject in keeping with his intentions and requirements, not the world's. He warns us not to talk about sex in any inappropriate context: But among you there must not be even a hint of sexual immorality, or of any kind of impurity, or of greed, because these are improper for God's holy people. Nor should there be obscenity, foolish talk, or coarse joking, which are out of place. (Ephesians 5:3-4) God designed sex for the sacred union of marriage and reserves it for that union. It is both how children are conceived (something very close to God's heart) and a means by which marital intimacy is expressed and cultivated.

- When it takes place in its proper context, God is pro-sex.

2. Like all good gifts from God, sex can be misused and perverted.

Water is a gift of God, without which we could not survive. But floods and tidal waves are water out of control, and the effects are devastating. Fire is an energy-producing gift of God that gives warmth and allows us to cook. But a forest fire or a house burning to the ground, or a person engulfed in flames is fire out of control-it is horrible and frightening. Water and fire are good things which, when they occur outside their God-intended boundaries, become bad. Likewise, God designed sex to exist within certain boundaries. When exercised in line with God's intended purpose, it is beautiful and constructive. When out of control, violating

God's intended purpose, it becomes ugly and destructive. Sex is a good thing which, when it occurs outside its God-designed boundaries, becomes bad. **The problem is not sex**; the problem is us. We are sinners who can pervert, abuse, and rip away from their proper place the good things God created. The greater the gift from God, the more power it has both for good and bad. Inside marriage, **sex has great power for good**. Outside marriage **it has equally great power for bad.**

3. The boundaries of sex are the boundaries of marriage.

Sex and marriage go together. Sexual union is intended as an expression of a lifelong commitment, a symbol of the spiritual union that exists only within the unconditional commitment of marriage. Apart from marriage, the lasting commitment is absent, and the sex act becomes a false expression, a lie. Every act of sex outside of marriage cheapens both sex and marriage.

➢ Sex is a privilege inseparable from the responsibilities of the sacred marriage covenant. To exercise the privilege apart from the responsibility perverts God's intention for sex.

➢ Sex is designed to be the joining of two persons of two spirits, not just two bodies. Sex should be giving to someone to whom I am 100% committed (as measured by the state of legal marriage), not taking from someone to whom I am uncommitted or partially committed. "But we really love each other" has no bearing on the ethics of sexual intimacy.

➢ Sex does not become permissible through subjective feelings, but through the objective lifelong commitment of marriage.

4. Your sexual purity is essential to your walk with God.

Sexual purity is not an option for an obedient Christian; it is a requirement. God's will is centered on our character and moral purity much more than on our circumstances, such as job, housing, and schooling. You want to know God's will? You do not have to wonder. Here it is: *"It is God's will that you should be sanctified: that you should avoid sexual immorality"* (1 Thessalonians 4:3). There is no sense seeking God's will in other areas when you are choosing to live in sexual impurity in your mind or body.

"Who may ascend the hill of the Lord? Who may stand in his holy place? He who has clean hands and a pure heart" (Psalm 24:3-4)

"If I had cherished sin in my heart, the Lord would not have listened." (Psalm 66:18)

"If anyone turns a deaf ear to the law, even his prayers are detestable." (Proverbs 28:9)

"When I called, they did not listen; so, when they called, I would not listen,' says the Lord Almighty." (Zechariah 7:13)

Sexual purity is inseparable from a committed Christian life. If you are not living in sexual purity, God will not hear your other prayers until you offer the prayer of confession and repentance and commit yourself to a life of holiness (1 John 1:9).

5. You are vulnerable to sexual immorality.

Do not deceive yourself that it can never happen to you. It can, and if you do not think it can, it almost certainly will.

"Pride goes before destruction, a haughty spirit before a fall." (Proverbs 16:18)

"So, if you think you are standing firm, be careful that you don't fall!" (1 Corinthians 10:12)

"Brothers, if someone is caught in a sin...watch yourself, or you also may be tempted." (Galatians 6:1)

If you think you will never be robbed, you will fail to take precautions to keep it from happening. If you think you will never fall sexually, you will fail to take precautions to keep it from happening.

6. You are targeted for sexual immorality.

Years ago, there was gossip about an international "hit list," a calculated plan for paid assassins to murder strategic world leaders. The Enemy, Satan, has maintained a moral "hit list" throughout the ages. Since God's children are close to God's heart, Christians are at the very top of that list. The more involved you are in serving Christ, the greater vested interests Satan has in destroying you and God's work in and through you. The evil one wants to take you down and to use your life as a bad example to other Christians, who will imitate your moral compromise. God requires that we be holy and pure instruments to be used by him (2 Timothy 2:20-21). More Christians including Christian leaders become useless and relapse from serving Christ due to sexual immorality than anything else.

Here is the reality; the forces of evil have taken out a contract on *you*. There is a price on your head. Satan has declared war on you: "Our battle is not against flesh and blood, but against principalities and powers of darkness, against spiritual forces of evil in the invisible realm" (Ephesians 6:12). These evil beings have vested interests in your moral collapse. They will do everything in their power to strike out at Christ and his church through enticing you into immorality. Satan is neither omnipresent nor omnipotent. There are only so many demons and none of them can be in two places at once. Therefore, fallen angels attack and tempt not indiscriminately but with strategic purpose. Satan does not have to waste his time on those who have already made the biggest messes of their lives. Rather, he specially targets those whose fall would have the greatest negative effect on the kingdom of God. That is why God's Word warns Christians:

"Be self-controlled and alert. Your enemy the devil prowls around like a roaring lion looking for someone to devour" (1 Peter 5:8).

The devil wants to derail you from serving God. He wants you imprisoned to sin. God wants you free. Only by exercising self-control and being alert can we expect to resist the enemy's plan to lead us into sin. Somehow, Satan knows the cracks in the armor of every Christian. His aim is deadly, he excels at tailor-made temptations, and it is at our points of greatest vulnerability that he will attack.

Do not forget that "the one [Christ] who is in you is greater than the one who is in the world" (1 John 4:4). As powerful as the evil one is to tempt us, God is infinitely more powerful to deliver us and has given us in Christ all the resources we need to live godly lives:

His divine power has given us everything we need for life and godliness through our knowledge of him who called us by his own glory and goodness. Through these he has given us his very great and precious promises, so that through them you may participate in the divine nature and escape the corruption in the world caused by evil desires (2 Peter 1:3-4).

7. Your body belongs to God, not you.

"You are not your own; you were bought at a price. Therefore, honour God with your body" (I Corinthians 6:20).

If it is my house, I have the right to do what I want with it. If it is someone else's, I do not. Sometimes when I am speaking, I ask to borrow a pencil from someone in the audience. Then I break it in half, throw it to the floor and stomp on it. There is always a wide-eyed silence and expressions of shock and discomfort in the audience. I ask them why they are bothered by what I have done, why they think I did something wrong. Someone always says, "Because it wasn't your pencil." Then I explain that it really was my pencil, that I gave it to the person ahead of time and asked her to hand it to me when I called on her. Suddenly it changes everything, because if it belongs to me, then (and only then) do I have the right to do with it as I please. If it belongs to someone else, I have no such right. When you came to Christ, when you affirmed him as Lord of your life, you surrendered your entire self, including your body, to God. The title to your life was transferred from you to God. Christ owns you and your body. You are bought and paid for. "Your body" is really *his* body. He paid the ultimate price for it. What price? The shed blood of God Almighty! We are his, by virtue of both his creation and his redemption. God has every right to tell me what to do with my mind and body. I have no right to do whatever I want with what belongs to God.

8. Sexual purity begins in the mind, not the body.

"As a man thinks in his heart, so is he" (Proverbs 23:7).

"For out of the heart come evil thoughts, murder, adultery, sexual immorality..." (Matthew 15:19-20).

"But I tell you that anyone who looks at a woman lustfully has already committed adultery with her in his heart" (Matthew 5:28).

You will inevitably adopt the morality of the programs, movies, books, magazines, music, Internet sites and conversations you participate in. GIGO: Garbage in garbage out, Godliness in godliness out. The cognitive is basic to the behavioral; you become what you choose to feed your mind on.

Sow a thought, reap an action.
Sow an action, reap a habit.
Sow a habit, reap a character.
Sow a character, reap a destiny.

Your future can be accurately predicted by what you allow your mind to dwell on. Sinful actions do not come out of nowhere. They are the cumulative product of little moral compromises made over time, which ultimately culminate in ungodly behavior. There is nothing new about sexual temptation. What is new is how it has invaded our homes. In the first century Corinth, there were prostitutes all over the streets, but when you entered your home, you had a sanctuary from the temptation. We live in a **technological Corinth**, where immorality can come into the privacy of our home through airwaves (television) and modems (the Internet). Most of us are only a few pushbuttons away from sexual immorality of the mind. Every choice we make to view and contemplate immorality desensitizes us to its evil.

Actions, habits, character, and destiny all start with a thought and thoughts are fostered by what we choose to take into our minds. Therefore, we should take extreme care about what we feed our minds on.

"Above all else, guard your heart [mind, inner being], for it is the wellspring of life" (Proverbs 4:23).

If someone wants to pollute water, he pollutes it at its source. If he wants to purify water, he purifies it at its source. **Our thoughts are the source of our lives**. All our lives flow from our mind and through the choices we make every day we program our minds, either for godliness or ungodliness.

"Turn my eyes away from worthless things; preserve my life according to your word" (Psalm 119:37)

Our minds are not a vacuum. They will be filled with something. It is necessary to turn our minds from the worthless, but it is not sufficient. We also must fill our minds with good thoughts that crowd out and combat the bad ones. It is not enough to say, "Do not think about anything bad." (If I say, "don't think about spiders," what do you think about?) We must also choose to think about the good. (If I say, "Think about your favorite dessert," soon you stop thinking about spiders.) Time in the Word, in prayer, and in conversations with Christ-centered friends reinforces our commitment to purity.

"Whatever is true, whatever is noble, whatever is right, whatever is pure...think about such things" (Philippians 4:8).

We cannot avoid every temptation, but we can avoid many of them, and we can certainly resist their attempts to take hold of us. Martin Luther said, "You can't keep the birds from flying over your head, but you can keep them from making a nest in your hair." Be careful what you expose your mind to. If you are on a diet, do not go to fast-food restaurants. If you do, your resistance will break down. If you want to abstain from lust, you do not go places and watch movies and programs and read things that stimulate lust. Your body will go where your mind allows it to. When it comes to your sexual purity, the ultimate battle is in your mind. Do not give your mind junk food. Be sure you are getting spiritual nutrition.

9. **Since God does not want you to have premarital sex, neither does he want you to do that which prepares your body for premarital sex.**

"How far can I go?" This is a common question, but it isn't the best question because usually it means "how close can I get to disobeying God without actually doing it?" If a parent tells his child "Don't step out on the freeway," an obedient child will not go dangle his leg over the freeway; he will stay far away from it. By putting himself close to the freeway, he subjects himself to unnecessary temptation to act on his impulses, disobey and put himself in grave danger. God made the body and mind with sex drives, and as those drives are stimulated, they move toward a climax. This is a simple fact of life that no one should be naïve about. Caressing each other in sexually stimulating ways is foreplay, and foreplay is designed by God to culminate in sexual intercourse. Since intercourse is forbidden outside marriage, so is foreplay. Since sexual intercourse before marriage is wrong, it is also wrong to engage in activity that propels mind and body toward sexual intercourse.

"Flee the evil desires of youth, and pursue righteousness, faith, love and peace, along with those who call on the Lord out of a pure heart" (2 Timothy 2:22).

There is a continuum of physical contact that begins with things like sitting close and handholding on the near side and moves to sexual intercourse on the far side. In between might be an arm around the shoulder, a brief hug, a kiss on the cheek, a kiss on the mouth, a longer hug, prolonged kissing, fondling, etc.

Scripture does not spell out exactly what "intermediate" behavior is permissible, but one thing is certain; the line must be drawn before either of you becomes sexually stimulated. This means that fondling and anything else that results in a "turn on" is forbidden. If one of you begins to be stimulated even by an apparently innocent physical contact, then, both of you should back off immediately. If you do not back off, you are choosing to stay on a canoe headed toward a waterfall. This is not just wrong, it is stupid. (Those who allow their minds to dwell on what is immoral and who engage in sexual stimulation together should not be surprised when they have sexual intercourse. It is simply the natural result of the choices they have made. If you want a different outcome, you must make different choices.) Guys are more quickly and easily stimulated than girls. A girl often thinks extended kisses and hugs are fine, naïve to the fact that the boy is sexually stimulated and is tempted to push for more. Again, make sure you draw the line far back enough that neither of you crosses it.

10. Once you let your body cross the line, it will neither know nor care about your Christian convictions.

Some Christians pray God will protect their purity, then willfully put themselves into temptation and wonder why God did not answer their prayer. This is like putting a book at the corner of a table and praying "God please don't let this book fall," when all the while you keep pushing it further and further off the edge. No matter how fervently you pray that the book will not fall, it will fall if you continue to choose to push it. No matter how fervently you pray that you will not fall into immorality, you will fall if you continue to make choices that feed your temptation toward immorality. Do not allow your choices to undermine and invalidate your prayers.

11. If you have sexual intimacy with someone outside marriage, you are stealing from God and the other person.

Since he or she belongs to God not you, which means you are borrowing this person for the evening. Be careful what you do with what does not belong to you. You will be held accountable to his or her Owner.

12. God has your best interests in mind when he tells you not to have premarital sex.

What is right is always smart, and always for your good. Sex is not just something you do. Sex is someone you are. It is linked to the welfare of your whole person. Having sex outside of marriage is self-destructive in every sense. Sexual purity is always for the best not only for God and others, but for you.

13. God would not tell you to abstain from impurity if it was impossible to obey him.

God is not cruel. He does not command you to abstain from necessities, such as eating or drinking or breathing. Sex is something everyone can abstain from. It is a strong desire, yes, but never an emergency, never a necessity. Christ has given us the resources to resist every temptation:

"The grace of God teaches us to say 'No' to ungodliness and worldly passions, and to live self-controlled, upright and godly lives in this present age" (Titus 2:12).

"His divine power has given us everything we need for life and godliness through our knowledge of him who called us by his own glory and goodness. Through these he has given us his very great and precious promises, so that through them you may participate in the divine nature and escape the corruption in the world caused by evil desires" (2 Peter 1:3-4).

You do not have to watch that movie. You can turn it off, walk out, go in the other room. You do not have to click on that link to an ungodly website. You do not have to fondle the person you are dating. You can and should draw upon your resources in Christ and say "no" to temptations to sin.

14. Satan will lie to you about sex, but Jesus tells you the truth.

Jesus said of Satan, "He was a murderer from the beginning, not holding to the truth, for there is no truth in him. When he lies, he speaks his native language, for he is a liar and the father of lies" (John 8:43-44).

Satan is an expert at telling lies, and he tells them smoothly and convincingly. He has persuaded many young people *"it's okay to touch her there, it's okay to let him touch you, it's natural, it won't hurt anything."* Soon there's lust, sin, devastation, disillusionment, loss of respect, conflict, insecurity and sometimes unwanted pregnancy and sexually transmitted diseases. Many young people end up angry and bitter at themselves and others because they bought the lie, the relationship is ruined and now they are paying the price! Satan is a liar, but Jesus is the truth and the truth-teller (John 14:6). He said, *"If you hold to my teaching, you are really my disciples. Then you will know the truth and the truth will set you free"* (John 8:32).

Those who believe Satan's lies about sex end up in bondage.
Those who believe Christ's truth about sex end up free.
Identify and meditate on the truths Christ tells you.
Identify and reject the lies Satan tells you.

15. You must learn to think long term, not short term.

Good or bad, you will always reap what you sow; you will always harvest the consequences of your choices.

"Do not be deceived: God cannot be mocked. A man reaps what he sows. The one who sows to please his sinful nature, from that nature will reap destruction; the one who sows to please the Spirit, from the Spirit will reap eternal life. Let us not become weary in doing good, for at the proper time we will reap a harvest if we do not give up" (Galatians 6:7-9).

It does not matter how smart you think you are. It does not matter whether you have a Ph.D in physics, if you step off the tenth story of a building, you will fall to your death. Gravity is law. There is just no getting around it. Likewise, God has set up spiritual laws that govern the universe, including laws concerning our sexual behavior. If we break his commandments, ultimately, we get broken. Scripture teaches two basic alternatives in life, the way of God and the way of men, the way of holiness and the way of sin. Proverbs speaks of the path of wisdom and the path of foolishness, and calls upon us to make right choices, which are also wise, and avoid wrong choices, which are also foolish. After laying out the blessings of obedience and the curses of disobedience, God said,

"This day I call heaven and earth as witnesses against you that I have set before your life and death, blessings and curses. Now choose life, so that you and your children may live" (Deuteronomy 30:19).

The lifelong consequences of sexual impurity are worse than we can imagine. The lifelong rewards of sexual purity are greater than we can imagine.

What You Need to Do (Guidelines for Protecting Purity in Dating)

1. Realize you do not have to date.

Much sexual temptation today is created by our social practice of coupling and isolating young people instead of doing what the Hebrew culture and many others have done requiring that single people spend time together only in a context supervised by parents and other adults. This structure of direct parental involvement and carefully overseen courtship has been the normal social structure; it is ours that is abnormal. In our culture, the unprecedented combination of young people's leisure time, money, transportation and being permitted to be alone for long hours and late at night and the large gap between the average age of puberty and marriage have proven overwhelming temptations to many, Christians included. (This is especially true in a culture that distorts teen sex, making it look romantic and healthy, when in fact it is usually unfulfilling, often emotionally devastating, and always morally wrong.)

Many people think that to be normal you have to date. But just because lots of other people do does not mean you have to. It is an option, not a need. With the upside comes the downside of definite risks and temptations. You can enjoy fun positive friendships with people of the opposite sex and be involved in all sorts of activities without coupling up with one person. If you do choose to date, the following guidelines can help you maintain a walk with God and guard your purity.

2. If you are a Christian, only date Christians.

Dating is the path to marriage. You will not marry every person you date. But the person you marry will be someone you dated. Therefore, every date is a potential mate. There is no such thing as "just dating" you do not "just" bungee jump from a helicopter, or "just" fight on the front lines of a battle and you do not "just" date. It is too important to say "just." Too much is at stake. God says, "Do not be yoked together with unbelievers...what fellowship can light have with darkness?" (2 Corinthians 6:14). Do not enter into any relationship that could compromise your convictions; the closer the relationship the greater the danger.

There are many contexts in which to do evangelism. Dating is not one of them. God does not call anyone to missionary dating. Far too much is at risk. For the same reason you would not marry a non-believer, you should not date one. If you would not eat poison mushrooms, do not put them on your plate. If that seems an unfair comparison to dating an unbeliever, reread 2 Corinthians 6:14. If you would not marry a person because they do not know Christ, that is a good enough reason not to date them. More young men and women are derailed from their walk with Christ by dating non-believers than anything else.

REMEMBER:

- The longer you allow a relationship to go on with a non-believer, the cloudier your judgment will become and the more likely you will commit immorality and turn your back on the Lord in other ways.

- Convictions waver when we place ourselves in the realm of temptation.

- There is only one way to be sure you do not marry an unbeliever: never date an unbeliever.

3. **If you are a committed disciple, only date committed disciples.** (and if you are not a committed disciple, why aren't you?)

It is necessary to date only Christians, but it is not sufficient. Many Christians lack moral fiber, convictions, maturity, and discipline. Just because a person is a Christian does not make him or her morally safe or a worthy partner. Let us face it; some Christians are still jerks, and a Christian jerk is still a jerk. Do not expect perfection in the person you date but, do expect character and godliness. Do not date someone with spiritual problems or character deficiencies that would cause you not to marry them. This assumes that you yourself are a growing Christian, that you are developing a strong character and strong convictions.

REMEMBER:

- If you are not a committed, growing disciple, then a committed, growing disciple should not be dating you.

- Do not only think about being out of God's will if you date the wrong person also think about whether someone else would be out of God's will dating you.

- The first key is being the right person; the second key is dating the right person.

4. Choose dates by character, not just appearance.

"The Lord does not look at the things man looks at. Man looks at the outward appearance, but the Lord looks at the heart" (1 Samuel 16:7).

Appearances change over time. You will find that out at your ten year and twenty-year class reunions! But even in the short run, a person who looks great at first glance but who lacks character and depth quickly becomes less attractive. A person with strong character quickly becomes more attractive. When we judge people by their appearances, often we turn out to be very wrong and meanwhile we may have made foolish choices.

5. Realize Christ is watching and is with you all evening wherever you go and whatever you do.

He is watching you because he is omniscient. He is with you because he is omnipresent, but as a believer he is with you in a very special way he indwells you; you are his holy temple. You are the holy of holies, the dwelling place of the Almighty: "Do you not know that your bodies are members of Christ himself? Shall I then take the members of Christ and join them to a prostitute (or anyone else in an immoral action)? Never! 1 Corinthians 6:15. Since the Holy Spirit of God is within us, when we do evil with our bodies, we bring God himself to the evil with us. This should be an unthinkable blasphemy for any Christian.

6. Realize where you go and who you go with will influence your sexual desires.

It is our nature to be influenced by our surroundings. When we put ourselves in a godly atmosphere with godly people, we are influenced toward godliness.

"Do not be misled: 'Bad Company corrupts good character" (I Corinthians 15:28).

"He who walks with the wise grows wise, but a companion of fools suffers harm" (Proverbs 13:20).

"Stay away from the foolish man, because you will not find knowledge on his lips" (Proverbs 14:7).

". . . Rash, conceited, lovers of pleasure rather than lovers of God... Have nothing to do with them" (2 Timothy 3:4-5).

7. Realize your date is your brother or sister in Christ not your "lover."

"Treat older women as mothers, and younger women as sisters, with absolute purity" (1 Timothy 5:2). Do not go into dating with the goal of romance, but the goal of spending time with your brother or sister. When you begin a relationship, a rule of thumb is, do not do anything physically you would not do with your brother or sister. If a Christ-centered and positive relationship develops, then you might move to cautious displays of affection such as handholding. But be alert to the difference between appropriate affection and intimacy.

REMEMBER:

- You must stay safely back from the line where either one is propelled toward sexual intimacy.

- It is very hard to move back once you have crossed a line. So, do not cross it in the first place.

- This person may end up being a lifelong friend or married to your best friend. Do not do anything with him or her that would cause you to be embarrassed or self-conscious if you end up being best man or maid of honor at his wedding.

8. Focus on talk, not touch; conversation, not contact.

Dating is a time to explore minds and souls, not bodies. Treat your date as a subject to listen to and understand and appreciate, not an object to experiment with, conquer or satisfy your desires.

9. Avoid fast moving relationships and instant intimacy.

Pace your relationship. Take it step by step; do not go into a free fall. A car moving too fast is likely to swerve out of control when it hits a slick spot. Keep your foot near the brake. Do not let this relationship get out of control.

10. Plan the entire evening in advance, with no big gaps.

Gaps always get filled, often with temptations to sexual impurity. Know what you are doing and either stay with the plan or go somewhere safe, where you are in the sight of others (particularly others who respect the need for purity). You can still have a private conversation even in a room full of people. But their presence will encourage you to focus on the conversation rather than on temptation to impurity.

11. Avoid setups like the plague.

Setups include such things as being alone on a couch or in a car late at night or in a bedroom. (Stay out of each other's bedrooms!) Learn not to trust yourself too much. Psychologist Henry Brandt's teenage son asked him, "Dad, don't you trust me?" Brandt responded, "Alone, late at night, in a car, with a girl? I don't trust me why should I trust you?"

REMEMBER:

- Determine to stay away from the setup, rather than putting yourself in the setup and having to call on your convictions when your resistance is at its lowest, and you are most likely to give in.

- In the moment of strength, make decisions that will avoid temptation in the moment of weakness.

- When you are on a diet, do not step foot in a doughnut shop. In fact, do not even walk down the street the doughnut shop is on.

12. Be accountable to someone about your physical relationship.

This should be a committed brother or sister in Christ, usually the same gender as you. It should be someone who takes sexual purity seriously, someone with wise advice, who will pray for you and help hold you accountable to high standards. Parents should talk openly with their children involved in dating relationships. They should go over these guidelines for purity and tell their kids, "Because we love you and it's our job to protect you, from time to time we're going to ask you how you're doing in maintaining purity in your relationship." It is not only a parent's right to ask such a question, but his responsibility. We all need someone to be honest with us. It's a great help just to have someone ask you, "How did it go last night? Did you honor the Lord? Did you maintain your purity?" If you know someone is going to ask, it is a great motivator to choose wisely.

13. Pray together at the beginning and end of each date.

REMEMBER:

- Commit the evening or day in advance to the Lord.

- Ask him to be pleased in everything you do.

- Plan to pray at the end of the date to thank him for the evening. If you know this prayer is coming, it will help you to be sure to control yourself and please God.

14. Imagine your parents and church leaders are watching you through the window.

Would that change how you behave? Then realize your life is not private; it is an open book to be seen by a watching world:

"What you have said in the dark will be heard in the daylight, and what you have whispered in the ear in the inner rooms will be proclaimed from the roofs" (Luke 12:3).

Meditate on the fact that someone much more holy than your parents and church leaders, and to whom you are even more accountable, is watching you, even when you tell yourself you are alone. God is omniscient and omnipresent. He is the Audience of One:

"Where can I go from your Spirit? Where can I flee from your presence? If I go up to the heavens, you are there; if I make my bed in the depths, you are there" (Psalm 139:7-10).

"Can anyone hide in secret places so that I cannot see him?" declares the Lord." Do not I fill heaven and earth?" (Jeremiah 23:23-24).

"The eyes of the Lord are everywhere, keeping watch on the wicked and the good" (Proverbs 15:3).

"My eyes are on all their ways; they are not hidden from me, nor is their sin concealed from my eyes" (Jeremiah 16:17).

God not only sees our actions, but he also knows our thoughts:

"You perceive my thoughts from afar. Before a word is on my tongue you know it completely, O Lord" (Psalm 139:2, 4).

"God knows the secrets of the heart" (Psalm 44:21).

"I the Lord search the heart and examine the mind" (Jeremiah 17:10)

In temptation, our theology becomes very cloudy. The truth is there is no such thing as a private moment. God is never in the dark. He is always watching. We may fool ourselves and others, but never God. He knows what we are thinking about and what we are doing. And it is his appraisal of our life that ultimately matters.

15. When you sense the temptation coming, before things start to get out of control, run.

"Flee from sexual immorality" (1 Corinthians 6:18). When it comes to sexual temptation, it always pays to be a coward. In this battle, retreat is always the first line of defense. He who hesitates (and rationalizes) is lost. Joseph demonstrated this with Potiphar's wife:

"And though she spoke to Joseph day after day, he refused to go to bed with her or even be with her...She caught him by his cloak and said, 'Come to bed with me!' But he left his cloak in her hand and ran out of the house." (Genesis 39:10, 12)

Joseph not only refused to go to bed with her but to "even be with her." He saw the danger signs and avoided her. And when she finally pushed herself on him, he did not trust himself to stay where he was but ran out of the house. Do not stay and try to "resist" temptation when you have the option of running from it. And do not choose to be near someone when that person is a source of temptation to you, or you are to her.

16. Write out your own standards and enforce them yourself. Never depend on your date.

You as an individual are responsible and accountable to God for what you do (Romans 14:10-12; 2 Corinthians 5:10). Someone else's convictions or lack of convictions, or self-control or lack of self-control is not the issue.

REMEMBER:

- You should never be dating someone who lacks convictions and self-control.

- You are fully responsible for your behavior.

- If you fall into sexual immorality, you have yourself to blame.

- Pointing the finger at someone else does not cut it.

17. Make your moral decisions in advance not in the time of temptation.

If you set your alarm clock at night and tell yourself you will decide in the morning whether you need to get up when the alarm goes off, you may as well not set it. Either you are committed to getting up or you are not. If it is left to your feelings in the moment of truth, you will make the wrong decision. Again: in the moment of strength, make choices that will serve you well in the moment of weakness.

18. Memorize Scripture on sexual purity and quote it when tempted.

"I have hidden your Word in my heart that I might not sin against you" (Psalm 119:11). When Satan tempted him, Jesus quoted Scripture to resist. Be ready to take up the sword of the Spirit, which is the Word of God, when the attacks come as they will (Ephesians 6:17). There are many Scripture passages in this handout. Choose some, then write each one on a note card and work on memorizing them.

19. Do not do anything with your date you would not want someone else doing with your future mate.

Somewhere out there is the man or woman you are going to marry. What do you want them to be doing now with someone else? Then live by that standard yourself. "Do to others as you would have them do to you" (Luke 6:31).

20. Look out for the "moral wear down" of long dating relationships and long engagements.

It is easy to peak out emotionally, to wear down in the battle for sexual purity, to begin to rationalize that you are really a couple, and after all you have been dating for years and maybe you think you are going to get married anyway, so you are "almost" or "sort of" married, right? Wrong. When it comes to the freedom to have sex, there are just two kinds of people; the unmarried, who do not have that freedom, and the married, who do.

Do not get engaged until you can put the wedding in sight. When you are engaged, people begin to treat you as no longer single, when in fact you are. You can be deceived into slipping into some of the privileges of marriage before marriage, especially sexual intimacy.

21. If you have violated some of these guidelines, confess, repent, and implement a plan to prevent future violations.

When you confess and repent of your sins, God will cleanse you:

"As far as the east is from the west, so far has he removed our transgressions from us" (Psalm 103:12).

"If we confess our sins, he is faithful and just and will forgive us our sins and purify us from all unrighteousness" (1 John 1:9)

A man once confessed to his priest, "Father, forgive me for stealing a half load of hay last night...no, make it a whole load." The priest said, "Which was it, a half load or a whole load?" The man replied, "Make it a whole load...I'm going back tonight for the other half."

Confession is not genuine when you are planning to repeat the same sin. There must be true repentance. Even if you are no longer a virgin you can and should commit yourself to secondary virginity to remain sexually pure from this day forward, preserving yourself only for your marriage partner, should God choose to give you one. You need more than good intentions to maintain your purity; you need a plan. The plan you formulate may incorporate a number of elements we have mentioned, but it should include avoidance and accountability. If you are committed to a relationship with a growing Christian, discuss it honestly and formulate a plan to prevent falling back into premarital intimacy.

22. Be radical; do whatever it takes to guard your sexual purity.

When it comes to causes of sin, do not wait for them to taper off on their own (they never will), take decisive steps to cut them off. Consider Christ's powerful words in Matthew 5 (repeated in 18:8-9):

"You have heard that it was said, 'Do not commit adultery.' But I tell you that anyone who looks at a woman lustfully has already committed adultery with her in his heart. If your right eye causes you to sin, gouge it out and throw it away. It is better for you to lose one part of your body than for your whole body to be thrown into hell. And if your right hand causes you to sin, cut it off and throw it away. It is better for you to lose one part of your body than for your whole body to go into hell" (Matthew 5:27-30).

I believe Jesus uses this shocking picture to persuade his listeners to do whatever is necessary to deal with temptation. (The hand and eye are *not* the causes of sin, but the eye is a means of access for both godly input and temptation, and the hand an instrument of action, either sinful or righteous. What the eye looks at and the hand touches is what we must carefully govern to guard our purity.) Removing a television from a home, getting rid of a computer, or going out of your way to never walk by a magazine rack may appear drastic measures, but they are nothing compared to gouging out an eye or cutting off a hand! Jesus is teaching us that we need to think much more radically and counter-culturally in our efforts to be sexually pure.

REMEMBER:

- Do not be casual or gradual but be decisive.

- If that means never going onto the Internet, never going into a video store, never being with a certain person, never listening to certain kinds of music, then make that resolution, no matter how radical or extreme it seems. (The Bible does not tell me I must watch TV or videos or send email, it *does* tell me I must guard my mind from impurity.)

- You might think "I should be strong enough to resist this temptation," but if you are not, take every step to avoid it.

- If these things seem like crutches, fine! Use whatever crutches you need to help you walk.

A Christian businessman who travels nearly every week told me his walk with God had been completely eroded because of one reason he stayed in hotels and had a long history of failing to resist the temptation presented by the "black box" on top of the TV set, which kept enticing him to view pornographic movies. After years of guilt and regret, followed by yielding again and again to this same temptation, he finally changed his strategy. One day when he checked into a hotel, he said "Please have the TV removed from my room."

When the desk clerk said, "Sir, if you don't want to watch TV, just don't turn it on," he replied, "I'm a paying customer, and I'd like the television removed." They sent in a maintenance man to remove it and he spent his late evenings reading Scripture and Christian books with no temptation toward viewing. In the moment of strength, he made a decision that kept him from temptation in the moment of weakness. He told me he has done this in every hotel he stays at for the last three years and said, "This single action has revolutionized my Christian life." If this means never being alone behind closed doors with your date, so be it. Do whatever it takes. Get creative, get radical, and do all you can to avoid temptation.

23. Count the cost of impurity.

Rehearse in advance the devastating consequences of sexual sin and you will be less likely to commit it. The consequences are serious and many of them are ongoing:

- ➢ Losing your virginity
- ➢ Disappointing your Lord
- ➢ Being a bad example to family or friends
- ➢ Having in the future to tell someone you love
- ➢ The strong possibility of unwanted pregnancy and serious sexually transmitted diseases
- ➢ The mental images of your sexual sin that can plague you

> ➢ The hindrances to marriage produced by premarital sex and

> ➢ The greater possibility of extramarital sex (adultery) among those who have had premarital sex.

Remember that if you do commit the sin of fornication, that can never be neutralized by the greater sin of abortion. Premarital sex is a sin; pregnancy is not a sin. Do not make a child pay the consequences for your wrong choice. Have the courage to make the right choice now. Do not tell yourself you may as well go ahead and sin since God will forgive you anyway. This cheapens the grace of God. Any concept of grace that makes sin seem unimportant is not biblical. God forgives when we sincerely repent, but if we sincerely repent, we will show it by taking necessary steps to avoid temptation.

Even a forgiven person must deal with many consequences to his sin. If I get drunk, drive recklessly, run over a six-year-old girl, and kill her, if I repent, God will forgive me. But his forgiveness will not bring the girl back to life, nor will it absolve me of legal and relational consequences of my sin. Sexual sin has lasting consequences. Do not presume upon God's forgiveness to take them all away. He removes guilt, but he does not always remove consequences. That is just how life works. "It is God's will that you should be sanctified: that you should avoid sexual immorality; that each of you should learn to control his own body in a way that is holy and honorable, not in passionate lust like the heathen who do not know God." (1 Thessalonians 4:3-5).

Final Thoughts

Are you ready to commit or recommit yourself to a life of sexual purity? Now is the time. Nothing is more fleeting than the moment of conviction. Respond now or you may never respond. Do not deny reality. God made a universe in which righteousness is always rewarded in the long run, and unrighteousness is always punished in the long run. What is right is always what is smart:

"I the LORD search the heart and examine the mind, to reward a man according to his conduct, according to what his deeds deserve" (Jeremiah 17:10).

"Does not he who weighs the heart perceive it? Does not he who guards your life know it? Will he not repay each person according to what he has done?" (Proverbs 24:12).

"For the Son of Man is going to come in his Father's glory with his angels, and then he will reward each person according to what he has done" (Matthew 16:27).

"Well done, my good servant!' his master replied. 'Because you have been trustworthy in a very small matter, take charge of ten cities" (Luke 19:17).

"God will give to each person according to what he has done" (Romans 2:6).

"Because you know that the Lord will reward everyone for whatever good he does" (Ephesians 6:8).

Live in such a way as to hear your Lord say to you one day, "Well done." Get on the right side of the universe's moral system. Honor God by living in sexual purity. If you do, you will experience his blessing and rewards not only today, tomorrow, and ten years from now, but throughout eternity. "I made a covenant with my eyes not to look lustfully at a girl. For what is man's lot from God above, his heritage from the Almighty on high? Is it not ruin for the wicked, disaster for those who do wrong? Does he not see my ways and count my every step? If I have walked in falsehood or my foot has hurried after deceit, let God weigh me in honest scales and he will know that I am blameless if my steps have turned from the path, if my heart has been led by my eyes, or if my hands have been defiled, then may others eat what I have sown, and may my crops be uprooted. If my heart has been enticed by a woman, or if I have lurked at my neighbor's door, then may my wife grind another man's grain, and may other men sleep with her. For that would have been shameful a sin to be judged. It is a fire that burns to Destruction; it would have uprooted my harvest." (Job 31:1-12)

LIVING IN A MODERN CORINTH: ACTIVELY PURSUING PURITY IN A SEX-SATURATED WORLD

1 Thessalonians 4:3-7

Randy Alcorn is a renowned pastor, speaker, and author of over 50 books who; very passionate about sexual purity was interviewed. The following is an excerpt from his response:

"How did you begin writing and speaking on the topic of sexual purity?" He replied: "I remember speaking at a Bible college as a visiting lecturer in the early 1980s. During one week of teaching, I had three different female students approach me and confess that they each were having an affair with a youth pastor or senior pastor in their church. It was like cold water thrown in my face. I think the Lord strategically brought those contacts into my life to help me realize I needed to address this issue. Now that was in the 1980s, when we did not yet have the internet. We were in the very early days of renting videos. At that point, I started comparing our culture to ancient Corinth, where you could go out into the streets and supposedly find a thousand priestesses of Aphrodite prostitutes who would throw themselves at men passing by. Today, with TVs, VCRs, DVDs, especially the internet, and now even cell phones, the immediacy and the amassing of pornography is greater than anything we could have imagined".

"As our culture becomes more sexually charged, why do leaders shy away from the topic of sexual purity?"

I think one of the main reasons is that Christian leaders have lowered the bar in their own lives, they feel like hypocrites, and they are desensitized to addressing it in the lives of their people. If a leader is not living a life characterized by sexual purity, how can that person teach others to be pure?"

"How can leaders keep standards high in their own lives and lead by example?"

"Leading by example starts in the home. I see the provocative clothing many young Christian women wear and say, "Moms, you are leading your daughters into immorality when you allow them to dress that way. How quick are our leaders to change the channel when impurity presents itself on TV? Do we lead by example in our personal lives and with our families? That's where discipleship and setting an example starts."

"How can leaders take a strong stand for purity without becoming legalists?"

"When I talk with pastors on this, I say, "This is not just about right and wrong; **this is about smart and stupid; wisdom and foolishness**." We must help everybody understand that this is not only about the glory of God; it is about our good. I take what some people would consider drastic measures to keep myself from sexual impurity. After many years of seeing the devastating consequences of immorality in the lives of person after person, including church leaders, I have come to say, "You know what, that could happen to me, too.""

THE PURITY PRINCIPLE: SUPERIOR SATISFACTION

A sexual image lures my mind toward lust. The world, the flesh, and the devil bombard me with messages: I will feel like a man or a woman; it will relieve my pain, disappointment, stress. I will be happier if I surrender. God's Word shows the lie for what it is. It tells me that real happiness can only be found in Christ. I am left with the choice; trust Satan or trust God. I must choose between sexual fantasies and intimacy with God. I cannot have both. When I see that God offers me joys and pleasures that sexual fantasies do not, this is a breakthrough. But that breakthrough will come only when I pursue God, making Him the object of my quest and when I realize that fantasies are only a cheap God-substitute. Running to them is running from God. When my thirst for joy is satisfied by Christ, sin becomes unattractive. I say no to the passing pleasures of immorality, not because I do not want pleasure, but because I want true pleasure, a greater and lasting pleasure that can only be found in Christ.

John Piper says, the fire of lust's pleasures must be fought with the fire of God's pleasures. If we try to fight the fire of lust with prohibitions and threats alone, even the terrible warnings of Jesus, we will fail. We must fight it with a massive promise of superior happiness. We must swallow up the little flicker of lust's pleasure in the conflagration of holy satisfaction. Those who drink of immorality are never satisfied (John 4:13). Those who drink of Jesus are fully satisfied (John 6:35). I can either have my thirst quenched in Jesus, or I can plunge deeper into sin in search of what is not there. The rest of your life will be largely determined by how you answer this question: Who will you believe?

The Purity Principle includes practical guidelines to protect purity, for singles, for married couples, and for parents who wish to train their children in purity. These include controlling the television and internet and offering alternatives for how to spend our time. It also includes confession, repentance and developing biblical accountability that does not just admit sin but prevents it.

Exercise: Sexual purity is not only for singles. It is also required of married people. How?

List and memorize at least 10 Bible verses that can help maintain sexual purity.

1. _____

2. _____

3. _____

4. _____

5. _____

6. _____

7. _____

8. _____

9. _____

10. _____

THE PURITY PRINCIPLE 2:

The Purity Principle is this: *Purity is always smart; impurity is always unwise.*

Does God really argue for sexual purity on the basis that it is the smart choice, while impurity is stupid? Judge for yourself:

Why be captivated, my son, by an adulteress? Why embrace the bosom of another man's wife? For a man's ways are in full view of the Lord and he examines all his paths; the evil deeds of a wicked man ensnare him; the cords of his sin hold him fast. He will die for lack of discipline, led astray by his own great folly. (Proverbs 5:20-23)

Why avoid adultery? Because God will see it and He will bring judgment but even before judgment day "the cords of his sin hold him fast." The adulterer will be ensnared; he will die. He is the primary victim of his foolishness. In contrast, the man who remains pure can "rejoice" and "be captivated" by his wife's love, enjoying their sexual union (Proverbs 5:18-19).

In the next chapter God asks, "Can a man scoop fire into his lap without his clothes being burned? Can a man walk on hot coals without his feet being scorched? So, is he who sleeps with another man's wife; no one who touches her will go unpunished. (Proverbs 6:27-29)

Haunting words: **no one who touches her will go unpunished.**

Proverbs also depicts the man who is seduced into adultery as "an ox going to the slaughter," and like a deer or bird being killed by a hunter (Proverbs 7:21-27).

A believer recovering from sexual addiction (which requires repentance from sexual sin) once said, "Addicts always think they can get away with it. You won't change until you realize you can't."

You can never get away with sexual immorality. God wants you to remember that...for your sake.

The Battle is in Your Mind

Brad was a seminary student preparing for ministry. One night he argued with his wife. Upset, he drove to Starbucks to think things through. Soon Brad was engrossed in conversation with a young woman. A few hours later, he was in bed with her. Brad came for counselling, ashamed and distressed. "How can I tell my wife?" he asked. "Will she ever forgive me? It was so sudden, there was no warning. It came out of the clear blue sky!" Or did it? Brad had worked nonstop to put himself through seminary. He had come to subtly resent his wife, seeing her and the children as obstacles to his goal of entering the ministry. He no longer dated her or communicated on a deep level. He had been looking and lusting at the magazine racks. He had watched lustful movies when his wife was gone. All of this culminated in the horrible episode that "happened without warning."

The truth is sexual sin never comes out of the blue. It is the predictable result of natural processes. Relationships are neglected and a mind is granted exposure to impurity. Today's thoughts form tomorrow's character. Temptation may come suddenly, but sin does not. Neither does moral and spiritual integrity. Both result from a process over which we do have control. We are what we think. We create our sexual morality through an ongoing series of choices and actions, including tiny indulgences and small compromises. The eye lingers here...the mind loiters there. Like a photographic plate accumulating light to form an image, our mind accumulates the light we expose it to, godly or ungodly. The battle is in our minds.

SETTING BOUNDARIES

To protect our purity, we need to set mental boundaries. On a scale of one to ten. Adultery or pornography addiction might be a ten, at the top of a ladder. But the question is, what were the bottom stairs of that ladder the ones, twos, and threes? When we identify those, disaster prevention can take place. Of course, prevention is not always easy, but it is a lot easier than the alternative misery.

DISASTER PREVENTION HAPPENS IN SMALL BUT SIGNIFICANT WAYS.

For years, I did not permit myself to go in a particular doorway to our local supermarket because of a magazine rack. Later, my mental discipline became strong enough that I could keep my eyes away. But until then I honored my boundary. It was inconvenient, but a small price to pay to guard my purity.

We have television, but we do not have cable. Rather, we use a satellite dish so we can censor the channels. Not because we believe it is wrong, but because we do not want more temptation in our home. Our TVs are in the living and family rooms which are common spaces. There is none in any of our rooms. I am not telling you what you must do. Boundaries will vary from person to person. A boundary may be:

➢ Not standing in a checkout line where certain magazines are displayed.

➢ Or not driving in a certain part of town.

➢ Or never going on a business trip alone.

➢ Or not watching a particular actor or listening to a particular musician.

Boundaries keep temptation from getting a foothold. They are based on the premise that *our* sexual purity cannot be strengthened if we keep doing what we have always done! We must change our habits. We are sentries charged with protecting something immensely strategic.

Our Commander says: "Above all else, guard your heart mind, inner being, for it is the wellspring of life" (Proverbs 4:23).

"Above all else" means it should be at the very top of our daily duty sheet. It is of the utmost importance that we protect our inmost being from new sources of temptation. We must not provide ammunition for our enemy to use against us. We must force our sin natures not to draw from old input (which fades as time goes on). Meanwhile, we make sure new input is pure and Christ-honoring. Of course, your flesh will demand that you give it new fuel. "Feed me," it will cry. But you refuse, praying this: *"Turn my eyes away from worthless things; preserve my life according to your Word"* (Psalm 119:37). You become part of the answer to your prayer by turning your eyes away. (Consider writing out this verse and posting it on your television.)

REMEMBER:

- We are not to be conformed to the world but transformed by renewing our minds (Romans 12:2).

- We are to deny lust and put it to death when it tries to get a grip on us (Colossians 3:5).

- We are to affirm that we are new creations in Christ, covered with His righteousness (2 Corinthians 5:17, 21).

- Your sanctified mind, fed on God's Word, nourished by His Spirit, polices your thought life. It says yes to what pleases Christ and no to what does not.

FILLING YOUR MIND WITH PURE THOUGHTS

Just for a moment, I would like you to carefully follow my instruction. Ready? Okay...do not think about snakes. Do not I repeat, do not think about big slimy snakes, slithering up from your bathtub drain at night and crawling into your bed. You heard me. Do not think about snakes. Have I kept you from thinking about snakes? No, I have encouraged you to think about them. Now, I want you to envision your favorite dessert. Perhaps it is your mother's Dutch apple pie, or chocolate chip cookies with a tall frosty glass of milk, or Almond Fudge ice cream, or a Butterfinger Blizzard. Just think about that mouth-watering treat. What has happened in the last few moments? You had forgotten all about those slithering snakes... until I mentioned them again.

"We take captive every thought to make it obedient to Christ" (2 Corinthians 10:5). When the wrong thoughts come, we correct them, replacing them with God's truth. In time, evil thoughts are not as much at home in us and become easier to evict.

While other urges exist for our physical maintenance, sex does not (1 Corinthians 6:12-13). We will die without food and water. We will not die without sex. No matter how strong the desire, sex is never an emergency, never a necessity. A friend told me, "Nobody has ever exploded due to toxic sperm buildup." As we learn to stop feeding lust, and say no to its demands, we begin to master it. In time its demands become less pressing, more manageable.

A COVENANT WITH YOUR EYES

Job says, "I made a covenant with my eyes not to look lustfully at a girl" (Job 31:1). Job made a commitment to guard his heart by guarding his eyes. The verses that follow spell out the terrible consequences should he not live by this covenant of purity (Job 31:2-12).

A covenant is an agreement between God and man. In this case, we make a sacred commitment to God and to our families and comrades. The agreement is to not look at, and to immediately turn away from whatever pulls us toward lust. Have you made a contract with your eyes, to not look where they should not? Are you practicing this purity covenant when you walk across campus? When you work out? When you drive? When you select television shows? When you are at church? Have you announced your covenant to others? Have you asked them to pray for you and hold you accountable to it? Have you restated your covenant before God? If not, why not do it now?

PARABLE OF THE DOUGHNUTS

Imagine someone whose weakness is eating doughnuts. His doctor says, "No more doughnuts." He vows to God, "No more doughnuts." He promises his family, "No more doughnuts." He calls the church and gets on the prayer chain. He even goes to a doughnut deliverance ministry to have the demon of doughnut desire cast out of him. Here is a guy who means business, right? But then what does he do? Well, if he is like a lot of us, he goes right on reading about doughnuts, listening to doughnut music, and watching television programs about making doughnuts. He spends his time with other doughnut lovers talking about doughnuts, joking about doughnuts at the office, where he often glances at the doughnut calendars on the wall. He looks through the newspaper for doughnut coupons and subscribes to Doughnut Desires, with its glossy, color photos.

It is not long before he is driving to work the long way that "just happens" to go by a doughnut shop. He rolls down the window and inhales. Pretty soon he is buying the morning paper from the rack right outside the doughnut shop. He is lingering just long enough to check out doughnuts through the window. Then he remembers he must make a phone call, and hey, what do you know, the doughnut shop has a pay phone. And since he is there anyway, why not have a cup of coffee? Now, remember, this man has no intention of breaking his vow and eating doughnuts. But the totally predictable and inevitable result is what? That he will give in and eat doughnuts! And can't you just hear his sad lament? "What went wrong? I prayed! I asked others to pray. I asked God for deliverance. Why try? I give up. You do your best and look what happens!"

THE FIRST AND MOST BASIC STRATEGY

If we learn nothing else from the parable of the doughnuts, we should learn that sincere intentions, and even prayers, are not enough. To have victory over temptation we must have clear goals and sound strategies, and we must diligently carry them out.

What is our first line of defense against impurity?

"Flee from sexual immorality" (1 Corinthians 6:18). When it comes to sexual temptation, it pays to be a coward. He who hesitates (and rationalizes) is lost. He who runs, lives.

Scripture puts it emphatically: "Do not set foot on the path of the wicked or walk in the way of evil men.

Avoid it, do not travel on it; turn from it and go on your way"
(Proverbs 4:14-15).

JOSEPH DEMONSTRATED THIS WITH POTIPHAR'S WIFE:

And though she spoke to Joseph day after day, he refused to go to
bed with her or even be with her...She caught him by his cloak and
said, '*Come to bed with me!*' But he left his cloak in her hand and
ran out of the house. (Genesis 39:10, 12) Joseph not only refused
to go to bed with her but to "even be with her." When she finally
pushed herself on him, he did not stay, he ran. Do not stay and try
to "resist" temptation when you can run from it.

ANTICIPATE AND PREVENT SEXUAL TEMPTATIONS

Those whose jobs involve travel get lots of sexual temptation.
Home, family, and community provide natural restraints that are
left behind. Anonymity, loneliness, and leisure time often spell
tragedy. I know godly men and women who travel frequently, yet
consistently have moral victory. But many others have long track
records of failure. They need to stop traveling, even if it means
finding another job that pays less. At a men's conference I once
asked those who travel to stand and share what they had found
helpful in resisting sexual temptation. The story has been told
of the man that for a long time had watched immoral movies in
hotel rooms. After years of this, he finally decided to do something.
"Whenever I check into a hotel, I ask them to remove the television
from my room. Invariably they look at me like I am crazy. 'But sir,
you don't have to turn it on.' Since I am a paying customer, I politely
insist, and I have never once been refused. Immorality is no longer
just a button push away. This is how I have said, 'I'm serious about
this, Lord.' I have done this for a year, and it is my key to victory.
Everything's changed." This man discovered a great principle: It
is always easier to avoid temptation than to resist temptation we
have already exposed ourselves to. **In moments of strength, make
decisions that will prevent temptation in moments of weakness.**

CULTIVATE YOUR INNER LIFE

There is a danger that a book like The Purity Principle can appear to be behavior modification. I understand simple guidelines and the "just try harder" exhortation are not enough to subdue the flesh, break the grip of lust, or minimize the power of deeply ingrained habits. There is no "easy little formula." I cannot emphasize enough the importance of drawing on the indwelling power of the risen Christ. Self-reformation is not enough. Yet, Scripture commands us to do and not do certain things that are within our power. And often, in doing these things, our hearts change.

So, we should take wise steps, knowing that they are necessary but not sufficient. Ultimately, the battle for purity is won or lost in quietness, on our knees with God and in collaboration with our fellow soldiers. Being busy wears down our ability to hear the promptings of God's Spirit, His Word, and His people. Fatigue makes us unaware of what is really happening. Healthy self-examination reveals to us our "triggers"; the situations that tempt us. We then take these to God and ask Him for strength and wisdom to avoid them. Time with God is the fountain from which holiness flows... and joy, and delight.

MEMORIZE AND QUOTE SCRIPTURE

Jesus quoted Scripture to answer Satan's temptations (Matthew 4:2-11). When the attacks on your purity come, be ready to take up the sword of the Spirit, which is the Word of God (Ephesians 6:17). This requires you to memorize Scripture:

"I have hidden your Word in my heart that I might not sin against you" (Psalm 119:11).

The Purity Principle and even this article contains many Scripture passages. Pick out several that really speak to you. Write them out, carry them with you, post them prominently. When you are tempted, talk back to the devil. The Bible gives you the words to say. Have them ready.

PRAY AND DO NOT GIVE UP

Jesus taught His disciples; *we should always pray and not give up* (Luke 18:1). We are often brought to our knees after losing a battle. But we need to fall to our knees *before* the battle begins. Too often we declare a truce with sin. We tolerate unrighteousness and let it claim more territory in our lives, and in our homes. Jesus says "Don't give up! Pray for God's help." Some readers will be suspicious of this because they have heard "Just read the Bible and pray, and that will solve everything." No, it will not solve everything, but nothing will be solved without it. Jesus knew what He was talking about. So did James.

"Resist the devil and he will flee from you" (James 4:7).

WOULD GOD TELL YOU TO ABSTAIN FROM IMPURITY IF THAT WERE IMPOSSIBLE?

Many men have been defeated so long they think victory is impossible. They have given up. That guarantees they will go right on losing. But God calls us and empowers us to be "overcomers" (Revelation 3:5); those who experience victory over sin. An overcoming friend told me, **"People never change until it hurts them less to change than to stay the same."** Many Christian men most of whom had to become desperate first are in sexual addiction recovery groups that have been great instruments of change in their lives. (Like everything else, these groups should be measured by their faithfulness to revealed truth. Some are biblically oriented, and some are not.) Tens of thousands of people are living proof that victory over sexual temptation is possible. And frankly, we need to hear their stories in our churches, to glorify God and bring this message of hope.

DRAW UPON YOUR SUPERNATURAL RESOURCES IN CHRIST (2 Peter 1:3-4). For the grace of God that brings salvation...teaches us to say "No" to ungodliness and worldly passions, and to live self-controlled, upright, and godly lives in this present age (Titus 2:11-12).

This is about the great themes of Scripture, redemption, and grace. Our sexual struggles should remind us of our need for grace and empowerment and make us long for our ultimate redemption (Romans 7:7-25). **If a lifetime of purity seems inconceivable to you, commit yourself in 24-hour increments.** Do you want freedom from the actions and obsessions of lust? Get help. Be wise. Avoid temptation. Go to Christ. Experience His sufficiency. Draw on His power. And when the first 24 hours are over, and you have tasted of the Lord and seen He is good (Psalm 34:8), commit to the next 24 hours. Depend on Him one day at a time. Never underestimate Christ. Sin is not more powerful than God. Do not imagine there cannot be victory until we get to heaven. God says otherwise. We are not to wait for victory. We are to live in it (1 John 5:4).

A FINAL QUESTION

Are you ready to commit or recommit yourself to a life of sexual purity? Now's the time. Nothing is shorter than the moment of conviction. God made a universe in which righteousness is always rewarded, and unrighteousness is always punished.

Purity is always smart; impurity is always unwise.

"I, the Lord search the heart and examine the mind, to reward a man according to his conduct according to what his deeds deserve" (Jeremiah 17:10). Live in such a way as to hear your Lord say to you one day, "Well done, my good and faithful servant." When we hear Him say those incredible words, we will know that any sacrifice we made was nothing compared to the joy that will forever be ours. (And that joy, by the way, starts now).

STRATEGIES TO KEEP FROM FALLING: PRACTICAL STEPS TO MAINTAIN YOUR PURITY AND MINISTRY

A sneak peek at the life of pastors and ministers of the gospel reveals something very disturbing. Terrible and abominable things are happening. Ministers of the gospel leave their wives/husbands and elope with other women/men. This is shocking, surprising, and heart breaking. These stories are heard time and time again. At Bible colleges and seminaries, pre-marital and extra-marital sex is very prevalent. Parents send their daughters to their pastors for counseling, and they end up sleeping with the girls. Church leaders violate their own daughters by having sex with them. Ladies have affairs with their pastors, regardless of whether they are married or single.

For every well-known Christian television personality or author whose indecency is widely publicized, there are a greater number of ordinary pastors, Bible teachers, and church workers who quietly resign or are fired for sexual immorality. Most of us can name several. The impression that ministers are morally secure should be changed as there is overwhelming evidence. But there has never been a mystical antibody that makes us immune to sexual sin. Even those of us who have not fallen know how fierce the struggle with temptation is.

Furthermore, ministry brings with it serious built-in hazards that can destroy us, our families, and our churches. Among them: our position of influence and that strange blend of ego-feeding flattery and debilitating criticism, which can fill us with either pride or despair. As a result, our perspective can be distorted, our resistance to temptation diminished. In addition, our endless tasks and the consequent disorienting fatigue can make us unaware to what is really happening to us.

MONITORING OUR SPIRITUAL PULSE

Often those who fall into sexual sin can point back to lapses in their practices of meditation, worship, prayer, and the healthy self-examination such disciplines foster. All of us know this, but in the busyness of giving out, we can easily neglect the replenishing of our spiritual reservoirs. Daily disciplines are important, of course, but I have found that for me they are not enough. God gave Israel not merely one hour a day but one day a week, several weeks a year, and even one year every seven to break the pattern of life long enough to worship and reflect and take stock.

I periodically take overnight retreats by myself or with my husband. In times of greater need I have been away for a weekend just spending time in God's presence. This is not a vacation but a time in which the lack of immediate demands gives clarity to the still, small voice of God so easily drowned in the activities of daily life.

GUARDING OUR MARRIAGE

It is a good practice to regularly evaluate your relationship with your spouse. Let us watch for the red flags of discontentment, poor communication, and poor sexual relationship. We should try to spend regular, uninterrupted time together to renew our spiritual, intellectual, emotional, and physical closeness. Many Christian leaders move so freely and deeply in the world of great spiritual truths and activities that unless they take pains to communicate daily, their spouses get left out. This development of two separate worlds leads to two separate lives and is often the first step toward an adulterous affair with "someone who understands me and my world." Communication is key because every adultery begins with a deception, and most deceptions begin with seemingly innocent secrets; things "my spouse doesn't need to know."

REMEMBER:

- At work, we are encouraged to surround ourselves with reminders of our spouse and children's pictures, drawings, and souvenirs.

- When traveling, contact your spouse as often as possible.

- If struggling with temptation, try to be honest and ask for prayer.

- Fierce loyalty to our spouses is also a key; try to speak highly of your spouse in public and never to downgrade him/her to others.

- We should be careful not to discuss our marriage problems with anyone of the opposite sex.

Further, we are to take advantage of many of the good books, tapes, and seminars geared toward improving marriage. When you attend Marriage or Couples Seminar, you will probably be surprised to discover some differences in perspective that, if left unaddressed, could have caused problems down the road.

TAKING PRECAUTIONS

One pastor found his thoughts were continually drawn to a coworker, more so than to his wife. After months of rationalizing, he finally admitted to himself that he was looking for reasons to spend time with her. Then his rule of thumb became *I will meet with her only when necessary, only if necessary, only at the office, and with others present as much as possible.* In time, his relationship with her returned to its original, healthy, coworker status.

QUESTIONS WITH WHICH TO CHECK ONESELF:

- ➤ Do I look forward in a special way to appointments with this person?

- ➤ Would I rather see her than my wife?

- ➢ Do I seek to meet with her away from my office in a more casual environment?

- ➢ Do I prefer that my coworkers not know I am meeting with her again?

An affirmative answer to any of these questions is a warning light.

DEALING WITH THE SUBTLE SIGNS OF SEXUAL ATTRACTION

There is a charm about spiritual ministry that some people find attractive. Their attitude toward the pastor can border on infatuation. It is flattering for a male pastor, who perhaps is nursing fresh wounds from the last board meeting, to receive attention from an attractive woman who obviously admires him and hangs on his every word. (The deacons jumped on his every word.) Often the woman's husband is spiritually dead or weak. Finding him unworthy of her respect, she transfers her affection to this wonderfully spiritual man, her pastor. This is usually unconscious and therefore even more dangerous. She may send notes of appreciation or small gifts; he may reciprocate. Expressions of affection may inch beyond the healthy brother-sister variety. The hands are held tightly in prayer; the arm lingers a bit longer on the shoulder; the embraces become frequent.

All this seems harmless enough, but a subtle, powerful process of soul merger can occur. If things are not good on the home front, the pastor will, consciously or unconsciously, compare this woman to his wife, who may be noticeably unappreciative and infatuated with him. This comparison is deadly and, unless it is stopped, can lead into covert romantic affection, which often leads to adultery. **A relationship can be sexual long before it becomes erotic.** Just because I am not touching a woman, or just because I am not envisioning specific erotic encounters, does not mean I am not becoming sexually involved with her. The erotic is usually not the beginning but the culmination of sexual attraction. Most pastors who end up in bed with a woman do it not just to gratify a sexual urge, but because they believe they have begun to really love her.

Once a woman was casually asked about her obvious interest in a married man with whom she worked. *"We're just friends,"* she responded with a defensiveness that indicated they were not. *"It's purely platonic, nothing sexual at all."* In a matter of months, however, the two friends found themselves sneaking off to be with each other, and finally their "friendship" developed into an affair that destroyed both of their marriages. Lust is not just unrestrained passion. Even when it is "bridled" it may lead us down a path that our conscience could not have condoned had we experienced it in a more obvious, wanton way. Thus, our enemies are not only lascivious thoughts of sex but "innocuous" feelings of infatuation as well.

BACKING OFF EARLY

Fortunately, when we align with and submit to the Holy Spirit, He will prompt us. Often, we justify our flirtations with logical, even spiritual, justifications. One pastor did not tell his wife about his frequent meetings with a particular woman on the grounds he should not violate confidentialities, even to his wife. Besides, he sensed his wife would be jealous (without good reason, of course), so why upset her? Under the cloak of professionalism and sensitivity to his wife, he proceeded to meet with this woman secretly. The result was predictable. Another pastor had been struggling with lustful thoughts toward a college girl in his church. Rather than deal with his struggles alone with the Lord, with a mature brother, or with his wife, he took the girl out to lunch to talk with her. Citing the biblical mandate to confess our sins and make things right with the person we have wronged, he told her, *"I've been having lustful thoughts about you, and I felt I needed to confess them to you."* Embarrassed but flattered, the girl began to entertain her own thoughts toward him, and finally they became sexually involved.

All this came from what the pastor told himself was a spiritual and obedient decision to meet with the girl. To misuse Scripture in this way and violate wisdom and common sense shows how undependable our thinking can become.

HOLDING MYSELF ACCOUNTABLE

Perhaps nowhere is more said and less done than in accountability. From talking with Christian leaders, I have come to understand that the more prominent they become, the more they need accountability and the less they get it. As a church grows, often the pastors come to know many people but on a shallower level, and those around them think, who am I to ask him if this is a wise choice he is making?

Many pastors in small churches also feel isolated, and even those in large churches with multiple staff members are usually Lone Rangers when it comes to facing their moral struggles.

A step in the right direction will be to create a safe space, perhaps during church staff meetings, to discuss personal "sufferings and rejoicings" (1 Cor. 12:26), telling each other the state of our spiritual lives, and seeking and offering prayer and advice. We make sure no one is left out. We ask, "How are you doing?" and if the answers are vague or something seems wrong, we probe deeper.

At first, this will feel risky as it involves entrusting our reputations to others and opening ourselves to their honest investigation. But the results are usually positive encouragement. The risks are likely to be small compared to the rewards. That way, we do not feel alone in the ministry. We know each other's imperfections, and we have nothing to prove to each other.

Pastors without other staff can find a lay person or two or a nearby pastor who will love them as they are and regularly ask the questions of accountability. This kind of accountability can produce amazing results.

GUARDING MY MIND

A battering ram may hit a fortress gate a thousand times, and it seems to have no effect, yet finally the gate caves in. Likewise, immorality is the cumulative product of small mental indulgences and tiny compromises, the immediate consequences of which were, at the time, invisible. **Our thoughts are the fabric with which we weave our character and destiny.** No, we cannot avoid all sexual stimuli, but in Martin Luther's terms, "*You can't keep the birds from flying over your head, but you can keep them from making a nest in your hair.*"

I like to put it another way: "**If you're on a diet, don't go into a doughnut shop.**" For someone, this could mean such practical things as staying away from the magazine racks, video stores, advertisements, programs, images, people, and places that tempt the person to lust.

REGULARLY REHEARSING THE CONSEQUENCES OF SIN

A man who had been a leader in a Christian organization until he fell into immorality was asked "What could have been done to prevent this?" He paused for only a moment, then said with haunting pain and precision, "*If only I had really known, really thought through, what it would cost me and my family and my Lord, I honestly believe I never would have done it.*"

WINNING THE BATTLE

We are in a battle far fiercer and more strategic than any Alexander, Hannibal, or Napoleon ever fought. We must realize that no one prepares for a battle of which he is unaware, and no one wins a battle for which he does not prepare. As we hear of Christian leaders succumbing to immorality, we must not say merely, "There, but for the grace of God, I might have gone," but rather, "There, but for the grace of God and but for my alertness and diligence in the spiritual battle I may yet go."

Exercise

What is your most memorable lesson from this book?

_____

_____

_____

_____

How do you intend to apply the lesson in your relationship with?

God

_____

_____

Your spouse

_____

_____

Your children

_____

_____

In your work/ministry/relationships?

_____

_____

PART 2

THE DIFFERENT COMPANIES

MODULE 2

ABRAHAM COMPANY

INTRODUCTION

IF THERE IS ONE THING THAT MANY MODERN people find difficult about the Bible, it is that stories written thousands of years ago can guide our lives today, such as the accounts of Abraham in the Bible. Abraham himself lived about four thousand years ago, and the stories about him were written nearly 3,600 years ago. Nevertheless, as followers of Christ, we are committed to the fact that these stories are part of the Scripture and therefore are profitable even for modern people.

If you have been around children and church, you may have heard the catchy praise song simply titled **Father Abraham**. It is delightful, entertaining and involves a repeated chorus and arms and legs and head movements. The lyrics are simple: *"Father Abraham had many sons, many sons had Father Abraham. I am one of them and so are you, so let us all praise the Lord!"*

Yes, this is the same Abraham whose son, Isaac, was born to Sarah when Abraham was 100 years old. Yes, the same Abraham whose first son, Ishmael, was born to Hagar his wife's maidservant 14 years earlier. In fact, Abraham had 6 other sons (Genesis 25:1-2) with his second wife, Keturah, after Sarah died. Note that it was Abraham's son Isaac who had 2 sons, Esau, and Jacob. It was Jacob, later renamed Israel, who had 12 sons whose descendants became the 12 tribes of the nation of Israel. Certainly, Abraham was a very real and historical person who lived a prosperous and active life. He was the first Hebrew and so considered the Father of the Hebrew nation. He lived to be 175 years old.

So, why does the song say that I am one of his many sons? And why praise the Lord over this? And what kind of Model Father was Abraham anyway?

A BLESSING TO ALL THE NATIONS

In Genesis 12, right after his father Terah's death in Haran, God said to Abram:

The Lord had said to Abram, "Go from your country, your people and your father's household to the land I will show you. "I will make you into a great nation, and I will bless you; I will make your name great, and you will be a blessing. I will bless those who bless you, and whoever curses you I will curse; and all peoples on earth will be blessed through you." (Genesis 12:1-3)

Quite a promise! Completely unearned! Abram was a mere man, son of Terah, who was chosen by God out of insignificance to play a key role in God's reconciliation plan. He proves worthy by being obedient to God and is reckoned as righteous by God by simply believing Him. Abram had an intimate relationship with God and through that, he could hear God speak to him at different times in his life journey. This is a very key component which guided most of his actions and decisions. Therefore, fathers are to develop a very close personal relationship with God, to enable them to receive clear directions from Him for the tough task of fatherhood.

In Genesis 17, the Lord appeared to Abram and asks him to walk habitually before God in integrity, righteousness, and complete obedience, knowing that he is always in God's presence. The Lord added that He will establish an everlasting covenant between Abram and Himself; God changed his name from Abram (exalted Father) to Abraham (Father of a multitude). I believe this change of name was very significant for Abraham to fulfill the purpose of God for his life.

At a point in our walk with God, it became very clear that we needed to change our names to align with what God ordained to accomplish in us. Therefore, my husband and I changed our names. God uses the call of Abraham to epitomize our call and mandate. It was a process of spiritual separation that was essential for us to posture ourselves to accomplish the Kingdom assignment God has for us. Furthermore, to ensure Abram sees his future through the lens of God,

He took him outside and said, "Look up at the sky and count the stars if indeed you can count them." Then he said to him, "So shall your offspring be." Abram believed the Lord, and he credited it to him as righteousness. (Genesis 15:5-6)

Abraham is forever identified as the one whose descendants are receivers of the promise. And all those who believe, Jews or Gentiles (non-Jews), are forever blessed. In his New Testament writings on the new Christian faith, Paul explains this extension of God's grace to all peoples/nations in his letter to the Christians in Galatia:

Understand, then, that those who have faith are children of Abraham. Scripture foresaw that God would justify the Gentiles by faith and announced the gospel in advance to Abraham: "All nations will be blessed through you." So those who rely on faith are blessed along with Abraham, the man of faith. (Galatians 3:7-9)

Yes, this is very good news for all of mankind. All peoples and nations on this created earth can be reconciled back to God merely by believing in God as revealed in His Word, the Bible.

DIVINE GRACE

In the first place, we have seen that God demonstrated much grace in Abraham's life. Of course, Abraham had to have personal grace because he was a sinner, but beyond this, God's mercy toward Abraham was also an objective display of God's kindness. By building a relationship with Abraham, God furthered the redemption of the entire world.

God's relationship with Abraham was based on his grace. God had entered Abraham's life long before Abraham had done anything in service to God. Abraham's call came very early in his adult life. He had not left for Canaan; he had not conquered enemies; he had not committed to covenant faithfulness; he had not prayed for the righteous in Sodom and Gomorrah; he had not passed any test of faith. On the contrary, God called Abraham as his special servant simply because it pleased God to be gracious to Abraham. God's grace was not only shown in the initial stage of Abraham's walk with God.

The grace of God is a theme that appears throughout the stories of Abraham because God also showed mercy to him at every moment of his life. As a sinner, Abraham needed God's mercy all the time. As Christians, we all know the importance of God's grace in our lives. We know that God initiates our relationship with Him by His grace and we know that He sustains us in our relationship with Him by His grace. Where would we be without the mercy of God? Well, the same thing was true for Abraham.

ABRAHAM'S LOYALTY

Initially, God required Abraham to fulfill the responsibility of migrating to the Promised Land, in addition to many other things throughout his life. He was loyal to God in very significant ways.

As Christians, when we read about the responsibilities Abraham faced, we should find our hearts and minds moving towards loyalty to our heavenly Father. So, every time we see the theme of Abraham's loyalty to God, we know that as Christians we can properly apply these devotions to the modern world only as we connect them properly to Christ. God did not merely choose Abraham to receive his mercy; he showed mercy to him so that Abraham would respond with faithful obedience.

God commanded him: "Leave your country, your people and your father's household and go to the land I will show you" (Genesis 12:1). This divine call obviously required enormous loyalty from Abraham. He was to leave his homeland and his father's estate behind and to go to a place he will be shown. Yes, God had shown mercy to Abraham, but Abraham was also expected to show deep-seated, loyal service to God. This is an important theme in Abraham's life, and it is highlighted in that God commanded Abraham to be obedient and loyal. He was to be faithful to God in every circumstance as an example of faith and trust in God. Perhaps the most remarkable example of his loyalty to God was when God commanded Abraham to sacrifice his son Isaac to prove that he loved God more than he loved his son. As followers of Christ, we understand that although salvation is a gift of God's grace, God expects us to show our gratitude to him by doing our best to obey his commands.

BLESSINGS TO ABRAHAM

God told Abraham that Israel would become a great nation, that prosperity would come to the nation in the land of promise, and that Abraham and Israel would have a great name worldwide. So, whenever we think about Abraham receiving blessings from God, we are to take hold of God's promises and enjoy God's blessings in even greater measure as co-heirs with Christ. God said this to Abraham, "I will make you into a great nation and I will bless you; I will make your name great" (Genesis 12:2). Abraham would become a great nation. His offspring would grow beyond number, and his descendants would become an empire, a great nation.

At that time, Abraham and those who were with him were relatively few, and he had no children of his own. Yet, God promised that the number of Abraham's descendants would one day be more than the stars in the sky. Likely, this expression means that Abraham and his descendants would receive the blessing of tremendous prosperity. Abraham and his descendants would live in abundance and wealth. As Abraham and his children proved faithful, they would enjoy great prosperity.

In other words, if Abraham would go to the Promised Land and serve God faithfully, the massive numbers and prosperity of his descendants would make him honored throughout the world. Great glory would come to him and his faithful descendants. As Christians, we have received so many blessings from God that we can hardly name them all. They had been delivered from slavery; they had increased in number; they had been protected and sustained throughout their journey and they were on their way to the land of promise, a land of great blessing in the future. We are sometimes like the Israelites, prone to forget all that God had done for them and what was in store for them.

BLESSINGS THROUGH ABRAHAM

God said that through a process of blessing and cursing, all peoples on the earth would be blessed through Abraham. Notice here that when God promised Abraham that he would bless all nations, he promised that this would come about by Abraham taking possession of all nations and spreading the kingdom of God to the entire world. Abraham and his offspring were to be heirs of the world, with all the nations under their leadership.

As Adam and Eve were originally told to subdue the entire earth, God promised that Abraham and his descendants would inherit the entire earth by spreading God's blessings to all the families of every nation. The promise that Abraham would be a blessing to all nations is ultimately fulfilled in the inauguration, continuation, and consummation of Christ's kingdom. "...and you will be a blessing. I will bless those who bless you, and whoever curses you I will curse; and all peoples on earth will be blessed through you" (Genesis 12:2-3).

These words explained that Abraham would not only receive blessings but that all peoples on earth will be blessed through him. God did not call Abraham to the Promised Land simply to enrich his life and the lives of his descendants. God called Abraham to be a conduit of divine blessings to all the families of the earth. According to this passage, Abraham would serve as a double-edged sword among human beings; because Abraham was favored by God, when people from other nations blessed Abraham, that is, when they honored him thereby honoring the God whom he served, then God would bless them.

However, when people of other nations cursed or attacked Abraham and thus despised Abraham's God, God would punish them. The fates of other peoples depended on how they treated Abraham. In his lifetime, Abraham encountered many people representing other nations such as the Philistines, the Canaanites, the Egyptians, and his nephew Lot, who was the father of the Moabites and the Ammonites. These interactions were significant because they showed specific ways in which God kept his word to bless and curse other people depending on how they treated Abraham. They also indicated that even in his own lifetime Abraham had begun to become a blessing to the world.

God's people tend to forget; the Israelites in Moses' day were like many Christians living today. We enjoy the blessing of salvation from God and life from God, but we forget why these blessings have been given to each of us. Each blessing God gave to Israel under Moses' leadership and every blessing he gives to his church today is designed for a greater purpose. We have been blessed so that we will spread the blessings of God throughout the world. God called Abraham to himself so that Abraham would lead the nations of the world into God's blessings. God called Israel to himself in Moses' day so that they would lead the nations of the world into God's blessings. And God has called the church to himself today so that we may lead the nations of the world into the blessings of God. This theme was so important for the Israelites who first received the stories of Abraham. And it is important for us too as we follow Christ in our day.

ABRAHAM EARNED GOD'S CONFIDENCE

For I know him, that he will command his children and his household after him, and they shall keep the way of the Lord, to do justice and judgment; that the Lord may bring upon Abraham that which he hath spoken of him. Genesis 18:19

Let us note that we are told here that God knows Abraham will instruct his children to walk in his way after him. First, there is instruction, and then what kind [of instruction] is noted. In other words, we are told the nature of that instruction and then how it extends beyond death. So, in the person of Abraham, we see what the responsibility of all believers is, principally the responsibility of the fathers of family whom God set up as heads of household and to whom He gave life, children, and servants so they would be diligent in teaching them. For when a father has children, his responsibility is not only to feed and clothe them, but his *principal* responsibility is to guide them so that their lives will be well regulated, and he will dedicate his full attention to that.

God values His servant Abraham's devotion which is shown in the effort he will make to serve and honour Him and to guide his family and those entrusted to his charge, for it is particularly stated that he will teach them to walk in the way of the Lord. Consequently, we see the nature of the right kind of instruction. For someone could be rather careful to give many rules and many laws without providing stability. There can be no foundation to build on unless God dominates and people obey Him and conform to His Word. That, then, is what we have to remember.

When fathers of family and those of some pre-eminence get ready to teach, they must not be presumptuous and say, "This seems good to *me*," and then try to subject everybody to their opinion and their concepts. "What? Shall I teach what I learned from God in His school?" What we have to remember from this passage is, briefly, that no one will ever be a good teacher unless he is God's pupil. So, let there be no teaching authority that advances what *we* invent and what our minds come up with, but let us learn from God so that He will dominate and alone have all pre-eminence; and may great and small bring themselves into conformity with Him and obey Him.

At that time, there was no written law and even less gospel; but Abraham still knew God's will to the extent necessary. So Abraham is without Scripture, but even so, he does not presume to or attempt to set up laws to his own liking. But he asks God alone to govern and show the way to everybody else and lead them, for he does not wish to say, "Let us go the way I say," but, "I am teaching you what I have learned from God. And may He alone have all mastery, and may I be a teacher only if I speak as by His mouth." That is the second point we have to remember here.

So, what is to be noted here is that heads of family must go to the process of being instructed in God's Word if they are to do their duty. If they do not know the basic principles of religion or of their faith and do not know God's commandments or how prayer is to be offered to Him or what the road to salvation is, how will they instruct their families? All the more, then, must those who are husbands and have a family, a household to govern, think, "I must establish my lesson in His Word so that I will not only try to govern myself in accordance with His will, but that I will also bring to it at the same time those who are under my authority and guidance."

LEGACY OF THE FEAR OF GOD

Now in the third place, Abraham will teach his family to walk in the fear of the Lord after his death, just as if it were said that the faithful man is not only to get honor for God and live tomorrow, but that he leaves good seed after his death. For God's Word is the incorruptible seed of life: it endures forever. And even though heaven and earth tend to corruption and will pass away, the Word of God must *always* retain its power (Mat 25:3; Isa 40:8; 55:11). Therefore, it is not without reason that it dies with us, is extinguished when God withdraws us from this world, and we carry everything off with us. But let us work, though we are weak and mortal and must depart this world, to leave the Word of God with a root here. And when we are dead and have turned to dust, may God be honoured and may His memory endure forever. That is what we have to remember.

Now, since God spoke that way, He is saying that Abraham's children, whom he will teach, will do *justice* and *judgment*. With those two words, Scripture comprises what concerns the second table of the Law. Moses says they will do justice and judgment. That shows us what the way of God is and how we will show we are obeying Him. For those two words involve uprightness and equity so that we may be kind, give ourselves to charity, help one another, protect everyone's right and not defraud, abstain from doing wrong and violence to one another, and even help those who need our help. Now, it is certain that in God's Law there is nothing but justice and judgment.

KEY ATTRIBUTES OF A GOOD FATHER MODEL AS EXEMPLIFIED BY ABRAHAM:

Respects, Honors, and Believes God – Abraham was not a high-performer or scholar; he simply respected God and honored Him through his obedient life. It was clear that he had been taught about Creator God by his own father. All of Abraham's life was one that reflected as an obedient servant of God.

Not Perfect – Abraham made several key mistakes and poor decisions that had terrible consequences: he allowed his nephew Lot (ultimately of Sodom/Gomorrah fame) to initially travel with him when told to leave his family; he lied about Sarah being his sister rather than wife (twice!) to protect himself from opposition; he forced the offspring promise (Ishmael born of Hagar) when he and Sarah misinterpreted God's promise. Nevertheless, God still accomplishes His purposes with imperfect people who believe.

Leads His Family – Abraham kept charging forward in leading and directing his family. His marching orders came from God, but he himself had to execute the work and directives, even if he experienced hardships and missteps along the way.

Teaches His Children About God – As Abraham was instructed by God, he passed this teaching and practices onto his children. While it is clear in reading about the mistakes and misfortunes of Abraham's family descendants, Abraham fulfilled his fatherly responsibility of passing on the ways of the Lord to the next generation.

Kind and Noble – While Abraham showed evidence of human shortcomings and self-serving behavior, he nevertheless was a man who proved to be kind, fair, and noble. He was generous in dividing land with Lot; he put himself and his men in harm's way to rescue Lot and his family when they were taken captive; he negotiated selflessly on Lot's behalf in the attempt to save Sodom from destruction. As an overarching characteristic, Abraham was a good, kind, and noble man; aspiring traits for all fathers. Being a good father is a developed skill. It takes work and comes with growth and maturity. Of course, this good father model is grounded in a faith and belief in God. Without God, fathering is merely behavioral and subjective to the cares and whims of man. Father Abraham lays down a humble example from which all of us can learn.

Does God give you his Spirit and work miracles among you by the works of the law, or by your believing what you heard? So also, Abraham "believed God, and it was credited to him as righteousness." Understand then, that those who have faith are children of Abraham.
– Galatians 3:5-7

Steps to Greatness

Abraham, "father of all nations," was the first true pioneer. He stood up to an entire selfish world and trail blazed a spiritual path to life, forever changing history. It was Abraham's embrace of a higher set of values of love, generosity and service that forged the standard for the basic human rights that we take today for granted.

POINTS TO PONDER... QUESTIONS TO ANSWER? ACTION POINT...

> ➢ What was Abraham's secret?

> ➢ What shaped this man?

> ➢ From where did he derive the power and courage to defy the tide of his times?

> ➢ How can we emulate Abraham and acquire his courage in our own lives?

To achieve greatness, every one of us may have to experience, in one form or another, these challenges. If you study your life and the life and history of your family, you will find glimpses of different trials and tribulations which may or may not be in the same order as they occurred in Abraham's life.

The challenge of childhood

The early formative years of a child are the most precious. They define the strengths the child will accumulate and the challenges the child will face throughout his or her entire life. It is therefore vital to create a spiritually nurturing environment for your child and protect your child, in these vulnerable years, from selfish and corrupting influences.

The challenge of commitment

Sometime in life, often early on, and perhaps more than once in a lifetime, you will be asked (with or without words) to make a choice: Either conform or disagree; which may not be literal today. But the price of choosing the "road less traveled," the path of virtue and faith, will be threatened by material pressures that consume us like "fire." Will you choose to bow and worship an "idol" – money, fame, superstars, whatever – or do you commit to a higher cause?

The challenge of change

As you mature into an adult, the time comes to psychologically leave your home and comfort zones to discover yourself and what you are capable of. This can be a tough challenge. More specifically, the journey consists of freeing yourself from the subjective forces that shape our lives: Our natural, biased tendencies; parental influences; and social programming. There is the need to find out from God *who* you are and what original contribution *do* you make, as opposed to being a product of others.

The challenge of deprivation

Then there will be those times when you may experience deep hunger and wonder whether your choices are worth it. You are committed to God and yet you have no "food on your table." You may need to wander to strange, hostile places to acquire some nourishment. Will you give up or trust God to see you through?

The challenge of sexuality

Pharaoh's abduction of Sarah. Your most intimate needs may be compromised or seized. Your heart challenged and your love denied. Will this break you?

The challenge of confrontation

No matter who you are and what your life space is like, you will be faced with confrontations. Even when you are not looking for an adversary, enemy forces will assault you. They may take on the shape of people; so-called friends, co-workers, neighbors, surrounding nations, or they may be inner fears, psychological phobias, or haunting imaginations of the past. But whatever form it takes, you can be rest assured that you will have to fight a battle or two in your life. These battles will either demoralize you or strengthen you.

The challenge of suffering

No one is immune to loss and some form of pain in our lifetimes. Even when God is merciful, we will, in our current condition as humans, experience the loss of a loved one, the break of a promise or the dissolution of a dream. We are mortals and fragile creatures. Health issues will come up, but the challenge is whether we can discover deeper resources to help us through the harder times.

The challenge of transformation

Abraham's circumcision at age 99 marked his metamorphosis to become spiritually complete, as God says to him: through circumcision you will "walk before Me and become complete." The covenant "in your flesh" will bond you with me forever. For Abraham, the challenge was compounded by the fact that he was 99 years old at the time. Today, the challenge is to ensure that our children from birth have engraved in their very heart Abraham's' Divine covenant. The challenge of transformation is not just a partial, limited commitment to a higher cause, but one that is complete and permeates every aspect of our lives, including the material and physical.

The challenge of discipline

Often, in the name of deep love and spiritual conviction, we can overwhelm ourselves and those around us. Abraham, the epitome of love, found it difficult to send away his son Ishmael. But this discipline was necessary for the welfare of Abraham's own home as well as of Ishmael and Hagar. We too will have the challenge in our lives, where we will need to exercise profound discipline lest we become consumed by spiritual and sensual passions.

The challenge of becoming Divine.

Finally, the ultimate challenge will be when you are asked to be ready to give up the single thing you love the most for God. Not with the intention of having to relinquish it but you cannot be aware of that at the time, or it will defeat the entire purpose; you will feel as though you actually will be sacrificing your most precious possession. Only to discover that when you are sincerely ready for such a sacrifice, you not only lose nothing; in return you gain immortality and an eternal connection to the very thing you love so much.

These are some general challenges that we may all face in our lifetime. How we will rise to these challenges will define our lives. Abraham was not just a man of distant history. His story is our story. His travels paved the way for our own. His endurance demonstrates and empowers us, his children, with the ability to not just survive, but to thrive and reach immortality. Over 3600 years of difficult history is a living testimony to a man's absolute dedication to a higher cause. Through all these millennia, and all of history's upheavals, Abraham remains the pioneering spirit that changed the world forever and is admired today perhaps even more than in his own time. If that does not instill in us confidence and inspiration that we too (with far less difficulties than Abraham's) can see it through, what will?

BREAKING THE CYCLE OF ABSENT FATHERS

A Family Legacy

George was a general in the army. In 1950, with the world wars over and prosperity booming, he enjoyed the benefits of his high rank. He had a wife and two sons at home but was constantly choosing his career, addiction to alcohol, and pursuit of women over his family. Eventually, George left his wife and sons and died, alone, from heart and liver failure caused by drinking. He had no idea that his choice to be an absent father would impact future generations and they would be faced with the choice to break the cycle.

His two sons John and Jeremiah grew up and found themselves facing the same choices their father had once faced. John chose to follow in the footsteps of his father. He held a prestigious title and made a financial fortune, turning to the material gains of the world to satisfy him. He married six times only to end up alone and never finding satisfaction. Jeremiah, however, chose a different path. His mother had taught him about God, and he decided to lean in to what God had planned for him, which was a family and children of his own. The lifestyle of the two brothers could not have been more different.

Today, John and Jeremiah both have children and grandchildren of their own. John's children grew up without their father present. They witnessed his marriages and divorces and watched their family fall apart time and again. And they struggle with the same choices their father and grandfather made to stay involved in their family. Jeremiah's children have had the opposite experience. They grew up with their father present. From his example, they have learned how to be present in their own kids' lives. They are thankful that their father, Jeremiah, chose to break the cycle and to give their family a legacy of redemption and love, rather than brokenness.

THE EFFECTS OF AN ABSENT FATHER

Many fathers over the years have made the heartbreaking choice to leave their families. However, the number of fathers leaving their children has seen an increase in recent decades. The impact that a father has on his children's lives cannot be understated. When a dad leaves his family whether physically or emotionally, the effect on his children can be damaging.

Research shows that children who grow up without a dad are more likely to:

➤ Have behavioral problems

➤ Drop out of school

➤ Face depression, anxiety, or other mental health issues

➤ Struggle financially

➤ Become sexually promiscuous and/or face teenage pregnancy

➤ Use drugs and alcohol

➤ Become aggressive or violent

➤ Leave their own children when they become parents.

There are many reasons that a dad might choose to leave his family. One significant reason may be that he did not have a present or positive example of a dad in his own life. He did not have anyone to teach him what it means to be a father or demonstrate to him the steadfast love and self-sacrifice that fatherhood requires. This lack of example impacted his confidence and ability to parent his children and may have caused overwhelming fear when facing fatherhood. How can we stop this growing trend of absent fathers? And how can we break the cycle of devastation that it leaves in its wake?

The Ripple Effect

When you drop a pebble into a pond, the stone will create ripples in the water. The ripples begin to multiply and spread across the water and can stretch over a long distance. Depending on the size of the pebble, the ripples can be damaging or cause erosion to things nearby. Just like the ripples in the water, a father's choice to leave his children creates a ripple effect. His choices will not only impact his children and cause damage in their family but will also influence everyone around them. These choices may even impact his grandchildren and great grandchildren in much the same way that George's choices impacted his descendants. If your father was not a part of your life, reflect for a moment on what his absence was like for you. What do you think your absence would be like for your children? And is this the ripple that you want to create?

Be the Author of Your Own Story

If you have experienced your father's absence whether emotionally or physically, you undoubtedly feel angry and hurt. Perhaps you feel as if you have been abandoned, or that you need to seek affirmation in different places. You may also feel fear: fear of failure, fear of rejection, fear of hurting your children in the same way your father hurt you. How does your father's absence and the things you experienced in the past tie in with the man you are today and what you are facing now? And how have those experiences shaped you and colored the way you see life? Our perceptions can turn into beliefs, and our beliefs then turn into behavior. Are there beliefs and behaviors that you wish you could change?

Breaking the Thought Pattern

How often have you heard a man, maybe even yourself, say, "*I don't want to be my dad, but I'm becoming my dad*"? Let us make a couple of lists. Grab a pencil and paper, your computer, or even your phone. First, write down which things about your dad or his actions that you do not like. What traits do you wish he had? What do you wish he had done differently?

Next, make a list of the qualities that you admired in other dads when you were growing up. Which qualities do you admire in other men now? What traits do you wish you had? Now look at the list of qualities you admire and wish that you had. What do you think that it would take for you to have those qualities? Are you willing to work to develop and build the skills necessary to have those things?

What Do You Want?

Studies have shown that our brains don't process the word "don't." Instead, they focus on the subject at hand. For instance, if you tell your son or daughter, "Don't eat those cookies," they are going to think about those cookies nonstop until they can have one. You need to tell your brain what to do, rather than what not to do. Rather than "Don't eat those cookies," you might say "Eat yogurt."

If you say that you do not want to be like your father, your brain is focused on "being like your father." You will start to behave like him unless you give your brain another directive. Take that list of traits you admire and tell yourself that you want to be like that. For example, "Don't leave your family" can be translated into "**I will spend time with my children each day.**"

Writing the Next Chapter of Your Life

You do not have to make the same choices in life that your father did. If your own father has left you, then you know that repeating that pattern is not the best choice. It can be a choice that is repeated in your family for generations to come. This does not have to be anyone's story. You can use your life story as a springboard to another path. You can choose how to write the next chapters in your story. Make the choice to break the cycle of absent fathers in your family.

You've Made the Choice — Now What?

What do you do once you have made the choice to break the cycle? Start by making a commitment to love and be present with your children. You do not have to be perfect. Your kids do not need your perfection; they just need you to be a part of their lives. Next, seek out God-fearing men to be a mentor to you. These should be men from different paths in life. For example, you might choose a pastor, a friend, an older person, and a neighbor. Instead of meeting with these men at the same time, schedule a time to meet one-on-one.

> ➤ Rotate who you spend time with each week. Setting up a schedule like this is a great way to be respectful of each other's time and will be less pressure with time commitments.

> ➤ Tell these men what you admire about them and what you want to learn from them. Your time together can be a place to vent but it should also be a time of focus and direction.

> ➤ Make sure that you structure your time together in order to make the most of it. For instance, you might choose to go through a Bible study together.

> ➤ Be sure to cling to God for guidance and help. Read the Word, spend time in prayer each day, and find a men's discipleship group through your church, if possible.

The journey will not always be easy, but God will honor it. He will teach you and grow you in amazing ways. He will be the Heavenly Father that you look to for hope and help if you will let Him fill that role.

Coming Alongside a Dad Who Once Had an Absent Father

If it has not been your experience to grow up without a dad, then you are in a situation where you can be a mentor to other dads who did experience this absence. Becoming a dad can be an exciting and terrifying experience all at the same time. Many fathers struggle with the need to be a perfect parent and to provide for their children in certain ways. They face a lot of fear and uncertainty in their parenting. They may struggle as they try to navigate the unfamiliar roads of parenting, especially if they did not have a good example to learn from when they were growing up.

A man whose father has been absent during his life has not had the opportunity to learn what it takes to be a dad. This may leave him feeling like he is stumbling around in the dark without a flashlight or a roadmap. A man who loves Jesus Christ and has some experience in fatherhood can be the perfect person to come alongside with a lantern and help guide another dad on his journey. You do not need a long list of qualifications or be the perfect dad to do this. All you need is a heart that is open to God and a willingness to step up and be present. God can take your willingness to do amazing things in the lives of others.

Being a Mentor

Being a mentor to another dad is so important. You have the opportunity to encourage them to make good choices and teach them the skills they may not know. Be present, talk through it, and walk life with them. Your encouragement can help them break the cycle in their families. Choose a time and frequency to meet that works with your schedules. It could be once a week, once every other week, or even once a month. Be sure to structure your time together so that you can make the most of it.

Discipleship

Men's discipleship groups at the Institute of Discipleship and Transformation are an amazing place for dads to disciple other dads on their walk with the Lord and in their parenting journey. After you have been trained and equipped, you will be supported to start one. This should be a group that gets together for more than breakfasts and fishing trips. It should be a group that gets into the Word and prays together and keeps each other accountable on a consistent basis. This can be an important step in helping others break the cycle.

Coming Alongside a Child Who Has an Absent Father

If you look around, you will notice the need for children to have excellent role models in their lives. You do not have to be a part of the family in order to make an impact in the life of a child whose father has left. You just need to be willing to step up and be present. God can take your willingness and open doors. Whether you are a father or not, you can make a difference in a child's life. So many children out there will never know their dads, but you can step up and show them what it means to be present and cherished. You can help grow a strong sense of worth and resilience in both boys and girls. You can teach boys how to be men in training. Investing time in a child and showing them that you are present can be a game changer for them and for their future families.

MODULE 3

DEBORAH ARISE COMPANY!

Who Was Deborah in the Bible?

EBORAH IS ONE OF THE MOST INFLUENTIAL women of the Bible. As a prophetess, Judge Deborah was said to hear God's voice and share God's Word with others. As a priestess, she did not offer sacrifices, as the men did, but she did lead worship services and preach. She is known for her wisdom and courage, and she is the only woman of the Old Testament who is known for her own faith and action, not because of her relationship to her husband or another man. Deborah was the wife of Lappidoth, a warrior, poet, songwriter, and singer.

INTRODUCTION

There seems to be a "cycle" in the book of Judges where Israel sins (idolatry, unfaithfulness to God, civil rivalry, etc.), God gives them over into the hands of their enemies in the land, they subsequently cry out for help, and God "raises up" a judge to act as a savior and deliverer for them. This is a repeated cycle in Judges 3:7–16:31, with different enemies and different judges but the same faithful God and same sinful Israel. So, while the title "cycle" is altogether appropriate, the book of Judges narrates this repeated habit in a way that looks more like a down-spiral. The classic "cycle" would portray the "judge" as an extension of God's own saving power and love (see Judges 6:9).

The era of the judges was marked by sin and more sin. The Israelites reverted to the ways of the ungodly in their midst and to idol worship. The pagan peoples they allowed to remain in Canaan after the conquest proved to cause turmoil in their life by their living amongst and association with them. It is apparent that God allowed the Israelites through their ungodly actions and deeds to become so oppressed by the pagans they assimilated with, to experience so much overwhelming distress, that they were forced to turn back to Him and pray for relief. An age-old lesson for us all is that we knowingly and unknowingly take on traits of those we associate ourselves with. As the book progresses, however, the actual judges of Israel appear to look less like proper representatives of Israel's God and more like the sinful people.

We read about Othniel, Ehud, and Shamgar, whose roles were not primarily legislative or judicial; they were not law-court "judges". The way the term is used in the book of Judges, it means something more like a leader of Israel who seeks justice for Israel, which often includes a strong protective component i.e., defending the nation from outside threats to Israel's *shalom* (peace). Under oppression from the Mesopotamian king, God raised up Othniel to be a "deliverer"; we know only a few small things about Othniel, but they are important.

"The Spirit of the Lord" was on him, which demonstrated that he was acting in the name and power of God. Following the military success of Israel under the judge, a certain period of "rest" came with Othniel. It was 40 years. When Othniel died, the people "did what was evil in the sight of the Lord" again. After that, the Lord "made strong" Israel's enemy the Moabites as punishment. When Israel called out to God remorsefully, the Lord "raised up" Ehud. Ehud betrayed the king of Moab in a sneaky plot and ushered in a peaceful period of 80 years. Then Shamgar was mentioned momentarily, who valiantly fought 600 Philistines with only a cattle nudge. Even after these signs of God's merciful presence and favor on behalf of his reckless people, they turned again to evil ways and God handed them over to the Canaanites and their military leader, Sisera. When the Israelites did earnestly turn back to God, God raised up a judge among them, who was strong, who would lead the Israelites, and continue to keep them faithful to the Lord their God. Deborah was this judge. Deborah would become the only woman to judge Israel. Not just a woman, Deborah was also described as a prophetess and a wife.

The story of Deborah is *the* highpoint of the whole book of Judges. The cycle from 4:1–5:31 shows the sure leadership of Israel's only female judge. Under the oppression of the Canaanites and their intimidating 900 "chariots of iron," Deborah served as "judge" over Israel (4:4).

A Prophetess and A Wife

We first read about Deborah in the Book of Judges as a...

"Prophetess, the wife of Lappidoth who was judging Israel" (Judges 4:4).

Apparently, according to this verse, being a prophetess and a wife are considered the two most important of her relationships. First, Deborah is characterized as a prophetess. In Deborah's Song, her love for the Lord is described as *"like the sun, when it comes in full strength"* (Judges 5:31). Most probably, this is why God chose Deborah to communicate His Will to the Israelites. Deborah was considered by the people as God's spokesperson, and this helped to establish her respect among them. Though Deborah was the only Israelite woman to become a judge; other Israelite women were prophetesses such as Miriam and Huldah.

In view of the distressing domination of the Canaanite leader Sisera, Deborah called for the Israelite warrior Barak to stand against the threat. Deborah promises to give Sisera into the hand of Barak if he is willing and obedient. When Israel battles against Sisera's forces, the Lord works mightily against the Canaanites and Sisera flees to what he knew to be an ally, Heber the Kenite (4:17). He was shown hospitality by Heber's wife Jael in *her* tent which apparently was a separate housing unit. At this point, the story is familiar to many: Jael makes Sisera comfortable, and he takes a nap. Then Jael hammers a tent-spike into his forehead. This assassination led to freedom from the relentless opposition of the Canaanites for a time. They had peace for 40 years.

Chapter 5 narrates the same story of Deborah and Barak's military success by the help of the Lord, but in poetic terms. Two themes encompass this "song." First, the victory belongs to God, the Divine Warrior. It was not primarily human strength and strategy that was victorious, but God's own power at work on behalf of his people. On the other hand, several of the tribes of Israel did not choose to go and fight Sisera, and their allegiance and bravery are called into question.

Deborah as a Wife

Deborah is described as the wife of Lapidoth. Though most Old Testament women were denoted as belonging to the household of a man, the implications here may have been two-fold. It, therefore, must be important to understand that while Deborah was a prophetess and a woman of great respect, she was also a woman that was a wife. Deborah belonged to a household, and we can rightly assume it was a household of faith. We read of no conflict between her and her husband with the role God had selected for Deborah. We do not read that Lapidoth had a problem with her putting God first rather than himself, nor do we read that he hindered her service to God in any way or was resentful of it.

Rather, we can assume because Deborah was a wife, she was of good character and had many social roles as a wife whom she capably fulfilled. Also, due to her position and love for God, she must have encouraged her husband to be Godly and ultimately won the Israelites' respect for her husband as well.

A Judge and Leader

Deborah was a judge that mainly settled disputes *"holding court under the palm tree of Deborah between Ramah and Bethel in the mountains of Ephraim"* (Judges 4:5). Being a prophetess must have helped Deborah to solve these disputes spiritually rather than simply politically or judicially. Also, we can assume that being a prophetess, the people who came to her to settle their disputes, which could not be resolved locally, would respect her opinion regardless of the outcome of the dispute. Being a prophetess and judge could have aided her as a female judge in a patriarchal society in a positive perspective as both a woman and judge by both the male and female population of Israel.

Deborah was not a military leader, nor did she pretend to be one to assert her judgeship or standing in the eyes of the Israelites. She was historically not characterized as one who demanded authority or as one who always insisted upon her own way. She had a mission to conquer the King of Hazor who commanded 900 chariots of iron. While the 900 chariots sound gloomy, the Israelites had not learned to work with iron; therefore, the number of chariots and what they were composed of forced the Israelites to go to battle by sheer faith in God.

Deborah called upon Barak, a known military man, in the name of the Lord to lead the Israelites in battle against the Canaanites of Hazor. She then passed down to him the instructions given to her by God. Barak willingly accepted the role of military leader with one provision; that Deborah would accompany him. She acceded to his request as she desired to carry out the will of God and destroy the Canaanites. She was disappointed in Barak's lack of faith in God alone, and that his faith needed bolstering by her presence at the battle.

Barak, described as a "military man" not a "spiritual man of God", needed her presence at the battle. Why? She must have represented someone whose relationship with God was so supreme that they knew God would not allow anything to happen to her or to them. Deborah's relationship with God must have been so great that it was recognizable to all those around her and so strong that they were willing to go to battle with her in the midst no matter the odds against them. Her femaleness must have been viewed as second to her love for the Lord.

The battle of the Israelites against 900 chariots of iron was a decisive one. The Israelites defeated King Hazor and he was killed while seeking refuge from the battle. The defeat was so strong that the city of Hazor fell within a few short years thereafter. The Israelites under Deborah's strong leadership would come to enjoy forty years of peaceful times.

Strength of Character

Deborah's relationship with God was first. She was also a wife, perhaps even could have been a mother, and she was a judge. She balanced many roles and with each role we are not told she did not have "the time" to fulfill a certain role. She served God faithfully and God provided Deborah a way to balance all her roles according to His calling. Deborah did not manipulate, use strong language or a loud voice to exercise her authority. She is not described as tough in her judgment of others. Worldliness was not a part of her lifestyle as she did not mix with the Canaanite culture, environment, or desire anything of their way of life. We can assume that her background and education were centered upon the teachings of the Lord. Deborah's spirituality, power, and inner peace were not disturbed by either adversity or prosperity. She was stable and of strong character.

"For the Word of God is living and powerful and sharper than any two edge-sword, piercing even to the division of soul and spirit, ad of joints and marrow, and is a discerner of the thoughts and intents of the heart" (Hebrew 4:12).

Some descriptors of good character are putting away worldly things and placing God first in our life. Instilling habits that will assist you to guard your emotions from worldly teachings and desires will help us to avoid the emotions associated with heartache and pain. Emotions help to shape how we are known by others. Emotions shape our thinking. Deborah is historically described as a woman who had a special relationship with God not a woman who allowed her emotions to overtake her.

"Let us hear the conclusion of the whole matter: Fear God and keep His commandment, for this is mans all" (Ecclesiastes 12:13).

Strength in character opposes sinful ways and does not participate in them. We can assume Deborah's strength of character helped her to overtake King Hazor who had earlier been defeated by a man, Joshua. But this man had not completely conquered King Hazor as he had regained power and rebuilt his army. Deborah's defeat would mean total destruction.

Modesty

With all the respect, acclaim, and power that go along with the denotation of prophetess and judge, Deborah remained modest. She was an obedient servant. She willingly without hesitation carried out the Will of God. She was Godly and used discernment of leadership. We are not told that she flaunted or "dressed up" to do the job. Rather, her perspective was one of a spiritual nature. We do not read that she usurped authority in her own home or that her home life was negligible. Rather, one can assume that Deborah, through the guidance of the Lord, balanced roles as only one that walked with the Lord could do. She used her gifts and talents as directed and it was not written that she failed at a single task. Rather, Deborah served the Lord competently, with capability, and with confidence in her abilities.

We also learn from Deborah's example that the role of prophetess and the role of judge were more significant than the role of military leader or fighter. Deborah would settle disputes, but she would not lead the army. Maybe the confines of women's roles in the Old Testament times or that Deborah neither needed nor wanted any credit for a battle victory to sustain her, helped to maintain the modesty within her.

Deborah was reluctant to go to battle with Barak, knowing that God chose Barak to lead the army. She may have been even uncomfortable with the role as a woman. Deborah would have preferred that Barak trusted in God and went off to battle without her. Maybe God's choice of Barak also indicated that women were not appropriate for every type of leadership role. Regardless of Deborah's personal felt limitations, she accompanied Barak and when the battle was won, in her song, "The Song of Deborah" she gave credit to God and the battle's leader Barak, omitting any role she may have played in the defeat of the Canaanites of Hazor.

May we all look to Deborah's example of her love for the Lord, using her gifts and talents, and the product of her obedience to the One she loved above all.

A Mother in Israel

Judges 5:7, in reference to the unique time of deliverance ushered in by Deborah, refers to her as "a mother in Israel." While this could be taken as a bare statement of fact that she had biological children, there is good reason to believe that she rose up as a national caretaker; or, as the New English Translation puts it, "a motherly protector in Israel." However, you look at her "motherly" role, the book of Judges sets her up to be a hero in Israel and a wise judge for the people. Deborah was chosen by God to serve as the Mother of Israel and lead His people to victory. Deborah's success was due to her faith in God. She served God by utilizing her values and Spiritual gifts. Due to her faith, God called her, a woman, to lead His people to victory. As in the Song of Deborah, those who love and obey the Lord will be renewed in strength and shine bright like the majestic sun.

Can you identify with Deborah? As you review the characteristics of her leadership, does your leadership reflect some of these traits? You were created to lead, and God is waiting for your faith, confidence, and obedience in His plans for you. Are you brave enough to step out in obedience and take the first step? I am looking forward to hearing from you and what action you will take today to step into your calling.

LEADERSHIP TRAITS OF DEBORAH

Deborah, a wife, prophetess, and judge of Israel, was chosen by God to serve His people at a very challenging time. Deborah showed her belief in God and her strength through God as she quietly and obediently stepped into her role.

Christian women leaders can learn quite a bit about leading others through an in-depth study of Judges 4 and 5. Let us look at some leadership traits reflected in Deborah's leadership.

> Deborah was **courageous**: She was called by God to lead at a difficult time. Deborah stepped forward with bravery in obedience to God to lead the Israelites in times of challenge and oppression. The old saying "God does not call the qualified, He qualifies the called" applies here. Doing something out of your comfort zone to glorify Him can be terrifying, but faith was never promised to be easy. Be bold, be courageous for His glory.

> Deborah **served with wisdom and knowledge**: She exhibited great listening skills, which were evident in her obedience to God. Deborah listened well, and when she spoke, she added value due to her wisdom.

> Deborah **supported** the people God called her to lead: She encouraged Barak and acknowledged his role in leading the Israelites to victory. Deborah's confidence in God's power gave the Israelites assurance that God was with them.

> Deborah was **trusted**: She earned her position due to her belief and faith in God. Her strong faith earned her the respect of the people, which allowed her to influence and motivate Barak and his men.

> Deborah was **genuine**: She spoke the word of God and no other. It was clear to the Israelites she shared God's message and not her own agenda. Never waiver in your faith. We may not always know what the road ahead will look like, but we only need to remember that God will faithfully guide us and lead the way.

> Deborah was **confident**: She placed her confidence in God. Deborah never hesitated to fulfill God's commands. Her reassurance and strong beliefs led the Israelites to victory.

> ➤ Deborah was **humble and obedient:** She gave praise and glory to God because the victory was God's. If God is telling you to do something or go somewhere, despite your fears, listen to His call. He has plans that we cannot begin to understand, and hearts and lives may be changed by our obedience.

> ➤ Deborah and Barak sang a song of thanksgiving and praise to God and the followers. And, they had peace for forty years due to their **belief** and **obedience.**

MENTORING

Deborah had spiritual and political leadership qualities like no other female recorded in biblical literature. Moses, Elijah, and Deborah are paradigms of relational Old Testament mentors. They were in a relationship with their followers and mentees. Mentoring is wisdom teaching from Proverbs 27:17, "Iron sharpens iron". Moses mentored Joshua; supporting, encouraging, and teaching him to lead Israel to the Promised Land (Deut. 34:9). Elijah inspired and taught Elisha, who assumed Elijah's ministry (2 Kings 19:16). Deborah motivated and supported Barak to fight Sisera, the captain of Jabin's army (Judg. 4:7).

In addition to their duties as prophets, the three leaders were successful in mentoring at least one person who would execute the will of God. Mentoring is one person giving advice and analysis in a reciprocal relationship helping another coordinate their ideas and methodologies to succeed in life. Both leader and mentor are suitable expressions for Moses, Elijah, and Deborah.

Deborah followed the work of Joshua, leading Israel when there was a void in Israel's leadership. Deborah's relation with God was respected by the people of Israel who would seek her as Israel's judge. She conveys God's authoritative word to the people of Israel as their prophetess. As judge and prophet of Israel, she called Barak to lead the army to battle and perceive that Barak respected the words of Deborah to fight the Canaanite army, and he asked Deborah to accompany him to battle.

There seems to be a parallel between the leadership of Deborah and Moses. Both leaders defeated their enemies through God's word, and both leaders formed excellent mentoring relationships with their mentees. Moses called his mentee, Joshua, to fight with Amalek. Deborah and Barak led the Israeli army to defeat the Canaanite army at Mount Tabor. Deborah confirmed the word of God to Barak that he might maintain his composure in crisis. God discomfited the enemy and his chariots by the sword. We can assert that God was in the fight with Moses when he parted the Red Sea drowning the Egyptian's army, and God was in the battle with Deborah and Barak killing the Canaanite men by the sword. Deborah, the relational leader, knew the needs of the people. She knew what Barak was able to accomplish with God's help. Deborah encouraged and inspired Barak to gather the army to defeat the enemy. She inspired Barak to implement the word of God. Deborah and Barak used their relational skills to sing a victory song about God as a warrior for his people Israel.

Transformational Leader

Deborah's story is exceptional since she is a woman, prophetess, and the judge in Israel. As a judge, she is a developmental leader who supervised Israel's dilemma of anguish by Jabin, king of Canaan. Deborah attained a solution to enhance Israel's oppression, using her prophetic gift as prophetess and judge to transform Israel from defeat to success. As a woman in the Old Testament, Deborah is a transitional leader, removing the old design of male leadership and developing a new model of female leadership. Deborah's position as a judge was an "image of accord" because the people came to her for decisions.

As Judge and deliverer of Israel, she was a liberator, who called the people to worship God. The people of Israel credited Deborah and Barak with obedience to God's word, and the land had rest for forty years. God's victory over the Canaanites through Deborah and Barak was the final blow to the Canaanite nation. We do not know why in this period of Israel's lifetime, the women (Deborah and Jael) had to enter the fight to defeat the Canaanites. Deborah did not hesitate to do what God ordained. Barak would not fight unless Deborah accompanied the men into battle. Even so, Deborah went with the ten thousand men and Barak to battle the Canaanites.

Mentors are intentional when encouraging, nurturing, and confirming those that are less experienced in achieving their desired competence to lead others. Leaders influence willing followers through concepts, behavior, emotion, and actions that foster the vision of the organization. Leaders and mentors share similar traits that help their followers and mentees succeed. Leaders and mentors are teachers with vision, trust, commitment, wisdom, expertise, and sound counseling skills that ensure those who follow will improve their personal and professional development. Leaders and mentors use leadership formation to help those that they mentor to develop the leadership skills that provide excellent performance in their chosen occupation or status in life.

The mentoring relationship is visible in the Old Testament through many leaders or mentors. God called the prophets, developed, directed, and mentored many of Israel's men and women, including Deborah. Joshua assumed the spirit and leadership quality of Moses, using strength and courage to finish the assignment that God gave him, leading Israel to the Promised Land (Josh. 14). God transferred Elijah's spirit to Elisha who assumed the prophetic duties of his prophet father, Elijah (2 Kings 2:9-25). Deborah was successful as an encourager, visionary inspiration, and the leader for Barak's army. Following the voice of God, Deborah and Barak brought success to Israel by defeating the Canaanites. Moses, Elijah, and Deborah were leaders and mentors who led their mentees successfully because the Spirit of God assisted the mentor and mentees in developing their abilities as leaders.

I also believe Deborah reflected many of the leadership qualities of the Proverbs 31 woman found in <u>verses 10-31</u> because Deborah served with honour, strength, and dignity. She quietly went about her role as a wife and leader. She was a humble and noble servant known as "a Mother in Israel."

Becoming a Proverbs 31 woman is not about being "perfect." It is about living life with purpose, diligence, forgiveness, and repentance. Let us take a look at the 10 qualities of the <u>Proverbs 31</u> woman below. **Oh, sweet friend, I've been there!** Being a wife and a mama is hard work and, sometimes, maybe oftentimes, you feel overwhelmed and frustrated and wish you could just get a break. *I have good news for you!*

Becoming a Proverbs 31 woman is not as hard as you think. In fact, Proverbs 31 is *not a checklist or a to-do list.* Instead, it is a beautiful representation of what it means to be a virtuous woman.

You sit there and think about your hectic morning, rushing about, trying to get the children ready for church on time, and no one can find their shoes much less get into the car without complaining, whining, and bickering. How in the world could you ever become a Proverbs 31 Woman?

THE PROVERBS 31 WOMAN TODAY

Often, women believe that Proverbs 31 does not really apply to our modern lives. However, I believe that God's Word stands the test of time, don't you? God's Word is still relevant today. These 10 Virtues of the Proverbs 31 Woman demonstrate how, as Christian women today, we can all be Proverbs 31 Women.

THE 10 VIRTUES OF THE PROVERBS 31 WOMAN

What does Proverbs 31 mean for the 21st Century woman?

The passage of Proverbs 31 was written a long time ago. So when you read about how she "holds the distaff and grasps the spindle with her fingers" you may feel like the words do not apply to your life in the 21st century. Let me show you how we can break down the verses, and how you can live out each verse in your own life.

1. Faith–She loves Jesus with all of her heart. A Virtuous Woman serves God with all of her heart, mind, and soul. She seeks His will for her life and follows His ways. (Proverbs 31:30, Matthew 22: 37, John 14: 15)

2. Marriage–She is a faithful bride. First and foremost, she is the bride of Christ; so, she does not necessarily need an earthly husband to be a virtuous woman. A married Virtuous woman respects her husband. She does him good all the days of her life. She is trustworthy and a suitable helpmeet. (Proverbs 31: 11- 12, 1 Peter 3:1-6)

3. Nurturing–She is a loving mother, and her children call her blessed. A Virtuous Woman teaches her children the ways of her Father in heaven. She nurtures her children with the love of Christ, disciplines them with care and wisdom, and trains them in the way they should go. (Proverbs 31: 28, Proverbs 22: 6)

4. Health–She takes care of her physical, mental, and spiritual health. A Virtuous Woman cares for her body. She prepares healthy food for her family. (Proverbs 31:17 & 15, 1 Corinthians 6: 19)

5. Service–She serves others with love and kindness. A Virtuous Woman serves her husband, her family, her friends, and her neighbours with a gentle and loving spirit. She is charitable. (Proverbs 31:20, 1 Corinthians 13: 13)

6. Stewardship–She is a wise steward of the gifts God has given her. A Virtuous Woman spends money wisely. She is careful to purchase quality items which her family needs. (Proverbs 31: 16, 1Timothy 6: 10)

7. Industry–She is industrious and works with willing hands.
A Virtuous Woman <u>works willingly with her hands</u>. She sings praises to God and does not grumble while completing her tasks. (Proverbs 31:24-25, Philippians 2: 14)

8. Homemaking–She is a good manager of her home. A Virtuous Woman is a homemaker. She <u>creates an inviting atmosphere of warmth and love</u> for her family and guests. She uses hospitality to minister to those around her. (Proverbs 31: 27, 1 Peter 4: 9)

9. Time–She spends her time on that which is good. A Virtuous Woman uses her time wisely. She works <u>diligently to complete her daily tasks</u>. She does not spend time dwelling on those things that do not please the Lord. (Proverbs 31:19, Philippians 4:8)

10. Beauty–She is creative and embraces beauty and godliness.
A Virtuous Woman is a woman of worth and beauty. She has the <u>inner beauty that only comes from Christ</u>. She uses her creativity and sense of style to create beauty in her life and the lives of her loved ones. (Proverbs 31:30 Psalm 139:14, Proverbs 3:15).

Are you beginning to see how you can apply these verses to your life? I hope so! Seeing God's Word come alive is so exciting to me.

What Does It Mean To Be A Proverbs 31 Woman? The passage of Proverbs 31 in the Bible was written by King Solomon, based on the advice his mother gave him. In reference, the passage begins: King Lemuel's mother wanted him to choose a wife wisely and she offered him a list of characteristics to look for in a Godly wife. The passage offers us a glimpse into what being a virtuous woman or being a Proverbs 31 woman might look like.

So, many people discount the idea that it is even possible to be a Proverbs 31 woman, or they feel discouraged by the seemingly exceptional standard set for women in this passage. I believe that all of God's Word is useful for instruction, correction, and reproof. I believe that God's Word is still relevant today. I do not believe that

God allowed the passage of Proverbs 31 in the Bible by chance. I do believe that it is possible to be a virtuous woman today.

Is it possible to live up to the idealistic portrayal of the virtuous woman?

Yes, but maybe not the way you think. Becoming a Proverbs 31 woman does not mean being a perfect, idealistic woman who can do it all and do it all at once. Rather, becoming a Proverbs 31 woman means that you live out God's will for your life daily and live each day with purpose.

A Woman of Noble Character and Valor

The Proverbs 31 woman is described as a virtuous woman or as a wife of noble character. She is also described as a woman of valour, which implies a strong woman who knows what she needs to do, and she sets about doing it. She has a purpose.

As women of valour, as Proverbs 31 women, we are fighting a spiritual battle. Remember, it is a woman's faith that makes her virtuous, not a list of tasks completed, or to-do lists checked off. It is her pliable heart in response to God's prodding.

"Be alert and of sober mind. Your enemy the devil prowls around like a roaring lion looking for someone to devour." 1 Peter 5:8

"For we do not wrestle against flesh and blood, but against the rulers, against the authorities, against the cosmic powers over this present darkness, against the spiritual forces of evil in the heavenly places." Ephesians 6:12

As virtuous women of valour, we are called to put on the armor of God and take every thought captive in obedience to Christ. Isn't that awe- inspiring? Do you see how God sees *you*?

Put on the whole armor of God that you may be able to stand against the schemes of the devil" Ephesians 6:11.

"For though we walk in the flesh we are not waging war according to the flesh; for the weapons of our warfare are not of the flesh but have divine power to destroy strongholds. We destroy arguments and every lofty opinion raised against the knowledge of God and take every thought captive to obey Christ" 2 Corinthians 10:3-5.

The virtuous woman of Proverbs 31 has great courage. She is a woman on a mission. She is ready, willing, and able to face each task and trial. She knows God is on her side. **And if God is on her side, who can be against her?**

"And those he predestined, he also called; those he called, he also justified; those he justified, he also glorified. What, then, shall we say in response to these things? If God is for us, who can be against us? He who did not spare his own Son, but gave him up for us all how will he not also, along with him, graciously give us all things? Who then is the one who condemns? No one, Christ Jesus who died more than that, who was raised to life is at the right hand of God and is also interceding for us. Who shall separate us from the love of Christ? Shall trouble or hardship or persecution or famine or nakedness or danger or sword? As it is written, "For your sake we face death all day long; we are considered as sheep to be slaughtered." No, in all these things we are more than conquerors through him who loved us. For I am convinced that neither death nor life, neither angels nor demons, neither the present nor the future, nor any powers, neither height nor depth, nor anything else in all creation, will be able to separate us from the love of God that is in Christ Jesus our Lord." Romans 8:30-39

The Proverbs 31 Woman is clothed with strength and dignity.
"Strength and honour are her clothing; and she shall rejoice in time to come." Proverbs 31:25.

Proverbs 31:17 says she, "...girds her loins and arms with strength." As a woman of valour, she is spiritually strong. She wears the belt of truth: "Stand therefore, having your loins girt about with truth." Ephesians 6:14. The New Living Translations says it this way: "Stand your ground, putting on the belt of truth and the body armor of God's righteousness."

She is ready to go to battle for those she loves, and she wears the armor of God.

Ephesians 6:10-18 says,

"Finally, my brethren, be strong in the Lord, and in the power of his might. Put on the whole armour of God that ye may be able to stand against the wiles of the devil. For we wrestle not against flesh and blood, but against principalities, against powers, against the rulers of the darkness of this world, against spiritual wickedness in high places. Therefore, take unto you the whole armour of God that ye may be able to withstand in the evil day, and having done all, to stand. Stand therefore, having your loins girt about with truth, and having on the breastplate of righteousness; And your feet shod with the preparation of the gospel of peace; Above all, taking the shield of faith, wherewith ye shall be able to quench all the fiery darts of the wicked. And take the helmet of salvation, and the sword of the Spirit, which is the word of God: Praying always with all prayer and supplication in the Spirit and watching thereunto with all perseverance and supplication for all saints."

We are talking about a woman who knows that she belongs to God and every good work comes from living a faithful life guided by Scripture. Proverbs 31:30 says, "Give her of the fruit of her hands; and let her own works praise her in the gates." She is not worthy of praise because of what she does but because of how she does them.

"For we are his workmanship created in Christ Jesus for good works, which God prepared beforehand, that we should walk in them." Ephesians 2:10

You can be a Proverbs 31 woman – you simply need to believe that Jesus is the Son of God that He came and died for you that you may have eternal life and ask Him to forgive your sins. Then, love Him with all of your heart, mind, and soul!

"...Love the Lord your God with all your heart and with all your soul and with all your mind." Matthew 22:37

Just as faith is what makes the Proverbs 31 a virtuous woman, it is your faith that redeems you. We can all be proverbs 31 women. You can be a proverbs 31 woman. You don't have to feel like a failure. You don't have to feel like you will never measure up. In fact, God says you are already His! All you have to do is believe

The Proverbs 31 Woman and Grace

She understands grace for herself and grace for others. Without Christ, we are nothing. We cannot be good on our own, but with Christ all things are possible. One of my personal favourite Bible verses is Philippians 4:13, "I can do all things through Christ which strengthens me." **I love this verse because it means I do not have to do it alone.** I have Christ on my side. It is His blood that covers my life with grace not because I deserve it, but because He loved me enough to die for me. When I stand before God on the judge-ment day, I do not have to stand there naked. Instead, the robe of righteous will cover my sins.

"*But he said to me, "My grace is sufficient for you, for my power is made perfect in weakness." Therefore, I will boast even more gladly about my weaknesses, so that Christ's power may rest on me.*" 2 Corinthians 12:9

Part of living out a life of Grace is also extending that grace to others.

"*Let your speech always be gracious, seasoned with salt, so that you may know how you ought to answer each person.*" Colossians 4:6

"Bear with each other and forgive whatever grievances you may have against one another. Forgive as the Lord forgave you." Colossians 3:13

"See to it that no one misses the grace of God and that no bitter root grows up to cause trouble and defile many." Hebrews 12:15

The Proverbs 31 woman does not fear the snow because her family is covered in scarlet. Jesus' blood covers us, and we have nothing to fear.

"She is not afraid of the snow for her household: for all her household are clothed with scarlet." Proverbs 31:21

"Do not fear, for I have redeemed you; I have summoned you by name; you are mine." Isaiah 43:1

It is about living with purpose, and your purpose ultimately, is to serve a risen Saviour.

How to Apply Proverbs 31 to Your Life Today

> ➤ **Commit your life to Christ.** Allow Him to come into your heart and lead, guide and direct your steps. You need

to give up your own selfish desires and ambitions and die to self.

> **Pray and study God's Word.** When you pray and study and allow your every thought to be taken captive, you are strengthening your faith and girding your loins, ready for battle. You can also study the 10 Virtues of the Proverbs 31 woman and determine how God would have you implement them in your own life.

"For the word of God is alive and active. Sharper than any double-edged sword, it penetrates even to dividing soul and spirit, joints and marrow; it judges the thoughts and attitudes of the heart." Hebrews 4:12

"Your word is a lamp for my feet, a light on my path." Psalm 119:105

"Blessed is the one who reads aloud the words of this prophecy and blessed are those who hear it and take to heart what is written in it, because the time is near." Revelation 1:3

"You will pray to him, and he will hear you, and you will fulfill your vows." Job 22:27

"Is anyone among you in trouble? Let them pray. Is anyone happy? Let them sing songs of praise." James 5:13

"Watch and pray so that you will not fall into temptation. The spirit is willing, but the flesh is weak." Matthew 26:41

> **Keep His commandments.** We are called to obey Him. As Christians, we will desire to live an obedient life. That does not mean we will never make mistakes. But it does mean that we will make it a priority in our life to grow and strive to improve. And when we do make mistakes, we will ask for forgiveness.

"Do your best to present yourself to God as one approved, a worker who does not need to be ashamed and who correctly handles the word of truth." 2 Timothy 2:15

"The one who keeps His commandments abides in Him, and He in him We know by this that He abides in us, by the Spirit whom He has given us." 1 John 3:24

"If you love me, keep my commandments." John 14:15

"I am the vine, you are the branches; he who abides in Me and I in him, he bears much fruit, for apart from Me you can do nothing." John 15:5

"But the fruit of the Spirit is love, joy, peace, patience, kindness, goodness, faithfulness, gentleness, self-control; against such things there is no law." Galatians 5:22-23

> ➤ **Study the virtues of the Proverbs 31 Woman and ask God to show you how you can implement them in your life.**

"Who can find a virtuous woman? for her price is far above rubies." Proverbs 31:10

"For this very reason, make every effort to add to your faith goodness; and to goodness, knowledge; and to knowledge, self-control; and to self-control, perseverance; and to perseverance, godliness; and to godliness, mutual affection; and to mutual affection, love." 2 Peter 1:5-7.

> ➤ **Accept God's grace in your life and let His love shine through you.** As women of virtue, we are called to share the Good News with others and be a light in a dark world so that others might experience His grace and love as well. Understand that grace is a gift and there is nothing you can do to earn salvation. Jesus came and died for you so that you might have everlasting life with Him for eternity. It is your choice to accept the gift of grace.

"Therefore no one will be declared righteous in God's sight by the works of the law; rather, through the law we become conscious of our sin. Now apart from the law the righteousness of God has been made known, to which the Law and the Prophets testify. This righteousness is given through faith in Jesus Christ to all who believe. There is no difference between Jew and Gentile, for all have sinned and fall short of the glory of God, and all are justified freely by his grace through the redemption that came by Christ Jesus." Romans 3:20-24

"But he said to me, "My grace is sufficient for you, for my power is made perfect in weakness." Therefore, I will boast even more gladly about my weaknesses, so that Christ's power may rest on me" 2 Corinthians 12:9.

"You are the light of the world. A town built on a hill cannot be hidden. Neither do people light a lamp and put it under a bowl. Instead, they put it on its stand, and it gives light to everyone in the house. In the same way, let your light shine before others, that they may see your good deeds and glorify your Father in heaven." Matthew 5:14-16

MODULE 4

DANIEL COMPANY

D ANIEL, WHOSE NAME MEANS "GOD MY JUDGE",
was a righteous man of princely lineage. He was likely a rel-
ative of King Zedekiah, as he was born into Judah's royal family.
Daniel and his God-fearing friends were forced to live in Babylon,
far from home and far from the land their Lord had promised
them. But Daniel remained true to Jerusalem. This was during the
reign of King Nebuchadnezzar of Babylon, whose attacks against
Jerusalem led to the capture of many young men, including Daniel

and his three friends, Shadrach, Meshach, and Abed-Nego. They were transported to Babylon while still children (Daniel 1:2–4, 6).

Daniel received special training in the royal court of Babylon. At an early age, he and his three friends received positions to serve the king as wise men. Daniel soon became known for his understanding of "visions and dreams." The prophecies that he interpreted or that were given to him include the following:

1. His own dream of four great beasts which are symbolic of world-ruling empires (Daniel 7).

2. The "handwriting on the wall," written by the finger of God, that prophesied the end of the Babylonian empire (Daniel 5)

3. The dream about the advent of the Persian Empire in which he saw a ram and a goat.

4. He also received the seventy weeks prophecy that foretold the birth and death of Jesus (Daniel 9), as well as the prophecy concerning the end time – the longest prophecy in the Bible (Daniel 10–12).

Eventually, Daniel became a chief advisor to the king, then the third ruler of the entire kingdom. Although he and his three friends held prominent positions in the government, they were not immune from persecution. Shadrach, Meshach, and Abed-Nego were thrown into a fiery furnace for not worshipping a golden image of the king. A conspiracy against Daniel led him to be thrown into a den of lions.

Daniel is one of the few books of the Bible that takes place during a period of judgment (many books foretell it and a few look back on it) and in a foreign nation. Whether it is in the contrast between the culture's idol worship and Daniel's faithful purity or in the account of the arrogant Nebuchadnezzar and his humbling encounter with God, the pagan backdrop in the book of Daniel makes the Lord's power shine through in a magnificent and majestic way that stands out in Scripture. The book makes it clear that the true God is the supreme ruler over heaven and earth (Daniel 4:17), even when all seems lost, and the consequences of sin seem overwhelming.

Many people today are still faced with daunting choices with regard to which God to serve, or which faith to adhere to, some at the risk of their lives. Religious bigotry is behind the many terrorist atrocities across the world, from Nigeria to Myanmar and from Israel to the Central African Republic.

In the case of Daniel and his comrades in exile, the absolute sovereignty of God, even over a multiplicity of self-absorbed foreign powers, is clearly portrayed. This theme of sovereignty occurs on numerous occasions, including Daniel's deliverance from the lions' den, his friends' rescue from the fiery furnace, and the future arrival of the Ancient of Days to save His people from the forces of evil.

Daniel and his three friends (Hananiah, Mishael, and Azariah) were likely 15 or 16 years old when the Babylonians took them into captivity and ushered them through a three-year education. So, they were likely teenage boys who were abruptly removed from their hometown and taken to a foreign pagan nation to serve a pagan king. These teenage Israelites entered a hostile environment which attempted to strip them of their identity, religion, and culture.

They received name changes (to Shadrach, Meshach, and Abednego) to stamp them with Babylonian identity in an attempt to erase any remnants of their Israelite history.

Sounds like high school! Teens, now more than ever, face a Babylon every day from 7 a.m. to 4 p.m. and beyond. Those wearing a Christian identity endure ridicule and attempts to stamp out their faith in everything – from the curriculum to peer pressure.

Daniel, however, was not shaken. Reading in chapter 1, verses 5 and 6 denote that King Nebuchadnezzar provided these Jewish captives with a daily supply of food, delicacies, and wine. Notice verse 8 however:

"But Daniel purposed in his heart that he wouldn't defile himself with the portion of the king's delicacies, nor with the wine which he drank; therefore he requested of the chief of the eunuchs that he might not defile himself." Daniel's example has key lessons we can learn from, especially for teens, just as he did thousands of years ago for the captives in Babylon. Let us see what we can draw from Daniel's experiences, and his whole life, and apply it to our lives today.

God was the central aspect of Daniel's life.

We find out later in the 6th chapter of Daniel that part of his daily routine was to kneel towards Jerusalem from his window and pray to God 3 times a day. Of course, this became the reason he was thrown into the lion's den. As illustrated earlier, there was nothing more important to Daniel than God. Everything in Daniel's life revolved around God. Christians today can learn from this example. Many have heard the analogy of a wheel on a bike. The case for far too many Christians is that instead of being the central part that all the spokes revolve around, God is merely another spoke. He is merely a part of our lives. Right along with sports, academics, hobbies, etc. This was not the case with Daniel, nor should it be the case for us in our Christian walks today. He should be the fundamental, most important part of our lives, with everything else revolving around Him. Unfortunately, it is easy for God not to be on the forefront of our minds most of the day. Sometimes, He simply enters our thoughts every now and then when we pray before a meal or when we sit through a Bible class. This is not the way we should treat someone whose incredible grace saves us each and every day. We are supposed to love God with all of our hearts, souls, and minds. Do not push God back to just being a part of your life. As shown in the life of Daniel, He needs to be the central part of your life that everything else revolves around.

Daniel was not willing to compromise his standards.

Look at the verse again. It says that Daniel purposed in his heart not to eat of the food Nebuchadnezzar had provided. The phrase "that he might not defile himself," suggests that the food King Nebuchadnezzar was serving was a kind of food that the Jews were not allowed to eat. Remember that the Jews had many dietary restrictions of foods that were declared unclean.

Here is my point: Daniel did not have to uphold his Jewish standards. He was away from home, in a foreign pagan kingdom, without his parents around. He could have eaten the food without a second thought. A modern day example of this would be if a child goes to a friend's house and they are playing a video game or watching a movie they are not allowed to watch. Since parents are not around, this child can easily get away with playing the game or watching the movie. That is the same thing going on here. Daniel did not have to maintain his Jewish standards, but he did. This young boy had the precepts of God as well as integrity so instilled in him that it mattered to him whether or not he pleased God. It did not matter what everyone around him was doing.

According to the text, only Daniel and his 3 friends refused the king's food. All the other captives ate whatever the king was offering. This did not matter to Daniel. He was not going to compromise. This is an extremely important lesson for young people (and adults) to learn.

Peer pressure is a powerful thing. It has been the cause of many young people losing their faith. As followers of Christ, we have to decide upfront, just like Daniel, so that we are not going to compromise our biblical principles, no matter what. Just as Daniel purposed in his heart, we must also determine that whatever comes our way, we are not going to forfeit what we know is acceptable in the sight of God when the pressure comes. Somehow, some way, you are going to get negatively influenced by your peers, coworkers, etc. However, if pleasing God and living according to His will truly is important to you, as it was to Daniel, it will be easier than you think. Decide right now that if something comes up you know is contrary to God's word, you are not going to participate or condone that behavior.

We now fast forward several years to bring us to the next point. Nebuchadnezzar and his son have both died and a new king Darius is ruling the Babylonians.

Daniel used his influence.

As Christians living in North America, we are influenced by so much every single day – some negative and some positive. Consequently, we also have the power of influence. We all influence in some way the people we come in contact with, whether it is the waiter at the restaurant or the visitors at church on Sunday morning.. Sadly, many Christians do not use their influence to further God's kingdom. Not all people are brought to Christ through direct evangelism. It starts with an example. If people cannot tell Christians apart from the rest of the world, we are missing the first major step. Just look at Daniel. In chapter 2, after he interpreted King Nebuchadnezzar's dream, the king proclaimed, "Truly your God is the God of gods, the Lord of kings…" How incredible that would be! Daniel used his influence to influence the king of Babylon! This is not the only time, however. In chapter 6, verses 25 through 27, after King Darius sees Daniel was spared from being eaten by the lions, he decrees that no one should worship anyone but the God of Daniel. Again, Daniel used his influence in an extremely positive and powerful way. As Christians today, we are able to have influence in changing laws like Daniel did, perhaps in different and little ways. Our influence should ultimately be used for God's glory.

Daniel did not waver when hardships arose.

Most people who know the story of Daniel know the reason he was thrown into the lion's den. The other administrators working under King Darius were exceedingly jealous of the king's favoritism towards Daniel, as well as his renowned success as a governor (6: 3-4). So, they tried to find something they could charge Daniel with, either in his ruling skills or his personal life that would diminish his influence with the king. Nonetheless, according to verse 4 of chapter 6, they could not find any error or fault in Daniel because he was faithful. So, these traitors and governors trick the king into signing a law basically forbidding anyone in the kingdom to worship anyone as God, besides Darius. Chapter 6 of Daniel, verse 10 reads, "Now when Daniel knew that the writing was signed, he went home. And in his upper room, with his windows open toward Jerusalem, he knelt down on his knees three times that day, and prayed and gave thanks before his God, as was his custom since early days."

It was not like Daniel was unaware of the new decree. He was completely aware, but that did not matter to him. Again, pleasing God was the most important thing to him. This is an example of political hardship, but the Bible makes it crystal clear that if we are following Christ the way we should, we are going to suffer persecution (John 15:20). It could be political; it could be personal. Either way, it is crucial that we do not succumb or yield to the enemy's advances. We are to put on the whole armor of God so that we will be able to quench the fiery darts of the wicked one (Ephesians 6:16). Just like Daniel, our first priority should be whether or not we are serving and honoring God.

There are key lessons we can learn from Daniel's example, especially teens, just as he did thousands of years ago for the captives in Babylon. Let us see what we can draw from Daniel's experiences, his whole life, and apply it to our lives today.

Daniel teaches teens to excel in all things.

Colossians 3:23 commands us to do everything as if we are doing it for God and not for men.

This includes situations which we hesitate or have no desire to endure. For instance, teens may struggle to roll out of bed to enter the hostile environment of high school. Daniel and his three friends exceeded in all areas of their Babylonian education, although they had strayed far beyond their comfort zone. They did so well that they surpassed the wise men in the land 10 times (Daniel 1:20). Because of this, the king took notice and favored them. The world has their eyes focused on Christians. If we submit a half-hearted effort on a project, cheat on an assignment, or give a lukewarm performance in an after-school club or sport, it reflects poorly on us and our Christian community. Even if we attend a Christian school or homeschool co-op, whenever we encounter a non-Christian school in a competition or event, they will hold us to the same standard. Daniel and his friends understood that their identity as God's people carried an extreme importance when they entered Babylon. They could get by, just learning the basics of the Babylonian language and hoping to fade in the background, and thus, affect no change for the kingdom. Or they could do everything to the best of their ability to catch the attention and favor of someone in higher authority. When someone in a lofty position takes notice of a person, they tend to give them a platform to speak, which means a greater chance to speak about the life-changing grace of Christ.

Daniel teaches teens to ask God for wisdom.

If you think a failed grade for not knowing an answer to a question sounds bad, try facing the death penalty for it.

King Nebuchadnezzar, disturbed after having a troublesome dream, consults the wise men in his land for an interpretation (Daniel 2). When no one can give a satisfying answer, the King decides to sentence all the wise men in the land to death, which included Daniel. Upon hearing the news, Daniel returned and let his three Israelite companions convey the gravity of the situation. He commands them to ask God to reveal the answer to the dream. God does so to Daniel after they asked. That wisdom saves thousands of lives.

Although, high school administrators do not threaten to kill teens if they cannot provide an answer to a problem, but sometimes God places teens in situations where they will need to rely on Him for wisdom. Perhaps a discussion arises at a lunch table about God, and friends bring up difficult theological questions such as the problem of evil or free will. As the Christian in the friends' group, they may expect the believer to provide answers which they have not arrived at themselves in their spiritual walk. In that moment, a Christian teen will have to rely on the Holy Spirit for what words to say.

The Book of Daniel teaches teens to stand up and stand out.

Literally, When Nebuchadnezzar constructed a 90-foot image of himself, he expected all of Babylon to bow and pay reverence to the idol. Those who disobeyed, in classic Nebuchadnezzar fashion, would face the death penalty and a fiery one at that. The problem was that no one could overtly disobey. With the whole kingdom falling down to worship the statue, if you refused, that required you to stay on your feet. Thus, in a very literal sense, standing up and standing out. The King would and could pick you out from the crowd. Although the Bible instructs us to obey the authorities placed over us (Romans 13:1), Christians will face situations in which they have to stand up and stand out for their faith. In high school, a Christian teen might have to decline an offer to partake in drugs or to take a relationship too far. This will cause them to stick out in a crowd that might make them face a social death penalty.

Daniel teaches teens to trust God in the fire.

The faith Azariah, Hananiah, and Mishael exemplify in the third chapter of Daniel is worth noting and emulating. They believe God will deliver them from the fiery furnace fate King Nebuchadnezzar has sealed for them for refusing to bow down to the statue. Nevertheless, even if He does not choose to deliver them, they still refuse to yield to the pressure of disobeying God. After the king increases the temperature of the furnace (Daniel 3:19), they enter the flames with the same attitude. Teens face fiery furnaces every day. They endure trials of bullying, pressures to perform well in sports, academics, extracurricular to attain scholarships, stress, and the list goes on. Like Daniel and his friends, they have to trust God. Often, He will deliver people in one way or another. However God chooses His deliverance, we have to enter the furnace with the same attitude that Daniel's friends did.

There are many lessons we can learn from the life of Daniel that go far beyond him being thrown into a lion's den. He was a faithful servant of God who did not waver or compromise when hardships arose. He put God first and foremost in his life and he was blessed for it. We can apply many of Daniel's principles to our lives today.

WILL WE CONFORM OR TRANSFORM? LEARNING FROM THE LIFE OF DANIEL ABOUT LIVING IN TODAY'S CULTURE

Daniel continues to be a model for how Christians should live in the world today. Let us explore his life in more depth. Like Daniel and the other Hebrew exiles, you may feel like a stranger in a strange land. If you take your Christian worldview seriously, you will find yourself at odds with the surrounding culture, just like Daniel. Yet, like Daniel, we must not withdraw from the world in which we live. We must engage it in obedience to God's call on our lives, working for his glory and the common good.

LEARNING FROM THE LIFE OF DANIEL

There are lessons to learn from the life of Daniel as a public servant in Babylon:

> ➢ Daniel sought to use his gifts to transform the culture around him.

> ➢ He wanted Babylonian life to be shaped by the values of the one true God.

> He worked for the flourishing of all of Babylon.

> Daniel was able to identify where his values and Babylonian values overlapped.

> Through Daniel's conscientious work, his Babylonian overlords became convinced of the excellence of Daniel's vision of their shared future.

There was a limit, however, to what Daniel was willing to do. When his government demanded ultimate loyalty, he refused, choosing instead what appeared to be certain death in the lion's den. God saved Daniel and continued to use him as a great witness within the empire.

WILL WE CONFORM OR TRANSFORM?

Like Daniel, we have a decision to make. Will we join those who conform, or those who renew and transform? Will we, like Daniel, embrace our biblical call to become agents, models, and witnesses to *shalom? During* the exile to Babylon, the best and brightest of Jerusalem were then taken into captivity and made to march almost 1,000 miles to the great city of Babylon. Even in their oppression, God was calling his people to take dominion by working for the restoration of the city of Babylon. Again, Daniel is the clearest example of this. Like Daniel, we are called to work for the transformation of the city, to do justice, love mercy, and walk humbly with God (Micah 6:8). We are to do this in everything we do, especially in our career calling. We believe in a coming age when shalom will be completely restored, an age without sin and injustice.

May we eagerly work in this world to bring about glimpses of that wonderful world to come.

Exercise

What attribute of Daniel do you possess, if any?

_____

_____

_____

_____

How can we use the story of Daniel to shape the attitude of the current generation of youths?

_____

_____

_____

_____

Write down some practical steps you will take to ensure God becomes the center focus of your entire life?

_____

_____

_____

_____

What does it mean to love the Lord your God with all your heart, all your mind, all your soul and all your strength?

_____

_____

_____

_____

How can you demonstrate that level of love towards God?

_____

_____

_____

_____

Do you agree that when you resolve and ask God ahead of time to help you not to give in to negative peer pressure that He will send you a way of escape?

_____

_____

_____

_____

MODULE 5

JOSEPH COMPANY

JOSEPH WAS ONE OF JACOB'S 12 SONS. HIS FATHER loved him more than any of the other sons and gave him a colored cloak. His brothers were jealous of him and sold him into slavery. He was taken to Egypt and eventually became a steward to Potiphar, one of Pharaoh's officials. Potiphar's wife tried unsuccessfully to seduce him and after false accusations were levelled at Joseph he was imprisoned. Due to his ability to interpret Pharaoh's dream he was made governor of Egypt. He wisely rationed the country's produce in preparation for a time of famine.

During the famine, Jacob's sons came to Egypt to plead with Joseph for supplies. They did not recognize him. But after he was satisfied that they were reformed, he identified himself with great joy. Joseph invited his father and brothers to come and settle in Egypt. The story is recounted in the Old Testament (Genesis 37, 39-45).

Joseph is often seen as an Old Testament equivalent, or foreshadowing, of Christ.

The story of Joseph in the <u>Bible</u> is one of my favorites because I feel like I can relate so well to him. Joseph had a dream from God as a youth and instead of beginning to walk out that dream as he imagined he would, he went through a bunch of what seemed like detours, and his life ended up looking a lot different than I am sure he had imagined. While I have never been sold into slavery or wrongfully imprisoned, I have had life go differently than what I had imagined, seemingly in the opposite direction of the dreams God had placed in my heart.

Let us take a deeper look at the life and story of Joseph and how his <u>faith</u> stands as a great example for us.

Joseph's pain was the key to his greatness.

Joseph was the favorite son because he was the first son born to Jacob's true love, Rachel. One day, Jacob gave Joseph a special gift in the form of a fancy robe, or tunic. This robe was beautiful, ornate, had long sleeves, and extended down to his ankles. In comparison, Joseph's brothers likely had shorter, sleeveless tunics that allowed them to do their manual labor more easily. Charles Swindoll writes in his book *Joseph: A Man of Integrity and Forgiveness*, "By giving Joseph this elaborate full-length coat, which was also a sign of nobility in that day, his father was boldly implying, 'You can wear this beautiful garment because you don't have to work like those brothers of yours.'"

I am guessing that this coat was not the first gift Joseph received that obviously pointed out the favor he had with his father. Joseph was likely spoiled and coddled his entire life, until that fateful day when he was forced to leave his father's favor and blessings. His brothers' jealousy built up and eventually overcame them so much that one day they threw Joseph into a pit and eventually sold him into slavery. Talk about the end of a spoiled childhood! Once Joseph belonged to foreign people who paid to own him, his days of being favored and coddled were over.

"The LORD was with Joseph, so he succeeded in everything he did **as he served in the home of his Egyptian master"** (Genesis 39:2, emphasis added).

Joseph had to learn to work because daddy was no longer around to let him off the hook. The beauty is that Joseph did work, and he worked hard. We see Joseph's gifts of administration and oversight start to bloom as *"Potiphar gave Joseph complete administrative responsibility over everything he owned"* (Genesis 39:6). We continue to see Joseph's hard work and his gifting developed as he worked hard and became in charge of the prison he was in and eventually over all of Egypt!

In the end, it was Joseph's God-given gift of administration and oversight that God used to save Jacob's family and the whole nation of Egypt from starvation. Going through the pain of losing his status of "chosen son" and having to work to earn his keep is the only reason that Joseph's gift was able to develop and grow in his life. If he did not experience the hardship of being sold into slavery, he never would have tapped into that gift and consequently never would have saved his family.

Joseph ministered to others in his darkest time.

Joseph's life was filled with what seemed to be setbacks on the surface, but in fact were the very situations that matured him, tested him, and ultimately set him up for God's plan to be manifested through him. In one of these major setbacks, we see the true, noble character that was the core of who Joseph was. After being wrongfully charged for an offense he did not commit, Joseph found himself in prison. One day he received two new cell mates, Pharaoh's chief baker and his chief cupbearer. Since Joseph was responsible and skilled, he was ultimately placed in charge of these two prisoners. Having this kind of authority, Joseph could have easily lorded it over them and been rude and disrespectful. Instead, we see that Joseph was kind and compassionate to them, acknowledging their feelings and reaching out to them.

While they were in prison, Pharaoh's cupbearer, and baker each had a dream one night, and each dream had its own meaning. When Joseph saw them the next morning, he noticed that they both looked upset.

"Why do you look so worried today?" he asked them (<u>Genesis 4:5-7</u>).

Can you imagine being wrongfully accused and thrown in jail when all you have been trying to do is serve God faithfully and honestly? Then some other prisoners, who were likely actually guilty of some crime, are moaning and complaining (that is my own interpretation, but that could have easily been the case) about their distress right in front of you? My first instinct would be to tell them they have nothing to complain about and explain the plight of my circumstances and show why I have it so much harder than they do.

Not Joseph! He reached out and basically offered himself as a shoulder to cry on. Then, not only did he listen to their distress, but he also offered to solve their problem by interpreting their dreams. What amazing character Joseph had, to put himself aside and help others during his own suffering!

3. Joseph did not try to push his own agenda in his life.

After Joseph interprets the baker's and cup-bearer's dreams, he asks the cupbearer, whom he knew would soon be promoted back to his job, to remember him and hopefully aid in getting him freed from his wrongful imprisonment. Joseph reached out and helped someone despite his suffering, so it seems right that he would receive a reward and a blessing from that. Nevertheless, once the cupbearer was restored to his position, he forgot all about Joseph, thus he remained in prison for two more long years. I bet it was really tempting for Joseph to try to manipulate and scheme things to get himself out of there. In contrast, it seems that he instead grew closer to God and grew in faith during this time. We know that by how he acted when we see him next.

Two years after Joseph interpreted his dream, the cupbearer did finally remember him when Pharaoh needed someone to interpret his dream. Finally, Joseph was brought out of prison to be able to share one of his God-given gifts and help someone in authority. After Joseph interpreted Pharaoh's dream about the forthcoming prosperity and famine, he told Pharaoh what he thought the best course of action would be.

Pharaoh should find an intelligent and wise man and put him in charge of the entire land of Egypt (Genesis 41:33). Joseph's suggestions were well received by Pharaoh and his officials. So, Pharaoh asked his officials, "Can we find anyone else like this man so obviously filled with the spirit of God?" (Genesis 41:37-38).

If I were Joseph, I would probably want to shout from the rooftops "Pick me, pick me!!!" Joseph was very capable of doing this job and he would do it well because he was experienced and gifted at it! But Joseph was quiet. He did not promote himself or try to prove that he would be the best at this. Instead, he sat back and watched as God promoted him, by only His grace and outside of any of Joseph's own efforts. And God did just that:

Then Pharaoh said to Joseph, "Since God has revealed the meaning of the dreams to you, clearly no one else is as intelligent or wise as you are. You will be in charge of my court, and all my people will take orders from you. Only I, sitting on my throne, will have a rank higher than yours." Pharaoh said to Joseph, "I hereby put you in charge of the entire land of Egypt" (<u>Genesis 41:39-41</u>).

Joseph was released from prison and put into a place of high authority in just one day and it brought glory to God instead of himself.

Joseph was an amazing man of patience, integrity, and character. So many of us have read his story repeatedly and marveled at how God brought justice and blessing to him, despite being treated unfairly.

Looking at Joseph more closely and analyzing his actions (and lack of action in certain circumstances), we can see a shining example of one of God's loyal servants whom God saw worthy of being promoted to the high calling he had. When we have times in our lives where we are being treated unfairly or things seem to be continually against us, we can look to Joseph for a great example of how to keep our eyes on God and continue to live in integrity and have confidence that God will come through for us at His perfect timing.

Joseph immediately went about the work to which Pharaoh had appointed him. His primary interest was in getting the job done for others, rather than taking personal advantage of his new position at the head of the royal court. He maintained his faith in God, giving his children names that credited God with healing his emotional pain and making him fruitful (Gen. 41:51-52). He recognized that his wisdom and discernment were gifts from God, but nevertheless that he still had much to learn about the land of Egypt and its agriculture industry.

Joseph's work as the senior administrator touched on nearly every practical area of the nation's life. His office would have required that he learn much about legislation, communication, negotiation, transportation, safe and efficient methods of food storage, building, economic strategizing and forecasting, record-keeping, payroll, the handling of transactions both by means of currency and through bartering, human resources, and the acquisition of real estate. His extraordinary abilities with respect to God and people did not operate in separate domains. The genius of Joseph's success lay in the effective integration of his divine gifts and acquired competencies. For Joseph, all of this was godly work.

Pharaoh had already characterized Joseph as "discerning and wise" and these characteristics enabled Joseph to do the work of strategic planning and administration.

As his first act, "Joseph...went through all the land of Egypt" (Gen. 41:46) on an inspection tour. He would have to become familiar with the people who managed agriculture, the locations and conditions of the fields, the crops, the roads, and means of transportation. It is inconceivable that Joseph could have accomplished all of this on a personal level. He would have had to establish and oversee the training of what amounted to a Department of Agriculture and Revenue. During the seven years of abundant harvest, Joseph had the grain stored in cities (Gen. 41:48-49). During the seven lean years that followed, Joseph dispensed grain to the Egyptians and other people who were affected by the widespread famine. To create and administer all this, while surviving the political intrigue of an absolute monarchy, required exceptional talent.

Joseph Relieves the Poverty of Egypt's People (Genesis 47:13-26)

After the people ran out of money, Joseph allowed them to barter their livestock for food. This plan lasted for one year during which Joseph collected horses, sheep, goats, cattle, and donkeys (Gen. 47:15-17). He would have had to determine the value of these animals and establish an equitable system for exchange. When food is scarce, people are especially concerned for the survival of themselves and their loved ones. Providing access to points of food distribution and treating people even-handedly become acutely important administrative matters.

When all of the livestock had been traded, people willingly sold themselves into slavery to Pharaoh and sold him the ownership of their lands as well. From the perspective of leadership, this must have been awful to witness. Joseph, however, allowed the people to sell their land and to enter into servitude, but he did not take advantage of them in their powerlessness. Joseph would have had to see that these properties were valued correctly (in exchange for seed for planting). He enacted an enduring law that people return 20 percent of the harvest to Pharaoh. This entailed creating a system to monitor and enforce the people's compliance with the law and establishing a department dedicated to managing the revenue. In all of this, Joseph exempted the priestly families from selling their land because Pharaoh supplied them with a fixed allotment of food to meet their needs adequately. Handling this special population would have entailed having a smaller, distinct system of distribution that was tailored for them.

Poverty and its consequences are economic realities. Our first duty is to help eliminate them, but we cannot expect complete success until God's kingdom is fulfilled. Believers may not have the power to eradicate the circumstances that require people to make hard choices, but we can find ways to support people as they or perhaps we ourselves cope. In our work, we may experience tension arising from feeling empathy for the needy yet bearing responsibility to do what is good for the people and organizations we work for. Joseph experienced God's guidance in these difficult tasks, and we also have received God's promise that "I will never leave you or forsake you" (Heb. 13:5).

Happily, by applying his God-given skill and wisdom, Joseph successfully brought Egypt through the agricultural catastrophe. When the seven years of good harvests came, Joseph developed a stockpiling system to store the grain for use during the coming drought. When the seven years of drought arrived, "Joseph opened the storehouses" and provided enough food to take the nation through the famine. His wise strategy and effective implementation of the plan even allowed Egypt to supply grain to the rest of the world during the famine (Gen. 41:57). In this case, God's fulfillment of his promise that Abraham's descendants would be a blessing to the world occurred not only for the benefit of foreign nations, but even through the industry of a foreign nation, Egypt.

In fact, God's blessing for the people of Israel came only after and through his blessing of foreigners. God did not raise up an Israelite in the land of Israel to provide for Israel's relief during the famine. Instead, God enabled Joseph, working in and through the Egyptian government, to provide for the needs of the people of Israel (Gen. 47:11-12). Nonetheless, we should not idealize Joseph. As an official in a sometimes-repressive society, he became part of its power structure, and he personally imposed slavery on uncounted numbers of people (Gen. 47:21).

Applications from Joseph's Management Experience (Genesis 41:46-57; 47:13-26)

The interest of Genesis in Joseph's management of the food crisis lies more in its effect on the family of Israel than in developing principles for effective management. Nonetheless, to the degree that Joseph's extraordinary leadership can serve as an example for leaders today, we can derive some practical applications from his work:

> ➤ Become as familiar as possible with the situation as they exist at the beginning of your service. Pray for discernment regarding the future so that you can make wise plans.

> ➤ Commit yourself to God first and then expect him to direct and establish your plans.

> ➤ Gratefully and appropriately acknowledge the gifts God has given you.

> ➤ Even though others recognize God's presence in your life and the special talents you have, do not broadcast these in a self-serving effort to gain respect.

- ➢ Educate yourself about how to do your job and carry it out with excellence.

- ➢ Seek the practical good for others, knowing that God has placed you where you are to be a blessing.

- ➢ Be fair in all your dealings, especially when the circumstances are grim and deeply problematic.

- ➢ Although your exemplary service may propel you to prominence, remember your founding mission as God's servant. Your life does not consist in what you gain for yourself.

- ➢ Value the godliness of the numerous types of honorable work that society needs.

- ➢ Generously extend the fruit of your labor as widely as possible to those who truly need it, regardless of what you think of them as individuals.

- ➢ Accept the fact that God may bring you into a particular field of work under extremely challenging conditions. This does not mean that something has gone terribly wrong or that you are out of God's will.

- ➢ Have courage that God will fit you for the task.

Believe that what you do will not only benefit those whom you see and meet, but also that your work has the potential to touch lives for many generations to come. God can accomplish abundantly far more than we can ask or imagine (Eph. 3:20).

BIBLICAL JOSEPH – LESSONS FOR ADMINISTRATORS

Like most of us, he had to learn administration and management the hard way, making many mistakes along the way.

Here are a few summarized excerpts, and what they might mean for modern behavioral administration.

Favoritism: Jacob gives Joseph, his favorite son, a "coat of many colors", which stimulates the envy of his brothers. Recommendation: Administrators should be very careful about showing such overt and dramatic favoritism.

Arrogance: Joseph tells his brothers of his dreams, which suggest they will later come under his domination. Recommendation: Would-be administrators should be careful about their ego and empathize with those they may pass by.

Failure: Joseph is sold into slavery by his brothers and ends up in an Egyptian jail; in jail, he becomes a valuable interpreter of dreams. Recommendation: Don't give up after even a major failure but learn alternative ways to use your strengths and skills.

Gratefulness: Joseph becomes so successful in interpreting dreams in Egypt that he is asked to interpret those of the Pharoah, but this time around attributes his success to God rather than solely or mainly himself. Recommendation: No matter how much our success seems to come from ourselves, be sure to acknowledge the help and support of others.

Planning: Joseph recognized that there were enough clues about future climate change to make controversial plans for periods of drought. Recommendation: Despite whatever immediate problems need attention, and how bad we are at prediction, always try to keep anticipated future needs and dangers in the picture.

Forgiveness: Near the end of the story, Joseph encounters his brothers after many years, and surreptitiously tests out whether they have changed for the better; the truth comes out, Joseph forgives them, and there is a heartwarming reconciliation. Recommendation: Forgiveness, after truthfulness and a sincere apology, along with some indication of real change, can help any organization move forward.

Practical Exercise: Choose one of these models and explain how it would help your work as an administrator.

_____

_____

_____

_____

_____

KINGDOM VERSUS CHURCH MINDSET

In the transition that churches and ministries are facing, there are many working to do "Kingdom" yet still battle old habits and a religious mindset. The old wine skin must be completely replaced with new wine skins. The old cloth cannot be repaired by patching it with a new piece of cloth; the entire garment must be made new. Sound doctrine of the Kingdom has ramifications in some very practical areas. Mind you, the goal is not to dismantle the existing church or criticize pastors. Rather, to move the ecclesiae into the new. Below are several key ramifications to help us make that shift and identify where the Kingdom is being applied in truth and in spirit.

➢ A kingdom mindset encourages all saints to be ministers in the marketplace (outside the religious establishment called church). A church mindset merely trains people to serve in a church building on Sundays (day of sun god worship and not the biblical Sabbath day). We can serve in church and enjoy it while our own vision and dream is taking shape.

➢ A Kingdom mindset creates wealth to transform a community and a nation. A "church-only" mindset motivates giving to build our own church programs.

➤ A Kingdom mindset is a holistic approach that integrates the Gospel of the Kingdom with politics, economics, and public policy. A church-only mindset insulates the gospel from politics and public policy (God's original intent was not religion but a nation).

➤ A Kingdom mindset views the Bible as a blueprint to structure every aspect of society. A church-only mindset views the Bible merely as a book that enables us to escape the world, enter heaven, and be spiritual (an exile mindset).

➤ With a Kingdom mindset, we embrace and love our surrounding unchurched communities. With a church-only mindset, we are prone to only embrace converted individuals within our faith communities.

➤ A Kingdom mindset trains all people for all of life. A church-only mindset trains people only for church life. We should honor those who labor among us in the local church and celebrate the exploits of "kings" in the marketplace at the same time.

➤ A Kingdom mindset nurtures leaders who are world changers and "culture creators" who articulate truth to society. A church-only mindset nurtures leaders who speak religious language relevant only to church people. We are prone to get way too introverted and stay within the four walls.

➤ A Kingdom mindset speaks of the rule of God over the entire created order. A church-only mindset speaks of the rule of God through deacons and elders over those in a church congregation. It is easy to get entangled in a bunch of rules that make us look irrelevant to our culture.

➤ With a Kingdom mindset, pastors encourage and value vocational callings of their people in the marketplace. A church-only mindset controls people by marginalizing their marketplace callings and emphasizing only Sunday ministries. Our job is to make disciples in church without being afraid to point them in the right direction someday when they mature, and we need to release them as "Kings" in the marketplace pursuing the desires God has placed in their hearts. No one can just plug into the church and tithe and listen to sermons for the rest of his life. If we do not release their hearts as "Kings", we lose them to boredom. Their dreams will wither and die.

➤ A Kingdom mindset applies a Spirit-empowered approach to the natural-world. A church-only mindset involves a spirituality that separates from the natural world. We practice in church to be equipped and do the real thing in the Kingdom-at work.

➤ Those with a Kingdom mindset are working toward a revival of Christianity, if you will. Those with a church-only mindset merely strive for a particular expression denomination of Christianity. Charismatics love revivals and conferences and worship. Now we need to learn how to multiply finances and convert money into ministry and impact our cities and regions.

➤ Churches with a Kingdom mindset equip 100% of the saints to fill up all things in every realm of life.

➤ Ephesians 4:10-12: He that descended is the same also that ascended far above all heavens, that he might fill all things.) And he gave some, apostles; and some, prophets; and some, evangelists; and some, pastors, and teachers; For the perfecting of the saints, for the work of the ministry, for the edifying of the body of Christ:

➤ Those with a church-only mindset have as their primary goal to equip the 2-3% of the congregation/community called to be "full-time" church pastors, ministers, and missionaries. It is fine to have 5-fold ministries in the church; just do not forget the goal to release the 95% of the congregation to do the real work of the ministry outside the church.

My heart longs for disciples who will release their hearts to embrace the wisdom and anointing required to create wealth and convert money into the work of the Kingdom. (Notice that Islam has done this very effectively...just for the kingdom of darkness...hint, hint). Let us teach the Lord's kings to do that in "church".

CAN I KNOW MY PURPOSE?

God created you to know him and to have an intimate relationship with him. In fact, God says that if a person is going to boast about anything in life, then he or she should "boast about this: that they have the understanding to know me" (Jeremiah 9:23). The Bible encourages us to seek God first, which is why Jesus encouraged his disciples by saying, "But seek first his kingdom and his righteousness, and all these things will be given to you as well" (Matthew 6:33).

We know God chose us; he is the initiator, and we simply respond to his invitation. Therefore, Jesus told his disciples, "You did not choose me, but I chose you and appointed you so that you might go and bear fruit that will last and so whatever you ask in my name the Father will give you" (John 15:16).

Humankind's relationship with God was lost in the garden when Adam and Eve sinned. Jesus' death on the cross, however, allows this relationship to be restored and to have intimate fellowship with the Father once again. The apostle Paul came to understand this when he said, "I gave up all that inferior stuff so I could know Christ personally, experience his resurrection power, be a partner in his suffering, and go all the way with him to death itself" (Philippians 3:10).

Establishing this relationship with God is vital to understanding your purpose in life. If you do not have this relationship with God, then you will seek to fulfill your purpose out of wrong motives, such as fear, insecurity, pride, money, relationships, guilt, or unresolved anger. God's desire is for you to be motivated out of love for him and to desire to worship him in all that you do. As you develop this relationship with God, he will begin to reveal his purpose for your life.

Your purpose in life is not something you decide to do; rather, it is chosen by God. It is non-negotiable. God had a plan in mind when he allowed your spirit, which was in heaven, to come into flesh and blood and be born on earth. "The Lord will fulfill His purpose for me," the psalmist said (Psalm 138:8). There is no changing God's purpose for your life, but you may not fulfill it because free will is involved.

The Psalms tell us that we have an assigned portion (purpose and destiny). For example, David wrote, "Lord, you alone are my portion and my cup; you make my lot secure. The boundary lines have fallen for me in pleasant places; surely I have a delightful inheritance" (Psalm 16:5–6). "He marked out their appointed times in history and the boundaries of their lands" (Acts 17:26).

Let us look at the stages God uses to bring many of his people into the larger story of their lives.

Stage 1: Crisis is Often the Front Door of Your Larger Story

Before we enter the first stage of our larger story, we often experience an event designed to usher us into the process of discovering our larger story. For Paul, it was being struck with blindness by Jesus Christ; for David, it was the battle with Goliath, for the disciples, it was when Jesus appeared to be a ghost on the water; for Joseph, it was being thrown into a pit. Like Joseph, there is often a dream or vision of what we believe God may be calling us to do. Joseph had a dream that indicated something was going to happen in his future. He did not totally understand his dream, but that dream had a devastating impact on his life when he publicly shared it with his brothers, who demonstrated that they could not handle it.

Joseph was immature and lacked wisdom at this stage of his life. His brothers perceived him as the favored son at their expense, he got a beautiful coat the others did not get, and so his brothers became jealous of Joseph's favoritism. His dream was from God, but his handling of it showed an immaturity that God was going to use to create a new Joseph and save a nation through him. God used this dream to usher him into the crisis stage. When Joseph was thrown into the pit, it ushered him into a crisis that must have created a level of fear Joseph had never known before. He was thrust from one place in life to a whole new place, with no rights or choices, and, no doubt, with questioning of God's love. "Where is my God? How could he let this happen to me? What happened to the dream I received from God?"

Oswald Chambers said, "Whenever God gives a vision to a Christian, it is as if He puts him in the shadow of His hand" (Isaiah 49:2). The believer's duty is to be still and listen. There is a "darkness" that comes from too much light that is the time to listen. The story of Abram and Hagar in Genesis 16 is an excellent example of listening to so-called good advice during a time of darkness, rather than waiting for God to send the light.

Friend, you may feel like you are in prison; you may feel stuck in your circumstances. Let God meet you in this place. Let this be a time of discovering the power and presence of God during adverse circumstances. Sometimes, the winds of adversity force us to adjust our sails to capture a different kind of wind. What should be our response when we are faced with a crisis?

Stage 2: Character Development

Joseph went through a thirteen-year season of character building and preparation. It was hardly an "assignment" that matched his purpose. His primary assignment to fulfill God's call included this painful process. God takes many leaders through a season of character building that often has little to do with their natural gifts, but it is a vital step toward developing the character that God requires for the assignment he has for that person.

If God has called you to some endeavor and you are frustrated that it has not manifested yet, know that times of preparation and simmering are required before the vision can be achieved. Seldom does God call and manifest the vision at the same time. There is preparation. There is testing. There is relationship building that must take place between you and God. Only once this is complete will you see the vision materialize.

Stage 3: Isolation

Stage three often leads us into isolation. Joseph was isolated from his family and all that he knew. David retreated to the Cave of Adullam to flee King Saul. The Apostle John was banished to the island of Patmos where he wrote the Book of Revelation. God turns messes into messages and messengers in the isolation stage of the call of God to our larger story.

This stage can also be described as the desert stage. When the Israelites were freed from slavery, they had to pass through the desert. The word desert comes from a Hebrew word midbaar, which means "to speak." Hosea 2:14 tell us, "Therefore I am now going to allure her; I will lead her into the wilderness and speak tenderly to her." God used the mess of the cave to turn David into one of our greatest messengers, who wrote much of the Psalms, which have comforted millions of people over the centuries.

We learn the lessons from tears he shed in these times, and they are a spring from which we deeply drink: "As they pass through the Valley of Baka (weeping), they make it a place of springs; the autumn rains also cover it with pools. They go from strength to strength, till each appears before God in Zion" (Psalm 84:6–7). We realize that it is only the Lord who can illuminate our path during these dark times: "You, Lord, are my lamp; the Lord turns my darkness into light" (2 Samuel 22:29).

If God calls us into darkness in order to enter his presence, then that darkness will become an entry to new levels of relationship with a God who longs for fellowship with us. God was testing David's mettle and preparing him for a new chapter in his life. God is calling forth his sons and daughters to step into their destinies: "For the creation waits in eager expectation for the children of God to be revealed" (Romans 8:19).

Stage 4: The Cross

The fourth stage to discover, navigate, and fulfill your purpose is the cross. There appears to be an unwritten spiritual law that God requires of leaders whom he uses significantly in his kingdom. I call it the graduate level test. This test contributes more to a leader coming to his or her own personal cross than any other activity. Many who have matured in their faith journey needed help to get to that maturity. There are certain experiences God allows that are designed to bring us to the absolute end of our carnal lives. This is so that Christ fully lives through us. Even the best of believers is unable to crucify the flesh by themselves. We might be able to put two nails into our own cross, but it always takes someone else to drive in the third one. And that usually involves some type of betrayal in the life of the leader. Most of the great leaders in the Bible experienced some form of betrayal:

- ➤ For Moses, it was Korah.

- ➤ For Job, it was his three friends.

- ➤ For Jesus Christ, it was Judas.

- ➤ For David, it was Absalom.

- ➤ For Joseph, it was his brothers and Potiphar's wife.

Betrayal is God's graduate level course for leaders. Joseph would have never been made prime minister of Egypt had he not passed the test of forgiveness from the betrayal of his brothers. Job would never have been restored had he not forgiven the betrayal of his three friends who wrongfully judged him. David would never have become the leader he was without the betrayal he experienced. Jesus Christ would never have become the Savior had he not forgiven our betrayal of him and taken on our sin. He also needed Judas to fulfill his role in putting Him on the cross. You are nothing in the kingdom of God until you have been betrayed and until you have come to know the fellowship of Christ's sufferings. This wounding must be experienced so that one can be acquainted with his grief.

Stage 5: Problem Solving

The problem-solving stage is a key component of the six stages. Once God has taken you through a process of maturity, then the fruit of that process often results in you solving some type of problem that ultimately gives you the authority in which God wants you to operate. For example, God raised up Pharaoh to demonstrate his power to him, his nation, and the people of Israel (Romans 9:17). Through Moses, God solved the problem of freeing the people of Israel from slavery, using as the catalyst a series of miraculous plagues. This is how God works through us to bring solutions that can solve problems in our world. We gain influence by being better and by providing solutions to culture's leaders and their problems. And when there are injustices, we tap into the power of God for the solution to the injustice, just as Martin Luther King Jr. did.

It may cost you your life when you stand up for righteousness and a cause that is bigger than yourself. When Satan throws bricks at you, let God use them to build his kingdom by tapping into heaven and letting God solve the problem. Jesus never fretted over a problem; He already has a solution; so do you, because Jesus lives inside of you. Solving problems will give you greater authority and influence. When Jesus told the disciples to feed the five thousand, he enabled them to fulfill the assignment.

George Washington Carver is one of the greatest inspirational stories of all time. Here was a man who should have been a victim to his circumstances. He lived during the worst time of slavery in America. He lost his mother to the slave trade; he was discriminated against continually. He could have become a victim to his circumstances. Yet he was a follower of Jesus who was gifted with an inventive mind. He discovered more than three hundred uses for the peanut and one hundred uses for the sweet potato that transformed the Southern economy. George Washington Carver was an American agricultural scientist and inventor who promoted alternative crops to cotton and methods to prevent soil depletion. He was the most prominent black scientist of the early 20th century.

What problem has God called you to solve?

Stage 6: Networks

The sixth stage of the call of God in the life of a leader involves networks. One of the great values of God we see in the Scriptures is the need for groups of people to come together in unity for a cause greater than any single person could accomplish by him or herself. God reveals this value for unity in diversity in the Trinity Father, Son, and Holy Spirit. Each member of the Trinity has a particular role to play. And when Jesus decided to start his worldwide mission, he recruited twelve disciples to accomplish this task. These were recruited from average men from the marketplace, not from the clergy of the day. Jesus spent three years pouring into these men and building unity among them for a common mission. David had his mighty men. Daniel had a small group of men he relied on to share the burdens they had as people living in Babylon serving an ungodly king. When Nebuchadnezzar told Daniel that he had to tell him his dream and interpret it or else he would die, Daniel immediately went to his core circle of friends Shadrach, Meshach, and Abednego to pray together.

God answered their prayer, and Daniel's life, and the lives of the men in his administration, were spared. God's name was uplifted in the whole kingdom as a result of this miracle. God revealed that there is incredible power in a unified vision of one group of people: "The Lord said, 'If as one people speaking the same language they have begun to do this, then nothing they plan to will be impossible for them'" (Genesis 11:6).

We usually cite this verse when describing the sin of the people trying to achieve something without God. However, God tells us that there is great power in a unified voice. An old saying goes, "There is strength in numbers." Not only that, but Scripture tells us five will chase a hundred, but a hundred will chase ten thousand (Leviticus 26:8). "Though one may be overpowered, two can defend themselves. A cord of three strands is not quickly broken" (Ecclesiastes 4:12). And again, Deuteronomy reminds us, "How could one man chase a thousand, or two put ten thousand to flight?" (Deuteronomy 32:30).

There is a dynamic multiplication factor in the unity of numbers. The Middle East saw this when hundreds of thousands gathered to stand for democracy. We are a hundred times more effective when we are a unified group. Ask God how and where you can best be used to work together with others to achieve a greater Kingdom impact.

MODULE 6

MARY COMPANY

MARY THE MOTHER OF JESUS CHRIST – BRIEF INTRODUCTION

YOUNG MARY WAS BORN IN A POOR FAMILY FROM the insignificant town of Nazareth. She did not appear to stand out from her peers and would probably not have been voted 'most likely to succeed.' Eventually, however, she was engaged to a man named Joseph who could not promise her affluence but was a kind man with a stable reputation.

While Mary was growing up unknown by the outside world, God had taken note of her and was delighted. One day, to Mary's astonishment, an angel appeared to her. "Greetings favored one! The Lord is with you," the angel said. "Do not be afraid for you have found favor with God." The angel proceeded to tell her she would conceive and give birth as a virgin to the Son of God himself. Instead of reacting in terror or objecting stubbornly, Mary submitted completely to a pregnancy she had to know would give rise to the ugliest of rumors and accusations. At that time, Mary went to visit her cousin, Elizabeth. The elderly Elizabeth was miraculously pregnant with a baby who was to become the mighty John the Baptist. When she saw Mary she cried, "Blessed are you among women! And blessed is the fruit of your womb. What an honor that the mother of my Lord should visit me!" Spontaneous joy overflowed from Mary's heart in those days.

Then, shortly after Jesus' birth, Joseph and Mary took him to the temple to be dedicated. That is when the godly Simeon told Mary, "This boy will be the greatest joy to some, but others in Israel will cruelly reject him. And a sword shall pierce your soul..."

Perhaps this was Mary's first omen of what was to come. But she did not shrink from forebodings, nor did she attempt to speculate to others of her son's future. As Jesus grew, and multiplied, events pointed to his unique identity, and his mother silently pondered and treasured up all these things in her heart. As the Son of God reached manhood and launched out into his public ministry, Mary ushered Him onto center stage and faded into the background. Little is mentioned of her throughout Christ's public ministry, but we do detect a few cases in which confusion about Jesus' words and actions appears evident.

This young girl showed unequalled bravery when she accepted the angel's message by saying, "... *may it be to me as you have said*" (Luke 1:38). But did she understand what she was agreeing to?

In Mary's famous song of praise, we find evidence that Mary knew the Old Testament teachings. As a Jew, she had been learning about biblical prophecy her entire life. Her song also bears a striking resemblance to Hannah's famous prayer (1 Samuel 2:1-10). Now, she would become part of the fulfillment of God's ultimate plan.

"He has helped his servant Israel and remembered to be merciful. For he made this promise to our ancestors, to Abraham and his children forever" (Luke 1:54-55).

Mary understood the magnitude of her decision to say yes when God chose her. Her knowledge of God's promise to send a Savior for His people showed through her worship.

Her Life Was Foreshadowed in the Old Testament

Mary's life and role in the history of salvation is foreshadowed in the Old Testament and the events of her life are recorded in the New Testament. The prophecy of Isaiah 7:14 speaks of the "Virgin-Mother of Emmanuel": "Therefore, the Lord himself will give you a sign. Behold, a virgin shall conceive and bear a son, and His name shall be called Emmanuel." Later in Isaiah, Emmanuel is referred to as the future Savior of His people. The prophet foretells an extraordinary future sign: that a virgin, without the copulation of a man, would give birth to a child who will be "God with us". This child would remedy the great trials of division facing the people of Israel. Isaiah's prophecy predicts the Virgin of Nazareth and the birth of Jesus.

She was a woman of great character and courage.

Mary loved God and wanted to serve Him with all her heart. But she was just a poor girl in an insignificant town, from a humble family, with little expectations that her life was going to be any different than most. When the angel Gabriel came to Mary to tell her she was chosen and favored by God to be the mother of His son, despite her own fear, she exhibited great courage and character: "I am the Lord's servant…May your word to me be fulfilled" (Luke 1:38). She also exhibited great courage and character during Jesus' earthly life and ministry. She pressed Jesus to provide wine when it ran low at the wedding in Cana, she approached Jesus when He was left behind at the temple, she went from Nazareth to Capernaum when she learned what was being reported there about Jesus, and she attempts to protect Jesus in some of the stickiest of situations. She was a person of discipleship and faith, and the first true follower of Jesus.

Why is virginity so important in the Bible?

When the Bible uses the word *virgin*, it refers to an unmarried person who has not had sexual relations (see Esther 2:2 Then the king's attendants, who served him, said, "Let beautiful young virgins be sought for the king. These are the ones who have not been defiled [by relations] with men for they are celibate. These are the ones who follow the Lamb wherever He goes. These have been purchased *and* redeemed from among men [of Israel] as the first fruits [sanctified and set apart for special service] for God and the Lamb). **Revelation 14:4**

In today's culture, many people use the word virginity to express sexual purity; however, many others use a technical definition to find loopholes in moral standards, limiting the word to mean only "the condition of never having gone all the way" thus, a couple can do anything and everything short of sexual intercourse and still technically call themselves "virgins." This is an unprofitable word game. Chastity should affect the heart, mind, and soul, not just certain body parts.

The Bible's emphasis is not so much on a technical or medical definition of virginity as it is on the condition of a person's heart. The morality we promote and the actions we choose give evidence of our heart's condition. The Bible's standard is clear: celibacy before marriage and monogamy after marriage.

There are three serious reasons to save sex for marriage:

1. First, as believers, we are to obey what God tells us to do. 1 Corinthians 6:18–20 states, "Flee from sexual immorality. All other sins a person commits are outside the body, but whoever sins sexually, sins against their own body. Do you not know that your bodies are temples of the Holy Spirit, who is in you, whom you have received from God? You are not your own; you were bought at a price. Therefore, honor God with your bodies." If we are in Christ, He has purchased us with the sacrifice of His life. He is our Lord, and we are to honor Him.

2. The second reason is that we are to fight our spiritual battles wearing the breastplate of righteousness (Ephesians 6:14). We are in a contest between our new nature in Christ and our fleshly desires. First Thessalonians 4:3–7 says, "It is God's will that you should be sanctified: that you should avoid sexual immorality; that each of you should learn to control your own body in a way that is holy and honourable, not in passionate lust like the pagans, who do not know God; and that in this matter no one should wrong or take advantage of a brother or sister. The Lord will punish all those who commit such sins, as we told you and warned you before. For God did not call us to be impure, but to live a holy life." Allowing your body (rather than the Spirit) to control your actions is an act of defiance against God. Godly, loving sex between a husband and wife is giving and unselfish. Using someone to fulfill a desire of the flesh is self-centered and abusive. Even if the partner is willing, you are still helping him or her to sin and negatively altering that person's relationship with God and others.

3. The final reason involves the "mystery" of marriage (Ephesians 5:31-32). When God spoke of two people being joined as one, He was referring to something we are only beginning to understand in a real, physiological way. When two people are intimate, the hypothalamus in the brain releases chemicals that induce feelings of attachment and trust. Having sex outside of marriage results in a person forming an attachment and trusting someone with whom he or she does not have a committed relationship. The definition of trust in the mind deteriorates. To have that kind of link with someone without the security of working together toward God is dangerous. Two individuals who are even mildly physiologically infatuated with each other, but not committed to growing in God as a couple can be torn from God and His plans for them.

Conversely, if two people make a conscious, deliberate choice to commit to each other in marriage, and then allow the intimacy that releases these chemicals, the body can reaffirm the connection the mind has made. The physiological feelings of trust and attachment are reinforced by the reality of the relationship. In this way, two people become one physically, and that reflects what God has done spiritually.

Marriage is to model the relationship between the church and Christ. A married couple is to serve God in a strong, unified partnership. Sex, along with procreation, was designed by God to strengthen that partnership. Sex outside of marriage creates bonds that tear apart people's hearts instead of joining them together.

Finally, we need to remember a few things about virginity, and the lack thereof, given God's grace. Those who come to Christ after engaging in premarital sexual relationships are not virgins; however, they are fully cleansed by Christ at the moment they are saved. God can redeem anyone, and He can heal those who have indulged their fleshly lusts. For those who engaged in premarital sex after becoming a Christian, there is forgiveness in Christ. He can cleanse us from all unrighteousness and bring healing (1

John 1:9). And, in the horrible case of persons victimized by sexual abuse or rape, who may feel that they, through no fault of their own, no longer measure up to the ideal standard of "virginity," Christ is able to restore their spirit, heal their brokenness, and grant them wholeness.

Why is virginity so important in the Bible?

Virginity is a very important concept in the Bible. The Bible defines sex outside of marriage as a sin because it is a form of sexual immorality (1 Corinthians 7:2). Therefore, Christians are not to engage in sexual relations outside of the boundaries of marriage. A person who chooses to remain abstinent is called a virgin. Mary, the mother of Jesus, is often referred to as the Virgin Mary because she became pregnant with Jesus as a miracle from God without having had sex. To many in modern culture, virginity is a negative thing. For others, "virginity" has become a technical delineation describing not "going all the way," yet still engaging in all sorts of other sexual acts. The Bible makes it clear, however, that any sexual act outside of how God created it to be within marriage is sinful. God desires sexual purity in body, mind, and heart.

The Bible emphasizes the importance of virginity because it is an act of obedience to God. First Corinthians 6:18–20 says, "Flee from sexual immorality. Every other sin a person commits is outside the body, but the sexually immoral person sins against his own body. Or do you not know that your body is a temple of the Holy Spirit within you, whom you have from God? You are not your own, for you were bought with a price. So, glorify God in your body." Practicing abstinence requires discipline, which can be very difficult when we face physical temptations. Sex was created by God; therefore, our sexual desire is part of how He made us. However, outside of marriage sex is defiled and can have negative consequences. When we choose to trust God, even if we do not fully understand His plan, we are obedient to Him. Our obedience is an act of submission to Him, acknowledging that we need Him as our Savior.

Virginity is also a physical sign of us being made into a new creation in Christ. When we accept Jesus Christ as our Savior, He forgives us for our sins and begins to make us more like Him (Ephesians 4:24; 1 Thessalonians 4:3–7). As a new creation, we begin to exhibit Christ-like characteristics such as self-control. By choosing to not have sex, we exercise control over our physical cravings and emotional impulses.

In addition, virginity is a symbol of commitment to God. The apostle Paul describes marriage as a relationship that symbolizes Christ's relationship to the Church (Ephesians 5:31–32). In this relationship both Christ and the Church are committed to one another in a monogamous relationship. In other words, as believers, we are to only have one God and to not put anything before God (Exodus 20:3; John 15:1–17; 1 John 5:1–4, 21).

It is important to note that although you may no longer be a virgin, you still have the opportunity to choose to be abstinent moving forward in obedience to God. When we are forgiven by Christ, He cleanses us from our sin and makes us new in Him (2 Corinthians 5:17–21; 1 John 1:9). Virginity is a physical condition, but more importantly it is the posture of our heart choosing to commit ourselves only to God.

What is consecration?

In religion, the word consecration is commonly used about the official ordaining of a person to be a pastor, priest, or missionary. This use implies that consecration is something that is reserved for a special category of people. But the New Testament reveals that it is something that every believer in Christ can, and should, experience. Consecration is also not something only for knowledgeable or spiritually mature Christians. Rather, we all need to consecrate ourselves to the Lord to deepen our personal knowledge of Christ and grow in the divine life, even if we have only just gotten saved. This is because consecration is the basis for every spiritual experience.

So, what is consecration? Consecration is giving yourself to the Lord to become "a living sacrifice," as Paul says in Romans 12:1:

*"I exhort you therefore, brothers, through the compassions of God **to present your bodies a living sacrifice**, holy, well pleasing to God, which is your reasonable service."*

In the Old Testament, sacrifices were set apart for God by being placed on the altar. In offering something to God, one relinquished ownership of that item. Instead, it belonged to God, for His use and His satisfaction. Today, when we consecrate ourselves to the Lord, we become a living sacrifice. This means we put ourselves completely in His hands. Before we consecrated ourselves, our life was for the pursuit of our own goals and satisfaction; now, it is for Him.

When we present ourselves to the Lord as a living sacrifice, we are simply telling Him: "Lord Jesus, my life is for you. I no longer belong to myself, the world, or anything else. I am here for you and for your satisfaction.

Four reasons why we should consecrate ourselves to the Lord.

To walk in the Lord's way

Before we were saved, we took our own way, made our own decisions, and chose the direction for our life. After we are saved, God wants us to walk in His way and be led by Him. But if we do not give ourselves to Him, how can we know what His way is? How can He lead us? Consecrating ourselves to Him keeps us in His way and saves us from taking our own way. We can pray, "Lord, I don't want to make my own decisions or take my own way. I want to be kept in your way. So, Lord Jesus, I give myself to you."

To grow in life

When Christ comes into us, we are regenerated with His divine life. His intention is for that divine life in us to grow. But any kind of life needs the proper environment to grow. Surrendering every part of ourselves and every aspect of our lives to Him creates the best environment for the divine life to grow in us.

Our experience of Christ is significantly affected by whether we give ourselves to the Lord. Without consecrating ourselves to Him, it is difficult to tell whether something is according to God's will, and whether it will please Him.

But when we surrender ourselves to the Lord, we spontaneously sense what pleases Him and what does not. This sensation is the result of God's divine life functioning in us, and it is activated by our consecration. As we follow God by obeying this sense, we grow in the divine life in a real and practical way.

To allow God to work in us

Before we can work for God, God first needs to work in us. Even though we are saved, He still must conform our thoughts, feelings, decisions, and disposition; our whole being to the image of His Son, as Romans 8:29 says.

God is omnipotent, but in His relationship with us, He is not a dictator. He respects our free will and does not force His work on us; rather, He needs our consent to work freely in us. Our consecration is our consent. God is patient, and He will wait until we give Him the permission to work in us to accomplish His purpose. Instead of resisting Him, we can pray, "Lord, I give you permission to work in me. I offer myself willingly to you. Lord, I open the door of my heart to you. Come into each room of my heart and conform me to your image in every way."

To enjoy the riches of God's salvation

Salvation is full of riches. Ephesians 1:3 tells us that God has blessed us with every spiritual blessing in Christ. These blessings include the divine life, Christ's perfect humanity and living, His effective death, His powerful resurrection, His victory over Satan, His ascension over all things, and so much more. The way we can enter the enjoyment of all these blessings is by consecrating ourselves to Him. We already possess them, but for us to enjoy them in our experience, we must consecrate ourselves to God.

In this respect, consecration is like a door. To enter a building, we must go through a door. If we do not, no matter what wonderful thing awaits us on the other side, we cannot enjoy or participate in it. Consecration is the door for us to enter through to enjoy all the riches of God's salvation. When we give ourselves to the Lord, He will lead us in our experience into the enjoyment of the rich blessings of God's full salvation.

We can pray, "Lord, I don't just want to know about the riches of your salvation; I want to enjoy them. Lord, here I am. I give myself to you fully. I belong to you. Lead me by Your Spirit into the experience and enjoyment of all you have for me in your salvation."

Exercise

Mary is described as the first true follower of Jesus. Why?

List the attributes of a true Christian, using Joseph, Abraham, Deborah, Daniel, and Mary as examples.

_____

_____

_____

_____

PART 4

INSTITUTE OF DISCIPLESHIP AND TRANSFORMATION

ENROLLMENT, CERTIFICATE, COMMISSIONING AND CALL TO ACTION

DEAR READER, MY EARNEST DESIRE AND HEART cry is that you will be sensitized to act right away. In conclusion, I would like to remind and invite you to enroll into The Institute of Discipleship and Transformation.

Here are a few quotes to empower you as a change agent to take small steps forward every day.

"Sometimes the smallest step in the right direction ends up being the biggest step of your life. Tiptoe if you must but take a step." Naeem Callaway

When you feel like procrastinating or making an excuse for not taking a step forward, let it remind you that the step that you are avoiding or putting off could be the biggest step of your life. So, you need to take it, without thinking about it too much, without delay.

"Do what you can, with what you've got, where you are." Squire Bill Widener

Be inspired as you do not need to be a different person, you do not need to have more, and be somewhere else before you can move forward with positive action in life.

"The journey of a thousand miles begins with one step." Lao Tzu

Life is an exciting journey but the things we want are rarely, if ever, handed to us on a plate. We have to work towards them, and we start by taking one single, small step. That step may frighten or terrify us, but that is okay. You will feel amazing once you have taken that small step.

"If you can't fly then run, if you can't run then walk, if you can't walk then crawl, but whatever you do you have to keep moving forward." Martin Luther King Jr.

There have been times in my life when I felt "stuck," as if I was a victim of circumstance. I did not feel like there was anything I could do to change any situation. By relying totally on the grace of God, I have always been able to crawl forward. The good news is that, over time, all your small steps will add up to a giant leap forward. You will be flying so high that no one will be able to stop you!

"Each step you take reveals a new horizon. You have taken the first step today. Now I challenge you to take another." Dan Poynter

If you don't know how to reach a goal, just take one step — the step that seems to be the best way forward, even if you are not sure if it is the best way forward. Once you have taken that step, you will be wiser. You will know what the next step should be. Even if you are still not sure, just take another step, so that you move forward.

The Institute of Discipleship and Transformation process will impact, influence, disciple, equip, add value, and create a lasting change in you. We will help you to develop the passion to make changing your world an intentional choice. Passion is a great energizer. Just gather a group of people that have like passion and invite us to mentor them. Keep in mind that transformation begins in you, which makes you a carrier of transformation. We care about you. We can help you. You can trust us. This is a safe environment where you can begin to learn, relate, connect, and care. We live in a world of no absolutes or standards; regardless, value is very important. Golden rule–treat others as you want to be treated. We are in this with you, and we will walk with you. We will walk before you to give you the vision, walk beside you to give you support. According to Mother Teresa,

"I can do things you cannot, you can do things I cannot; together we can do great things."

Be a part of this transformation company today! Sign up now for a 4-Week Certificate Course and get 50% off for a limited time. Do not miss out! We are just a phone call away +1905 232 2457

Looking forward to connecting and working with you:

Email: fruitfulrehoboth@gmail.com

LinkedIn: http://linkedin.com/in/uche-ezechim-a41416105

Website: www.transformation-company.com

Instagram: www.instagram.com/ucheezechim/

Twitter: @uchetransformation

Facebook: https://m.facebook.com/fruitfulrehoboth

Subscribe YouTube: https://m.youtube.com/channel/ UCPE2pUkp8LW9rA54Wu02-Ng

THE FRUITFUL VINE AND OLIVE SHOOTS
BY UCHE EZECHIM.

Infertility is something that affects many people but is often not discussed out of fear or shame.

This book urges readers to:

Find encouragement and hope in author's story, as well as the testimonies included from her children and others who have shared their experiences with her.

Aggressively and diligently take hold of God's promises, until they are realized physically.

ABOUT THE AUTHOR

U CHE EZECHIM IS A KINGDOM AMBASSADOR, A pioneer, motivational speaker, consultant, and a multi-gifted mentor of mentors. She has earned postgraduate degrees from York University, Toronto, Canada. As a certified and experienced educator with extraordinary passion to positively impact the Education sector, she has established a number of initiatives.

Uche works closely with associates and stakeholders, harnessing their strengths, attributes, and growth opportunities, to appropriately empower everyone to be a part of the big picture in a way that will be meaningful to them.

At the Institute of Discipleship and Transformation, the author coaches and inspires active followers of Christ to become leaders, and leaders to become agents of change through mentorship and personal development programs.

Uche is a trailblazer with great apostolic unction and grace who disciples and raises leaders across nations. Travelling extensively across many nations, her ultimate desire is to extend the blueprint of what a transformed person, marriage, family, professional, business, nation, Kingdom, and globe look like. She serves as a

Wailing Women Worldwide American Continental Coordinator, with strong prophetic and administrative gifts.

Uche and her husband, Engr. Ezekiel Ezechim, the Founders of Grace Apostolic Ministries, an Interdenominational Missionary Intercessory Outreach within Canada and beyond, are involved in teaching at seminars, ministering with sensitive hearts, and propagating an international vision.

They are joyful parents of three 'Godly Seeds' residing in Toronto, Canada.

BIBLIOGRAPHY

Amy Desai, J.D. 2007. "How should a Christian view marriage and divorce?" Focus on the Family (blog), January 1, 2007. https://www.focusonthefamily.com/marriage/how-should-a-christian-view-marriage-and-divorce/

Behavioral Healthcare Executive. 2021. The Biblical Joseph: Lessons for Administrators. https://www.psychcongress.com/blog/h-steven-moffic/biblical-joseph-lessons-administrators

Bible.com. n.d. 6 Stages Of A Call Of A Change Agent. https://www.bible.com/reading-plans/4837-6-stages-of-a-call-of-a-change-agent/day/1

Bibles For America. 2021. "What is consecration?" biblesforamerica.org (blog), January 12, 2021. https://blog.biblesforamerica.org/what-is-consecration/

Bob, Waliszewski. 2007. "The influence of media." Focus on the Family (blog), January 1, 2007. https://www.focusonthefamily.com/parenting/the-influence-of-media/

Carrie, Gordon Earll. 2021. "What the Bible says about the beginning of life." Focus on the Family (blog), April 19, 2021.https://www.focusonthefamily.com/pro-life/what-the-bible-says-about-the-beginning-of-life/

Christopher, Allen. 2020. "Joseph Arise – Doing business in 2021 and beyond." christopherallen.net (blog), December 18, 2020. https://www.christopherallen.net/joseph-arise-doing-business-in-2021-and-beyond

Compelling Truth. n.d. "What does the Bible say about sexual purity?" https://www.compellingtruth.org/sexual-purity.html

Compelling Truth. n.d. Why Is Virginity So Important In The Bible? https://www.compellingtruth.org/Bible-virginity.html

Coptic Orthodox Diocese. n.d. "Deborah the Judge: Godliness Produced Strength of Character and Modesty." https://suscopts.org/resources/literature/265/deborah-the-judge-godliness-produced-strength-of-c/

Cortni, Marrazzo. 2021. "Joseph in the Bible: '3 Things You Didn't Know about His Life & Story.'" crosswalk.com (blog), January 18, 2021. https://www.crosswalk.com/family/career/3-things-you-didn-t-know-about-joseph-in-the-bible.html

Danny, Huerta. 2020 "Breaking the cycle of absent fathers: Focus on the family." Focus on the Family (blog), June 16, 2020. https://www.focusonthefamily.com/parenting/breaking-the-cycle-of-absent-fathers/

Diane, Shirlaw-Ferreira. 2020. "God uses broken people – 4 reasons god uses broken people to do amazing things." Worthbeyondrubies.com (blog), December 15, 2020. https://www.worthbeyondrubies.com/god-uses-broken-people/

Doug, Britton. 2021. "Commit to your marriage – Do not divorce." Doug Britton Books. Focus on the Family. n.d. "Biblical perspective on homosexuality and same-sex marriage." https://www.focusonthefamily.com/family-qa/biblical-perspective-on-homosexuality-and-same-sex-marriage/

Got Questions. n.d. Why is virginity so important in the Bible? https://www.gotquestions.org/Bible-virginity.html

BIBLIOGRAPHY

Grace Church. n.d. Divorce and Remarriage. https://www.grace-church.org/about/distinctives/divorce-and-remarriage

Hope, Bolinger. 2019. "4 Relevant Ways the Book of Daniel Equips Teens." crosswalk.com (blog), May 7, 2019. https://www.crosswalk.com/church/youth-ministry/4-relevant-ways-the-book-of-daniel-equips-teens.html

Hugh, Whelchel. 2016. "'Will we conform or transform?': Learning from the life of Daniel about living in today's culture." Institute for Faith Works and Economics. https://tifwe.org/learning-from-the-life-of-daniel/

Jerusha, Drummond. n.d. Leadership Formation Through Mentoring In The Old Testament. https://www.regent.edu/acad/global/publications/jbpl/vol9no1/Vol9Iss1_JBPL_20_Drummond.pdf

Jim, Wolstenholm. 2017. "3 simple steps to change your world." Jimthefollower.com (blog), December 5, 2017. https://jimthefollower.com/2017/12/05/transformational-love/#page-content

John, Calvin. 2021. "A father's main responsibility." monergism.com. https://www.monergism.com/father%E2%80%99s-main-responsibility-genesis-1819

Lech-Lecha. n.d. "Ten Steps to Greatness." Meaningful Life Center. https://www.meaningfullife.com/lech-lecha-ten-challenges/

Lynn, Copeland. 2020. "What God's word says about abortion." Living Waters (blog), January 9, 2020. https://www.livingwaters.com/gods-word-says-abortion/marriageinformationandadvice/bibleandchristiandivorce01-committoyourmarriage/

Mary, K. Pratt and Joseph Flahiff. n.d. "What is change agent (agent of change)?" Whitewater Projects Inc. https://searchcio.techtarget.com/definition/change-agent

Matt, Henslee. 2020. "3 Ways to harness social media to the glory of God." Lifeway Research (blog), January 27, 2020. https://lifewayresearch.com/2020/01/27/3-ways-to-harness-social-media-to-the-glory-of-god/

Melissa, Ringstaff. n.d. "The 10 Virtues of a Proverbs 31 Woman." avirtuouswoman.org. https://avirtuouswoman. org/10-virtues-of-the-proverbs-31-woman/

Michael, Griego. 2017. "Abraham – the good father model." Biblicalviewpoint (blog), June 16, 2017. https://biblicalview-point.com/2017/06/16/abraham-the-good-father-model /

Munroe, M. 2007. The Most Important Person on Earth: The Holy Spirit, Governor of the Kingdom. USA. Whitaker House.

Nijay Gupta. n.d. "Deborah – Judge, Prophet, and 'Mother in Israel.'" Seattle Pacific University. https://blog.spu.edu/lectio/deborah-judge-prophet-and-mother-in-israel/

Pastor, Joe. 2017. "Ministry of the Holy Spirit." Freedom Life Church (blog), February 23, 2017. https://freedomlifechurch. net/ministry-holy-spirit-agent-change-pastor-joe/

Randy, Alcorn. 1996. "Strategies to keep from falling: Practical steps to maintain your purity and ministry." Eternal Perspectives Ministries (blog), June 1, 1996. https://www.epm.org/resources/1996/Jun/1/strategies-keep-falling-practical-steps-maintain-y/

Randy, Alcorn. 2010. "Guidelines for sexual purity." Eternal Perspectives Ministries (blog), January 18, 2020. https://www. epm.org/resources/2010/Jan/28/guidelines-sexual-purity/

Randy, Alcorn. 2010. "Living in a modern Corinth: Actively pursuing purity in a sex-saturated world." Eternal Perspectives Ministries (blog), March 22, 2010. https://www.epm.org/resources/2010/Mar/22/living-modern-corinth-actively-pursuing-purity-sex/

Randy, Alcorn. 2010. "The purity principle: Chapters 5 and 6." March 6, 2010. https://www.epm.org/resources/2010/Mar/6/ purity-principle-chapters-5-and-6/

Randy, Alcorn. 2011. "When and how should I teach my kids about sex?" Eternal Perspectives Ministries (blog), May 2, 2011. https://www.epm.org/resources/2011/May/2/q-when-and-how-should-i-teach-my-kids-about-sex-vi/

Randy, Alcorn. 2020. "The purity principle: Superior satisfaction." Eternal Perspectives Ministries (blog), January 20, 2010. https://www.epm.org/resources/2010/Jan/20/ purity-principle-superior-satisfaction/

Redeeming the Arts. n.d. "The restoration of the arts to God's creational intention." (LOP 46). 2020. Laussane Movement. https://lausanne.org/content/lop/redeeming-arts-resto-ration-arts-gods-creational-intention-lop-46

Richard, Bumpers. 2020. "10 evangelistic ways to share your faith on social media." The Christian Index (blog), June 29, 2020. https://christianindex. org/10-evangelistic-ways-share-faith-social-media/

Robin, Ravis Pyke. 2019. "7 leadership traits of Deborah: A mother in Israel." robinravispyke.com (blog), March 17, 2019. https://robinrevispyke.com/2019/03/17/7-lead-ership-traits/#:~:text=Deborah%20was%20 courageous.,now%20that%20Ehud%20was%20dead.

Steve, Fortosis. 2016. "Mary the Mother of Jesus biog-raphy." inspirationalchristians.org (blog), August 11, 2016. https://www.inspirationalchristians.org/bible-characters/ mary-the-mother-of-jesus-biography/

Stewart Kabatebate. n.d. "Alice Bailey 10 point plan to destroy Christianity." Inspired Walk. http://www.inspiredwalk. com/6297/alice-baileys-10-point-plan-to-destroy-christianity

Susan, J. Nelson. 2021. "Who Was Deborah in the Bible?" Christianity.com. https://www.christianity.com/wiki/people/who-was-deborah-in-the-bible.html

The Christian Working Woman. n.d. "The transforming power of love." https://christianworkingwoman.org/broadcast/the-transforming-power-of-love-part-i/

Theology of Work. n.d. Joseph's Successful Management of the Food Crisis. TOW Project. https://www.theologyofwork.org/old-testament/genesis-12-50-and-work/joseph-genesis-372-5026/josephs-successful-management-of-the-food-crisis-genesis-4146-57-4713-26#toc

Tim, Kight. 2019. "A Kingdom worldview." A Call to Excellence (blog), April 24, 2019. https://www.acalltoexcellence.com/a-kingdom-worldview

Tyrone Grandison. 2018. "5 steps to being an effective change agent." govloop.com (blog), March 16, 2018. https://www.govloop.com/community/blog/5-steps-effective-change-agent/

Will, Harrub. 2015. "4 lessons from Daniel for today's Christians." Renew Your Mind Focus Press (blog), August 24, 2015. https://www.focuspress.org/2015/08/24/4-lessons-from-daniel-for-todays-christians/

CPSIA information can be obtained
at www.ICGtesting.com
Printed in the USA
LVHW111227240721
693545LV00002B/97